There's Got To Be A Better Way:

DISCIPLINE THAT WORKS!

By Dr. Becky Bailey

Loving Guidance, Inc.

Published by: Loving Guidance, Inc.

                 P.O. Box 622407
                 Oviedo, FL 32762 U.S.A.

Publisher's Note
This book is designed to provide information in regard to the subject matter covered. It is sold with the understanding that the publisher and author are sharing ideas and activities, and the success of those ideas and activities contained within vary from individual to individual.

Cover Design by Aardvark Productions

Publisher's Cataloging in Publication Data
Bailey, Becky Anne
        There's got to be a better way : discipline that works! / Becky Anne Bailey.
        p. cm.
        Includes bibliographical reference.
        Library of Congress Catalog Card Number: 97-70596.
        ISBN 13: 978-1-889609-03-4
        ISBN 10: 1-889609-03-X

        1. Discipline of children--United Sates.   1. Title

HQ770.4.B35 1994   649'.64
                                          QB194-1141

CONTENTS

Part Three

"*I'll give you something to complain about.*"
Creating an Environment Where
Children Choose to Cooperate

Part Four

"How many times do I have to tell you?"
**The Basic Discipline Techniques and Skills of Discipline
Every Adult Must Know**

ACKNOWLEDGMENTS

Recently the phrase,"It takes a whole village to raise a child," has become very popular as a metaphor for the need and power of working together. I believe the same is true in any creative process. It indeed takes a whole village to write and publish a book!

I gratefully acknowledge the contributions of those who have worked to make this book a reality: Virginia McIntyre, Carolyn Brookes, Vi Nemec, Lisa Fenn and Penny Leggett, who were kind enough to read and *reread* the manuscript and offer suggestions; Sarah Whalen,the talented editor; Lorrie Cabral for typesetting; Jeff Jones, the imaginative artist who created the delightful drawings throughout the book; Daryl Gagliano for her translation into Spanish; Raymond Merten for the photograph on the back cover and Mary Gayle Guidon for her beautiful book jacket design.

With any endeavor there are those driving forces that keep you going. Keith McIntyre is one of those forces. Not only did he encourage and support me during the process, he is also responsible for the layout of the book. His creative and loving spirit are on every page.

During the writing of this book my parents, Talmadge and Frances, and dear friend Kate O'Neil have given me the psychological support that is so very important. And to my constant companion, Bo, who loves me unconditionally, your supportive spirit is always with me.

For this village I am eternally grateful.

*This book is dedicated to you
and the journey of love we are
all taking together.*

INTRODUCTION

I truly believe that we teach what we most need to learn about. Therefore, this book is about my journey to understand myself and those around me. Specifically, it is about my journey to understand how to love myself and extend this love to the people I encounter each day.

The title of the book represents a place I believe many of us visit. It is a place of *almost* change. " There's gotta be a better way," is a phrase I say when I become aware that my old patterns of behavior are not effective. It is a phrase I say when I am ready to seek help and look for new alternatives. It is a phrase that represents a transition time in life. It becomes a feeling that ultimately moves me to take new action.

The name, *There's Got To Be A Better Way: Discipline That Works,* represents my transition and the transition I am seeing in schools, homes and our society. This transition is a shift from placing power outside ourselves in the form of status symbols—like cars and clothes or behavior patterns, such as blaming others for our life choices—to a power that lies in each of us. Our source of strength comes from the love we feel for ourselves and each other.

The guiding motto for myself is "Teach only love for that is what you are." As I began using this creed to guide my perception, my thoughts and my behavior, I recognized I really had no true concept of what love entailed. I had confused love with guilt, shame, control, fear and even hatred at times. In this confusion, I justified my behavior. I reasoned it was okay to treat children certain ways for their own good. I reasoned it was okay to use fear to motivate and guide children—how else would they learn? I reasoned control was the answer to create obedience, order and sanity. I reasoned punishment and guilt were essential if children were to be moral. I finally realized the devastating effects of such beliefs and brought myself to a changing point.

Maybe you're at that same point in your life. You may be looking for a new belief structure to guide your interactions with children. This book is then for you and dedicated to you and the journey to love we are all taking.

The book is divided into four major sections. Section one is probably a section you will not find in any other discipline book. It is a section that begins where we must always start—with ourselves. The first four chapters ask you to explore yourself, your beliefs about yourself, and your beliefs about children. Section two gives information about understanding children. Many of us are aware that children develop in a rather orderly sequence. I chose to describe the development of children in a slightly different format. I wrote about the development of misbehavior in young children. It is important to understand that children, by nature, will create conflict for us and within us as adults. Being aware of this process will assist us in being better guides for them. Section three begins a more focused journey as you are guided even further from control to structure. The specifics of how to structure environments and situations for young children are delineated with concrete examples. The final section of the book is entitled, "Discipline Techniques and Skills". These last chapters will take you through specific skills that can be utilized with children in specific conflict situations.

Each section of the book offers you exercises to complete. These exercises will provide you with insight and skill in working with young children. You are invited to actively interact with the book. Throughout the book you will experience many delightful and humorous pictures drawn by a very talented artist, Mr. Jeff Jones. These pictures are to remind us we tend to take life too seriously. The book asks you to look at yourself, learn new skills, yet delight in the process. So, this book is a joyous journey from control to structure, from perfection to acceptance, from resentment to forgiveness, from apathy to action and from fear to love. Thank you for sharing it with me.

Becky Bailey

Part One

"When I grow up I will never _____ to my children!"

Understanding Why We Act and React to Our Children the Way We Do

The more we idealize the past and refuse to acknowledge our childhood sufferings, the more we pass them on unconsciously to the next generation.

—Alice Miller

Chapter 1

This is for your own good:
The Development of Beliefs

The Boundaries of Our Lives

Have you ever watched children play in a fenced yard or playground? If so, you have witnessed that if there are fences, children are more likely to use the entire space. If there are no fences, they are likely to avoid the perimeters and restrict their area of play. The limits teachers and parents set on a child's behavior are like the fences around a playground.

With boundaries, children feel secure. They gradually learn to set their own boundaries and develop healthy self-discipline. Such self-discipline builds within the child a sense of control and a confidence that their world is predictable and safe. They can freely explore with an awareness of what they are and are not permitted to do.

Without appropriate boundaries a child's life lacks protection. When there are no boundaries, no limits and no rules, the number of choices becomes overwhelming. Under these circumstances children limit their spontaneity and become reckless about their own welfare and the welfare of others. Children will rebel or passively accept the world as a hostile place from which to retreat.

As you develop or revamp boundaries for the classroom or home, think seriously about what type of fence you will erect. Will it be one that helps children feel secure and cared for or one that will make them feel limited and reckless?

• •

Boundaries, like fences, are not solely physical, they are also psychological.

• •

Boundaries, like fences, are not solely physical; they are also psychological. They are built from a combination of spoken and unspoken rules that have been designed by adults. Think back to when you were a child. There were rules reiterated so loudly they were often actually shouted—rules like, *Don't run in the hall* or *Don't talk with your mouth full.* Then there were silent rules never really spoken by anyone but realized by everyone, *Don't question authority* or *Only speak when you are spoken to.*

If a brave soul musters up the courage to ask why, the adult simply dismisses the child as a wise guy or, worse yet, a trouble maker. Whether rules are spoken out loud or picked up by osmosis is usually irrelevant. Spoken and unspoken rules are internalized by the child.

As external boundaries are established for children through rules, an internal belief system begins to develop that they will use to govern their own lives. Some children come to school with a set of internalized rules that prompts them to be seen and not heard.

Others may arrive with the internal rule system that to get attention you have to act out. Whatever the belief system, it has been developed in response to the child's awareness of his or her own needs and the awareness of the needs of others.

A good example of this is a young mom who wanted her baby to sleep more. She considered her child's needs too demanding, and wanted her baby to sleep almost *all* the time. The three-month-old boy was sleeping through the night but only napping during the day. This mom had a need for the child to sleep more in the daytime, so she could have a break. She was unable to meet the needs of the child and was frantically trying to get her own needs met. Little did she know she was modeling for her son to be aware of one's own needs and not be aware of the needs of others. He is now five years old and seeks desperately to get his own needs met without any concern for the needs of the others. He learned this from his caring but stressed young mother.

Some children are taught boundaries by adults who are judgmental and critical. Mistakes are treated harshly as the adult attacks the esteem of the child. Comments like the following are often heard:

"How many times do I have to tell you something?"

"I'm sick and tired of your sorry excuses! You never listen!"

"You're mean to treat people like you do! You're just like your father."

Other boundaries are set up by inference, with children never really being told what is expected; they are just expected to magically know: "Remember to be nice to your friends." What is nice? The child will never learn the meaning of this abstract concept unless the meaning is repeatedly demonstrated. Too often the child breaks an unwritten rule, such as being nice, and is reprimanded, "I thought I told you to be nice." The child is not given any usable information that helps him or her understand and learn what nice means.

Some boundaries are taught with extremely rigid rules that when broken, are punished in ways unrelated to the action, as children are threatened with physical harm or loss of love:

"I said to put away one toy before you get out another; you are just asking for trouble!"

"You talk back to me again and you are off to the principal's office for a paddling. Do you hear me?"

"That's better. Now sit down so Ms. Nora can be proud of you."

Others are taught boundaries with threats of abandonment or actual abandonment.

"If you aren't ready by the time I count to three, I'm leaving without you. 1...2...3..."

The external boundaries we have experienced shape who we are and what type of world we see. The boundaries ultimately create an internal structure called beliefs.

Creating Beliefs

For a child to build any kind of internal structure belief system there must be external structure. External structures are provided for young children by parents, caregivers and teachers. The type of external structure we choose to utilize with young children will substantially influence the internal structure that children build for themselves.

A basic understanding of child growth and development is imperative when planning the external structure for young children. Expectations must be realistic. What is appropriate for older children may not be appropriate for younger children. For example, as part of structuring a school morning routine for young children, many kindergarten teachers choose to use the Pledge of Allegiance.

A young girl was asked, "Why do you put your hand over your heart when you say the Pledge?" The youngster responded, "So the witches can't get in."

The teacher thought she was teaching the beliefs of patriotism, but the little girl was simply protecting herself from the witches.

A five-year-old responded to the same question by saying, "So that my mother loves me."

"... and to the public from witches stands ..."

One way children build internal structures is partly from the experiences we allow them to have or impose upon them. If the experiences are beyond their level of development, what they internalize may instill false anxieties. The young girl who protected her heart from witches said the Pledge of Allegiance also on weekends. Her parents were so proud, telling family and friends about their patriotic daughter. Little did they realize the young girl was scared if she didn't say the pledge, the witches could get her at home.

Another way children build internal structure is from values and skills adults teach and model. Watch how travelers respond to a police car on the highway. If the speed limit is 65 miles per hour and the police officer is driving 75 miles per hour, people often ignore the limit and stay right behind the police car. The police officer sets the boundary. The 65-miles-per-hour rule is irrelevant with a powerful model. Teachers and parents are like the police car on the highway. Their actions, more powerful than their words or rules, model for children what is acceptable behavior and what is not. Adult actions provide structure.

Structure is essential for survival. It defines how we function. Since young children cannot provide it for themselves, they must first have it provided by adults. Giving structure to infants means meeting their emotional and physical needs in consistent ways -- feeding them when they are hungry, changing them when they are wet, cuddling them when they are in need of human contact. As children mature, adults must expand the ways they provide structure for children.

Adults can provide structure by helping children learn how to perform tasks skillfully; to think clearly; to collect and assess information; to identify options; to set goals; to start, work and complete tasks; to manage materials, tools, time, ideas and feelings. Structure involves teaching children to be responsible; to honor commitments, and other people; eventually to develop morals and values (Clarke & Dawson, 1989). Creating structure means to safely plan environments and events so that children will be successful at fulfilling adult expectations *and* have their own needs met at the same time. It helps children problem solve as well as say yes to healthy relationships and no to destructive ones.

Without structure there is chaos. Young children from chaotic environments may spend their day creating chaos at school in an attempt to establish some continuity between home and school. People living in chaos, whether young or old, have little energy left over for the growth and the joy of truly connecting with others. In this extreme isolation, loneliness, pain and negativity become the only predictable elements.

Because children need to develop their own structure for survival reasons, they will build an internal structure system with whatever materials are offered at home, at play and at school. Appropriate external structure can provide sturdy building blocks for children as they develop self-discipline and their own internal structure system. In order to provide sturdy building blocks for healthy internal structure, a teacher must avoid what Alice Miller, a well-known psychologist, terms the "poisonous pedagogy."

Structure helps children problem solve and say yes to healthy relationships and no to destructive ones.

The Poisonous Pedagogy

Pedagogy is the art and science of teaching. The poisonous pedagogy values obedience above all other characteristics, closely followed by orderliness, cleanliness and the control of emotions and desires. It advocates controlling children at all costs.

In the poisonous pedagogy, children are considered good when they think and behave the way they are told to think and behave. Children are virtuous when they are meek, agreeable, considerate and unselfish. The more a child is seen and not heard and speaks only when spoken to the better. Children are believed to exist only to meet the needs of adults around them. Many parents and teachers believe that the purpose of early childhood education is to get the children under control. Once children are tamed into being quiet, sitting still and raising their hands to speak, then they are considered ready for school.

Alice Miller (1990) summarizes the beliefs of the poisonous pedagogy:
1. Adults are the masters of the dependent child.
   "This is for your own good."
2. Adults determine in a godlike fashion what is right and wrong.
   "Speaking without raising your hand is wrong. You know the rules."
3. The child is held responsible for the anger of the adults.
   "Now just look what you made me do! Don't make me have to send you to time out!"

4. Parents, teachers and adults in general must be shielded from the actions of children.
    "Just what is the matter with kids these days? They should be sent off until they are civilized."
5. The child's feelings pose a threat to the autocratic parent or teacher.
    "If you are going to cry, just go to your room."
    "I will not tolerate these outbursts in my room. Either settle down or you can go to the principal."
    "I'll give you something to have a tantrum about!"
6. The child's will must be broken as soon as possible.
    "Start out tough the first day of school. Come down hard on them so they know who's boss. They'll walk all over you. Mark my word."
7. All this must happen at a very early age.
    "You better get control of that two-year-old; he will be a teenager before you know it."
    This poisonous pedagogy belief was never clearer than when I first started teaching. I received warnings from the more experienced teachers such as "You better get control and get control fast." I received looks from other teachers when my children *appeared* to be out of control. Many of the teachers patronized me. I heard tail ends of conversations such as "She will learn." I knew there must be a better way than trying to control children, but I had no idea what to do. The more I experimented with techniques other than control, the more judgmental looks I encountered, and the worse I felt!

If Not Control, Then What?

If not the poisonous pedagogy, then what? Without discipline we cannot truly be free. M. Scott Peck, author of *The Road Less Traveled (1978)*, views discipline as a coping strategy. This is a far cry from the deep-seated beliefs perpetuated by the poisonous pedagogy, which equates discipline to pain. Appropriate childhood management involves beliefs that encourage children to be themselves. Such beliefs enhance our being and protect uniqueness.

The poisonous pedagogy upon which many of us were raised will prevail in our classroom and home unless we adopt a more developmentally appropriate set of structuring and nurturing rules. The following are developmentally appropriate beliefs from which we can structure the environment for young children:

☛ It's okay to feel what you feel. Feelings are not right or wrong; they just are. There is no one who can tell you what you "should" feel.

☛ It's good and necessary to talk about feelings.

☛ It's okay to ask for what you want.

☛ Your perceptions are valid.

☛ It's okay and necessary to have lots of fun and play.

☛ It's important to know your limits and to be able to delay gratification.

☛ It's crucial to develop a balanced sense of responsibility. This means accepting the consequences for what you do and refusing to accept the consequences for what someone else does.

☛ It's okay to make mistakes. Mistakes help us learn.

☛ Other people's feelings, needs, and wants are to be respected and valued.

☛ It's okay to have problems. They need to be solved.

☛ It's okay to have conflict, both within yourself and with others. It needs to be resolved (Bradshaw, 1990).

There is a big difference between the controlling beliefs that are basis of the poisonous pedagogy and the structuring, nurturing beliefs listed above.

Controlling Beliefs
Thou Shalt Not Feel

Nurturing Beliefs
Feelings Are Valued

As a teacher or parent, you have the wonderful opportunity to examine where you stand in relationship to these two approaches. Has your upbringing and training placed you in the poisonous pedagogy camp? Are you working to place yourself in a nurturing environment? What do you believe? For some of us, we once believed in the poisonous pedagogy as the correct way to manage and control children. Now, with new information and understanding many teachers and parents are rethinking those traditions. The following exercise asks you to reflect upon your own beliefs. Your answers will help you discover where you are and, knowing that, will help you decide where you want to go.

Examining Your Beliefs

Exercise: In the activity that follows ask yourself two questions: Is this a statement I grew up believing? and Is this a statement I presently believe? Rank your answers from 0 to 10 with 10 being a strong yes.

Here's an example:

The statement is: **Children should be seen and not heard.** Since I was exposed to this belief a great deal while growing up, I will rate this a 10 under <u>Grew Up Believing</u>. However, I no longer believe this statement to be valid, so I rate this as a 3 under <u>Present Belief</u>. (Note: I gave myself a 3 even though I no longer believe the statement to be valid, yet during times of stress I find myself reverting back to old patterns.)

	<u>Grew Up Believing</u>	<u>Present Belief</u>
Children should be seen and not heard.	<u>10</u>	<u>3</u>

	Grew Up Believing	Present Belief

1. **A feeling of duty produces love.**
   "Well, young man, you just need
   to learn your place in life. Do
   what is expected of you and all
   will be well."   _____   _____

2. **Hatred in children can be
   abolished by the adult
   forbidding it.**
   "Name calling and hitting is
   not allowed in my classroom!
   Stop this minute!"   _____   _____

3. **Parents and teachers deserve
   respect because they are parents
   and teachers.**
   "These children are going to have
   to learn respect."   _____   _____

4. **Children must earn respect by
   behaving correctly.**
   "Those who sit quietly will
   get a sticker. I like the way Kesha
   is sitting. She may line up first."   _____   _____

5. **Obedience makes a strong child.**   _____   _____
   "It is good for you to do what
   you're told."

6. **A high degree of self-esteem is
   harmful.**
   "You should be ashamed of your-
   self for bragging."   _____   _____

7. **A low degree of self-esteem makes
   a person altruistic and humble.**
   "Wouldn't want to get a big head
   now, would you?"   _____   _____

	Grew Up Believing	Present Belief

8. **Tenderness (doting on the child) is harmful.**
   "You are going to spoil every last one of your children in that classroom!"

9. **Responding to a child's needs is wrong and will spoil the child.**
   "She just wants attention, ignore her!"

10. **Strong feelings are harmful. They interfere with thinking.**
    "My job is to teach them. Children need to leave their personal problems at home."

11. **Parents and teachers are always right.**
    "When you get older, you will see it my way."

12. **A pretense of gratitude is better than honest ingratitude.**
    "Tell her you are sorry."

13. **The body is something dirty and disgusting.**
    "No one wants to see someone with dirty hands."

14. **The way you behave is more important than the way you truly are.**
    "Everyone sit up straight and look busy; the principal is coming."

	Grew Up Believing	Present Belief
15. **Severity and coldness toward a child is good preparation for life.**	_____	_____

"She wants to be held and cuddled. That is not the way it is in first and second grade. That is not the way life is."

TOTALS

Grew Up Believing _____ Present Belief _____

Add your totals for each column and determine whether your scores are low (0-45), moderate (46-90), or high (91-150).

What Does All This Mean?

High totals on grew up believing and low totals on present. Either you have done a great deal of work becoming more aware of yourself and loving yourself or you are in constant conflict between your "shoulds" and "wants." You may be struggling to be the person you want to be so desperately that you constantly feel like you go one step forward and two steps back.

High totals on grew up believing and high totals on present. 1) You are getting pressure from your school or spouse to change; 2) the students are not responding to anything you are doing so you are desperate; or 3) you were coerced into buying this book and plan to stop reading it now.

High totals on grew up believing and moderate totals on present. You are just starting to question some practices and are looking for some concrete answers and direction.

Moderate totals on grew up believing and low totals on present. You feel successful and peaceful with some of your practices but are ready to be challenged and acquire new ideas.

Moderate totals on grew up believing and moderate totals on present. This is required reading for some class you are taking. You probably find it interesting and if time permits, you will continue to read onward.

Moderate totals on grew up believing and high totals on present. You are stressed beyond belief. You are willing to try anything to survive, including reading this book.

Low totals on grew up believing and low totals on present. You are constantly trying to learn and grow, and this is just one of the many books you selected to continue your personal journey.

Probably no modern parent or teacher holds all the above poisonous pedagogy beliefs to be true. Some may have carefully developed belief systems that incorporate most, if not all of the structured nurturing values. Still others may want to turn their backs on the poisonous beliefs and feel frustrated that they can't erase all traces of the poison. Maybe you're coming to grips with your beliefs. No matter where you are on the continuum, we all have a lot to learn!

The Fantasy Bond

Many of us who work with young children know that when children do not meet our expectations, they think they are bad. The classic example is when a family breaks up through divorce. Many times the children believe they caused this to happen. If adults are abusive, the children believe they caused the abuse— deserving pain for being bad. Children blame themselves for almost everything that happens to them. Young children view their parents and teachers as invulnerable. To think otherwise would create unbearable anxiety for the child, since they are totally de-pendent upon these adults for survival.

Robert Firestone (1985), a psychologist, hypothesizes that children develop, as a defense mechanism, what is termed a fantasy bond. The fantasy bond is the illusion of connectedness we create with our major caregiver whenever our emotional needs are not adequately met. Since no mother, father or other caregiver is perfect, all humans develop this fantasy bond to some degree. The more emotionally deprived a person has been, the stronger the fantasy bond. Paradoxically, the more a person has been the victim of the poisonous pedagogy, the more that person tends to idealize the way he was raised and to accept, legitimize and defend the poisonous pedagogical rules and fear the nurturing ones. Teachers and parents with the most abusive histories may tend to set up their classroom or home environment based on the poisonous pedagogy. These same adults vehemently deny certain strategies are harmful to children and resist any or all suggestions for change. Common comments such as "If it was good enough for me, it is good enough for my children" represent this resistance. Check yourself to make sure that your picture of the past has not been distorted by the lens of the fantasy bond.

The Poisonous Pedagogy in Action

In the morning session of the School Readiness Academy Preschool, the four-year-old children sit silently at their desks as Mrs. Bernard demonstrates the proper way to raise one's hand in order to be called upon before answering a question. Several children are asked to demonstrate the skill for the remainder of the class. Mrs. Bernard then holds up an object in her hand and asks the class, "Who can tell me what this is?" Several children, in the excitement of recognizing the object, call out "Cupcake!" Mrs. Bernard gives them *the look* and says, "Now, now, what did we just talk about? Good boys and girls raise their hands to speak." Sherry, who has sat patiently through Mrs. Bernard's reprimand of the other children, has her hand high in the air. Mrs. Bernard looks slowly around the room and says, "Sherry, what do you think this is?" "A cupcake" says Sherry, sedately. "That's right! For being so polite and waiting for me to call on you, you may have the cupcake. Those of you who can't learn to follow the rules will do without."

Ouch! Mrs. Bernard is more concerned with her need to be in control than the children's need to be actively engaged with their environment. She seems to be unaware of the pain she has inflicted. Mrs. Bernard, the victim of years of training by the poisonous pedagogy herself, is also the carrier of its lethal poison. With such incidents, she is infecting the next generation with the poisonous pedagogy. And so, it goes on.

Summary

Children need boundaries and structure to make it in this world. Setting boundaries involves setting safe, consistent limits on children's behaviors. Structuring is basically planning, organizing and arranging surroundings and events in such a way that children have the greatest chance of being successful. In an effective environment the adult is responsible for providing the necessary boundaries and structure so children may try out new behaviors, safely explore their world, and learn the boundaries of what are acceptable and unacceptable ways of getting one's needs met.

The external structure provided for young children becomes internalized. The external structural building blocks provided by parents and teachers become the values, beliefs and skills children will possess and use. Developmentally appropriate structure provides children with nurturing rules that help to establish and maintain relationships with objects, people and events. Structure organizes the environment so that children are more likely to meet the expectations of the adult and meet their own needs at the same time. Structure always focuses on safety.

. . . .

Moving out of control and into structure requires the courage to let go of fear.

. . . .

Developmentally inappropriate structure, such as the poisonous pedagogy, provides children with a sense of control. Since controlling the world, the environment and others is impossible, the child will use external control rules to develop an internal belief system based on comparisons, competition, judgments and blame as she or he constantly strives to be good enough. Control always involves fear. It is fearfully doing whatever is necessary to meet the needs of the teacher, the principal and the parents. The poisonous pedagogy can easily be passed on from generation to generation, creating internal belief systems that cripple people and prevent them from leading full, productive lives.

I look back on my early years of teaching and realize most of my decisions were driven by my fear of what other teachers were saying or thinking about me. I had been exposed all my life to the poisonous pedagogy. This external structure system taught me fearfully to try and meet the expectations of others. I would come home from teaching school and constantly talk of what *they* were thinking of me. I would obsess about how my classroom looked because *they* might not like it. I would punish children, really for just being children, because of what *they* wanted. I was afraid they would find out what I was really doing in my room. I was out of control in my insane attempt to control.

Moving out of control and into structure requires the courage to let go of fear. This book is a journey from control into structure. I'm glad you've decided to join me. Let's get started!

Chapter 2

Don't make me have to send you to time out:
The Development of Power

Looking in the Mirror : What Do I Expect?

Mirror, mirror on the wall, who has the healthiest children of them all? Everyone wants what is best for children. No matter what methods are utilized, the goal is always the same—the best possible environment for children. What constitutes the best possible environment for children? What do teachers, parents and caregivers expect from children? If adults are to "structure classrooms" as opposed to "control children," it is imperative that adult expectations are very clear. Many times children are asked to meet the "unconscious expectations" of adults. For example, Ms. Capri wanted the best for the three-year-old children in her classroom. She wanted the parents and children to love her program. Whenever children refused to do what they were told, Ms. Capri was devastated. She felt hurt and rejected, as well as guilty for not being a better teacher. On some days when the children were especially rowdy, she *knew* she was a failure.

• •

Structure environments instead of trying to control children.

• •

Ms. Capri is unaware that she is expecting the three-year-old children to meet her self-esteem needs as a teacher. She is expecting the children to provide *her* with approval, support and encouragement. She is unconsciously using the children to get her needs met as opposed to truly being able to meet the needs of the children. When teachers unconsciously use children to get their own needs met, they must control the children to ensure at least some of those adult needs will be met.

To move from control to structure we must first "realize" (make real or stop denying) what it is we expect from ourselves and others. In order to do this, it is imperative we get in touch with our own internal structure system from which we operate. Our internal structure guides our expectations of others. This guidance will be conscious or unconscious depending on our willingness to look within. Once we become aware of our internal structure, then we can make our expectations clear to the children in our care.

The Building Blocks of Internal Structure: I and We

Our internal structure system was built from childhood with the external building materials offered by the family and culture in which we were raised. The core of our internal structure was actually developed during the first three years of our life. Each of us was born with two innate needs. One was to be a unique individual. This drive can be called a desire to become an "I". The other innate need was the drive to be a person who belongs and feels connected to others. This drive can be called a desire to become a "We".

Meeting these simultaneous needs to be an "I" and a "We" is a lifelong journey. Meeting these needs in the relationships we form has been called the human dilemma. The human dilemma basically asks how we develop a connected "We" without losing our sense of self (I) and how we develop a sense of self (I) without feeling disconnected and separate. This human dilemma of how to be close without losing our individuality and to be unique without feeling alone is a constant balancing act many adults continually play. The following is a situation that demonstrates this dilemma.

Ms. J, as the children call her, ends the majority of her teaching days in a prekindergarten class frustrated with her aide. She finds herself leaving school in conflict. Her thoughts go something like this : "It's my aide, she just does things different then I would. I don't want to sound mean or anything. She *is* a nice woman, don't get me wrong. Well, it's just—I don't know. Well, I do know, but what can I do? She is friends with the principal. She has been at this school for twenty years. She knows everyone. This is my second year and I just don't fit in. Yet I can't let her treat the kids poorly, can I? We just differ. It is okay to be different, isn't it? But it is not okay to make those children sit in the bathroom alone until they stop crying. I think that is abuse! I hate it at work. I feel so isolated."

Her husband, who once again sat patiently through Ms. J's tirade, responds, "It has been eight months, I am really tired of hearing about this same old problem! Why don't you talk to the woman and work things out or change jobs?"

Ms. J wants to be more connected to the school. She is feeling out of control in her relationship with her aide. She has created a great deal of fear surrounding her relationship with her aide. She does not feel connected enough (We) to have a conversation and share her feelings and thoughts At the same time, she does not feel strong enough in her own beliefs (I) to stand up for them. The conflict repeats itself daily as Ms. J hopes for another aide next year. Little does Ms. J realize that the problem is not with the aide or the job, but within herself.

How do we meet these dual needs of being a unique "I" and a connected "We"? We meet these needs with Personal Power. Personal Power is defined as the ability to cause an effect on the environment in order to get one's needs met. Ms. J, in the above situation, is missing Personal Power. She is unable to meet her own needs. How well then is she able to meet the needs of the children in her class? She will more likely expect the children to meet her needs. What could have happened in Ms. J's life to leave her unable to utilize Personal Power?

The Development of an Internal Structure

Infants are born with varying degrees of Personal Power, depending on genetics and temperament. Infants generally have a built-in system to call out to the world, to signal the world they have discomfort. As they utilize their Personal Power through crying, the world responds to their signals, their needs are met, and their Personal Power grows. The infants begin to develop a visceral sense that they can get their own needs met and that the world is a safe place. Trust is being formed.

Some infants signal to the world and the world does not respond. The baby cries and no adult is available to remove the child's discomfort. The child continues to cry, to scream, to cry, to scream, and to cry until someone attends. This child learns that the world is not a safe place, but a place you cannot trust. The child learns that in order to get one's needs met, she must act out in an attempt to control the behaviors of others. This is called Power Over instead of Personal Power. The child learns to exert force on others to get needs met. The child begins developing beliefs such as: If I can control other people I can be safe; if I can control what happens in my life I can get needs met; if I can be the boss I can force the world to respond to me. This child develops a big egocentric " I" and gives up being a "We". A Power Over internal structure core is being formed.

On the other hand, some infants signal the world by crying, fussing and screaming. When no one responds, the child ultimately just gives up. This child learns that the world is not a safe place, that it cannot be trusted. Yet the child still must get needs met to survive. The child over time learns that Power Under others is necessary to get needs met. The child begins developing beliefs such as: If I take on the needs of other people as my own then I can get my needs met; if I want what they want, I can cause the world to respond to me; if I submit my will to others, if I become passive and compliant, I can be safe. The child becomes the perfect child as he constantly strives to please everyone. This child develops a big "We" and gives up being a unique "I". A Power Under internal structure core is being formed.

Personal Power	Power Over	Power Under
Safe World	Fearful World	Fearful World
Able to Interact	Need to Control	Need to Please Others
Strong Sense of Identity	Sense of Self Depends on Power	Sense of Self Depends on Others
I ___ WE ▲	WE ◢◣ I	I ◢◣ WE

People who possess Personal Power believe deep down inside they can get their needs met. Power Over people believe that in order to get their needs met, they must be in control of others and the situations. Power Under people believe that in order to get their needs met, they must totally and constantly please others.

Remember Ms. Capri and Ms. J at the beginning of the chapter? What building blocks do you think they received? Ms. Capri is definitely building her life on a big connected "We". She can only feel safe and confident when everyone is happy and pleased with her. She is threatened by the children's and parents' individuality. Each expression of uniqueness is viewed by Ms. Capri as a rejection of her. Ms. Capri is operating from a Power Under internal structure. Day after day, she becomes a victim to everyone else's individuality. Ms. J is not that cut and dried. She vacillates. She has developed a little individuality but not enough to balance her ever-present need to be connected and approved of by others. Her struggle within herself and with the aide continues.

The Bully and the Victims

People who grew up with Power Over belief systems are generally called bullies, while people who grew up with Power Under belief systems are called victims. Bullies seek out victims and victims seek out bullies in order for both parties to get their needs met. This can be seen in marriages, in friendships, between siblings and in classrooms.

A car full of Power Under people might have a difficult time deciding where to go for lunch. Each person would respond to the question, "What would you like to eat?" with similar answers: "I don't care. Whatever you want is fine with me" or "It really doesn't matter to me; it's up to you." A person with a Power Over belief system might not even consider the wishes of anyone else in the car and take everyone to a steak house. If a Power Over person did ask for input about where to go for the meal, he might put down the suggestions of others or try to persuade the others a good steak is just what they need.

In the classroom, the bullies (Power Over) find the victims (Power Under) and become "best friends" in a dependent love/hate relationship. The victim cries to the teacher, the teacher separates the victim from the bully, and at the first possible chance the victim is right back attempting to play with the bully. They believe they need each other to get their needs met. Battered spouse syndrome is the extreme case of this type of dysfunctional bonding.

Looking at Everyday Situations

The following four first grade teachers demonstrate a Power Over internal structure system. Mrs. Smith has a stiff body and doesn't show much emotion. She attends discipline and guidance workshops reluctantly and has trouble validating the feelings of children. She believes children should be seen and not heard. Children should obey the rules and do it pleasantly. Any sign of emotion produces even harsher punishments in her classroom. Mr. Bantam holds a tight jaw and is overly judgmental of others. Ms. Carline has set beliefs and ridicules other points of view. Ms. Kayley constantly complains about the kindergarten teachers who refuse to "teach the children properly." Grade level meetings are disastrous and decisions are usually made to appease Ms. Carline. Can you recall any teachers you know who you believe hold Power Over beliefs? Power Over internal structure utilizes the poisonous pedagogy in its expectations and beliefs about children.

The Dreaded Weekly First Grade Team Meeting

The next group of teachers have developed a **Power Under internal structure.** Mrs. Kendra is a second-grade team leader. She expects the rest of the team to do all the work, using the excuse, "My efforts might not be what they want." Mr. Cain, who has never missed a day of work, is constantly confused about the new programs the principal wants to implement. He wants to do it "right" but feels anxious trying to mind read what is expected. The preschool teachers complain that Ms. Howstader hogs all the materials. They feel there is nothing that can be done to stop her and reason, "Why rock the boat?" Mrs. Waters is unable to make decisions and think for herself. When Mrs. Waters was asked what she felt about the new nongraded report cards, she responded, "I am sure it is wonderful or it would have not been implemented." She gave the same answer two years ago about corporal punishment. Power Under internal structure, like the Power Over internal structure, utilizes the poisonous pedagogy as acceptable beliefs from which to operate. The only difference is that with Power Under the poison is aimed within one's self and with Power Over the poison is projected onto others.

Then there is a group of teachers at the school that has developed a Personal Power internal structure. Ms. Davis is the creative spark on the kindergarten team. She feels confident in her curriculum and feels comfortable sharing new ideas at group meetings—and they are met with interest and respect. Mr. Frazier has developed a layout for the weekly newsletter and is asking for suggestions and input. He has put the layout on computer disks so everyone can access it easily. Mrs. Johnston brings new ideas to the group. She is firm in her beliefs but will negotiate on things when a different strong case is presented. The team works well together, is flexible, is confident in their skills, and is open to new ideas. These teachers utilize more beliefs in the nurturing and structuring paradigm than those in the poisonous pedagogy.

Where do you fall? It is not always easy to know. The rule of thumb is that we parent as we were parented, discipline as we were disciplined, and teach as we were taught, unless we consciously do something to change. Since your life involves young children, it becomes imperative to get in touch with the internal structure in which you were raised. Here are a couple of exercises that will help give you some insight.

Uncovering Hidden Beliefs

Exercise: After reading the following scenario, write down how you would handle the situation. To obtain the most insights, include the exact dialogue you would use.

You are presently a preschool teacher or parent supervising 20 four-year-old children on the playground. Suddenly two children are fighting at the water fountain over who was first. What do you do? _____

_____

_____

_____

Your response to this situation can give you insights into your beliefs about children and ultimately your beliefs about yourself. If you use your position of authority to exercise control over the situation, you value domination and being dominated and probably were disciplined in the Power Over control model of discipline. You see your job is to teach the children right from wrong. For example, you might have approached the children and said, "Stop that right this minute! Fighting is not allowed at this school. You both go over and sit out from playing until you learn to get water without hurting each other. I don't care who was first. Now go sit by the tree."

If you approached the situation with, "You two know the rules. It is not nice to fight with your friends. I am sure you can find a way to solve the problem." You value a more permissive Power Under style. You may rationalize your use of the Power Under approach by saying they need to learn how to solve their own conflicts.

If you facilitated the children in solving *their* problem at the water fountain by saying, "Stop! Hold up! I see you have a problem. The problem is that you both want to get a drink at the same time. What could you do to solve your problem?" then you value Personal Power. You believe that children can think, negotiate, and initiate their own learning in a consistent understanding environment, provided you structure the situation and ask the children to be responsible.

Looking Within

Exercise: Think of an authority figure in your life, such as your father or boss. Now say , "When it comes to dealing with _____ ," and finish the sentence by circling a statement from each column below. For example:

1. I know what he
    needs & wants

    (I know what I need
    & what I want)

    I don't know what
    I need & want

Column 1	Column 2	Column 3
1. I know what he needs & wants	I know what I need & what I want	I don't know what I need & want
2. I trust nobody but myself	I trust in myself explicitly	I trust the other person
3. I don't care about my impact on him	I understand I have an impact on him	I rarely have an impact on him
4. I would never allow him to infringe on my rights	I am aware when he infringes on my rights	I do not know when he infringes on my rights
5. I order him to do just what I want	I initiate behaviors to get things done	I allow things to happen to me
6. I never need help	I have the ability to ask for help when I need it	I expect him to help me without my asking
7. I never make mistakes	I accept my mistakes and learn from them	I put myself down when I make a mistake
8. I usually know all the answers	I know how to problem solve	I am confused

9. I blame him for the discomfort in my life	I accept responsibility for my own discomfort	I accept responsibility for his discomfort
10. I am critical of him	I am accepting of him	I am self-critical
11. I have the right & responsibility to choose for him	I recognize I have choices and I can make decisions	I have no choices a lot of the time
12. He must agree with me to resolve conflict	I have the right to my own beliefs and negotiate to solve problem	I agree with him to resolve conflict
13. I have an obligation to take care of him	I can take care of myself	I feel important when I take care of him
14. I exaggerate & boast about my achievements	I can recognize my achievements	I have few achievements worth recognizing
15. I share what I'm thinking or feeling when it suits my best interest	I have the ability to share my thoughts, beliefs & feelings	I am so afraid of rejection I don't share my thoughts, feelings or beliefs

Column 1 Total _____   Column 2 Total _____   Column 3 Total _____

Results: Column 1 is Power Over, column 2 is Personal Power, and column 3 is Power Under. Repeat the exercise using different authority figures. Are the results the same? Different?

What Does All This Mean?

Let's review these examples in light of expectations. What does the Power Over adult expect? She probably expects there should be no conflict. Conflict is disruptive, and if children would just do what they are told and follow the rules, all would be well.

What does the Power Under adult expect? Children should magically know how to solve their problems. They should be able to work it out "nicely" so no one is hurt and everyone returns to a happy state. Conflict from a Power

Under or Power Over perspective means somebody wins and somebody loses. Conflict is therefore determined to be bad and to be avoided or punished.

What does the Personal Power individual expect? Children will function within the structure provided. Children are to be responsible and utilize the information and framework offered to assist them in solving their problem. Conflict in the Personal Power belief system is necessary and natural. It represents growing individuality and a win-win situation.

Summary

The core of your internal structure system consists of feeling safe or not safe. If your core is based on Power Over or Power Under structures, your foundation is built on fear. Down deep in your heart you believe your social interactions to be unsafe and scary. The more intimate the interaction, the more unsafe you become. If your core is based on Personal Power, your foundation is built on love or trust. You believe that you are safe and the world is a safe place from which to grow.

Most of us were raised with a combination of Power Over or Power Under methods. Our parents were told, "Do not pick up that baby because you will spoil it." We still carry around the notion that if we meet the needs of children, they will be weak, dependent or in some way "spoiled." To many of us, the thought of the world being a safe place is bizarre. A typical response might be, "Don't you read the paper or watch TV?"

Many of us developed a large "We" and seek to please others to create safety in the world. Others of us developed a large " I" and seek to create safety by attacking first and being right no matter what. Some of us vacillate between the two. And yes, some of us are finding the balance between the two and learning Personal Power.

Our internal structure core then is projected out onto the world and becomes our expectations of others, the set of principles and values we use when working with children. In reality, whatever beliefs you hold true for children (consciously or unconsciously), you hold to be true about yourself. To move from control to structure we must consciously be aware of what expectations of ours we want the children to meet *and* what needs the children have.

An internal structure core creates the belief system or philosophy from which we make external choices. Our external choices become the boundaries and structure system that creates the internal system of the next generation. Our core either consists of a fear base (Power Over or Power Under) or a love base (Personal Power). If we truly want to pass love onto the next generation, then we must become aware of our internal structure and how that structure forms a scaffold for a philosophy that guides our every step.

• •

Whatever you believe about children, you believe about yourself.

• •

Chapter 3

These children are driving me crazy:
**The Development of a Philosophy of
Guiding Young Children**

Too Strict: Punitive Guidance System
Too Lenient: Permissive Guidance System
Just Right: Responsibility Guidance System

Philosophies

I remember the first time I heard a mother say, "My child is to defend himself. If anyone hits him, I teach him to hit back. My boy is not going to be a sissy." Malcolm's mother gave me the scare of my life. I thought she was going to hit *me*. I tried to convince her she was wrong and I was right. She reported me to the principal and even though he backed me, I went home crying. I just didn't know if I was cut out to be a teacher at all. These were all the skills I had: defend ... attack ... cry!

It took me years to realize fully the importance of having a philosophy. The word had no concrete meaning for me. It didn't become clear until that day Malcolm's mom showed up in my classroom ready to knock *me* senseless for not letting her boy hit.

There are three basic philosophies in guiding the behavior of young children: If you have a Power Over internal structure core, you probably believe in a **punitive guidance system;** if you have a Power Under structural core, you probably believe in a **permissive guidance system;** and if you have developed a more Personal Power internal structure, you might believe in a more democratic approach, or a **responsibility guidance system.**

Each guidance system represents a different set of beliefs and translates a different view of the world to children. Each reflects the values transmitted from the teacher or parent about boundaries or limits, and the ability to get one's needs met. Each of the three philosophies of guidance transmits and perpetuates its own distinct culture as it disciplines children. Each type of structure affects the way in which children form an image of themselves.

It all came together the day Malcom's mother showed up in my classroom. I realized I must become better informed about how people develop their beliefs about their world and themselves. I must understand how these beliefs guide the day-to-day transactions between adults and children. I was convinced this type of understanding would help me interact more effectively with Malcolm's mom. The following is what I learned over the years. These philosophies grow out of the Power Over, Power Under and Personal Power internal structure cores discussed in Chapter 2.

The Punitive Guidance System
(Power Over Internal Structure)

The goal of the punitive system is unquestioning obedience to those having authority. Punishment is sanctioned and relied upon. Inflicting pain is believed to be effective, fair and necessary. Disobedience must be stamped out for order to prevail. Might makes right. Right is defined by the person with the authority. Those in control are not held accountable; adults are allowed to lose control, children are not. For example, the child makes *you* spank or suspend him or her. Wrongdoers must be punished, and justice is satisfied only when punishment has occurred. Another example, is that many people advocate that child abusers should be beaten. The sad fact is the abuser was beaten as a child and is now the abuser.

Society becomes defined as having two unequal classes: those in power who have privileges (referred to by adults as the rich, by teenagers as the in-group and by children as the good guys) and those who are subservient and may be exploited (referred to by adults as the poor or lazy, by teenagers as the out-group and by children as the bad guys). Many of us were raised in this two-level system. In youth I thought, "Just wait until I become an adult." In essence I was waiting to get into the privileged group with power because I was feeling subservient or powerless. Just think how many potential problems are set up in the lives of children when we model this powerful/powerless paradigm. Powerless children may grow up to join powerful groups. We call these gangs.

The punitive guidance system encourages the development of people whose primary purpose is to avoid punishment and guilt. Lying, evasion, withdrawal, repression of feelings, displacement of rage, blaming others, or submission to aggressors are all acceptable and necessary since they enable a person to avoid punishment.

You know better. What are you - stupid?

How we dominate children . . .

teaches them how to . . .

Now look what you made me do.

dominate others.

The punitive guidance system requires and demands external control for stability. These external controls can be through fear, such as humiliation, embarrassment or shame, or through rewards such as special foods, treats, stickers or extra hours of video games.

Without the constant monitoring of the external controls by adults, children can become recklessly out of bounds. Or with the constant monitoring of adults through external controls, children can become fearful they will lose the love of the very significant adult they adore.

The punitive guidance system encourages the development of people who use other people for personal gain and pleasure, and/or people who compulsively seek praise and approval from others (Snyder, 1982).

In addition to obedience, the goal of many punitive authoritarian adults is to ensure that children will fit into society. The children are actually being groomed to fit into their place in a sexist, classist, racist, homophobic society that neglects and excludes many of its gifted and disabled members. Ms. Tucker is a good example: Ms. Marty Tucker, a single parent, is looking for a kindergarten classroom she believes will offer her son the most advantages in our world. She wants him to learn to respect authority the good old-fashioned way. She is looking for a school that truly teaches the children something: reading, writing and arithmetic. She wants academics, none of this play-based curriculum she's heard so much about. But most of all she wants her son to be ready for first grade.

Ms. Tucker, like many parents, values obedience-oriented academic programs. These programs reflect more of her own value system. She wants a program for her son so that he will fit into the next grade, then into second grade, and ultimately fit into society.

Here's another example: Ms. Fisher has her room organized for the children to enter. She has spent the better part of her weekend cutting patterns for the valentine art project. She wants the children to have a product the parents will appreciate. When the bell rings, each child is to file into the room and go directly to his or her assigned seat. She then will call each child by name to walk quietly to the cubby area and put lunches and back packs away. Children who wait patiently until their names are called receive star stickers on their behavior chart. Children with ten stars on Friday will get popcorn at the class party.

The Messages We Send

Once all items are stored properly, the good-morning song is sung, the pledge is recited, and the children report to the circle on the rug for calendar. Ms. Fisher spends time telling the children about the classroom rules, the consequences of those rules, and firmly expresses her expectations that ignorance is no excuse. She does not allow nor tolerate forgetting. She feels confident and proud her children will be ready for first grade.

Ms. Fisher values following the rules and fitting in. She values obedience above independence and conformity over creativity. She is comfortable with the children depending on her decisions, her answers and her commands. Her classroom reflects the family system in which she was raised and therefore feels more comfortable to her. Countless numbers of workshops are given at her school to assist teachers in making their rooms more developmentally appropriate. However, Ms. Fisher discounts these efforts as just another educational fad. She knows what is best for children.

Punitive Guidance System

Goal:	obedience; conform to society as it currently exists
Strategies:	rewards and punishments
Justice:	set of rules to be obeyed; justice is served with revenge
Society:	two unequal classes— powerful/powerless
Feelings:	guilt and shame
Morality:	based on fear

The Permissive Guidance System
(Power Under Internal Structure)

The child permissive culture consists of adults who attempt to remove all children's discomforts. The adults are overprotective and give children what they want, when they want it. The children are usually not forced to do anything against their will. The adults utilizing a child permissive culture are usually overly identified with their children and unconsciously believe if they can prevent their children from experiencing pain, their own internal pain will dissipate. An example would be a parent who is sitting on a sofa and the child tells the parent to get up because he or she wants to sit in that spot and the parent moves to accommodate the child's command. The child learns that his or her needs are more important than the needs of others.

The child permissive culture allows children to terrorize, exploit, deprive, or abuse weaker siblings, other children and often adults. Dependency, passivity, and selfishness are sanctioned. Parental guilt and self-denial are encouraged. Children come to understand justice as getting one's way and anything that works is permissible. Rules are seen by the child as applying to others but not to him or her. Society and parents are believed to owe children total care and comfort. Society becomes defined as being composed of two classes, the privileged children and their adult caregiving servants.

Structure (schedules, behavioral standards, rules, expectations regarding self-discipline and development toward behavioral maturity) and challenges (intellectual, social, emotional, physical) are seen as a threat to children's individuality and independence (NAEYC, 1992). Good, in the permissive culture, is not defined. The goal is not obedience nor is it independently ethical behavior. There is no goal or role for adults in regard to providing the guidance and structure for children. The following example is typical of the child permissive guidance system.

Mr. and Mrs. Connoly are searching for just the right preschool for their child. They want a place where their little flower, Katie, will be allowed to bloom. They want a stress-free environment where the children make most of the choices and are free to explore and interact with each other as they desire. They are looking for a laissez-faire, just-let-them-play program. They want loving, kind adults who will perform the normal housekeeping chores involved with the care of young children and who will be available in case the child should run into any conflict or frustration.

Mr. and Mrs. Connoly are part of the child permissive culture and are looking for a program that matches their view of children and their view of themselves. Unfortunately, such total play programs generally teach children in socially unguided and intellectually unchallenging environments.

Ironically, Mr. and Mrs. Connoly both grew up in a punitive Power-Over family system. When they married and had children, they both agreed, "We don't want to discipline our children the way we were treated." So instead of using a punitive system, they utilized a permissive guidance system. Little did they know the outcomes were the same. Both systems rely on a powerful privileged group and a powerless submissive group. The only difference is that in a punitive system the adult is in control and in the permissive system the child is in control.

Punitive

Permissive

The Responsibility Guidance System
(Personal Power Internal Structure)

The goal of discipline and structure in this guidance system is to develop fully functioning, caring, creative, and responsible people. The individual is believed to have basic worth. Adults understand that some rules are negotiable and some rules are nonnegotiable. Nonnegotiable rules deal with safety issues including physical, mental and emotional safety. Negotiable rules are determined through group input. The rights of individuals to have a say in their own governing process is a strongly held principle. There is equality of law, thereby creating only one class within society. The structure and intention of justice is an environment that is *safe, fair, and caring.* All people have the right to physical and emotional safety. This system uses fair consequences that correct injustice and restore the wrongdoer to healthy functioning. The primary goal of justice is to assist people in successfully functioning within the group. Democratic skills are taught and encouraged: listening to one another; trying to understand other perspectives; having empathy; recognizing and defining problems; looking at alternatives to solve problems; selecting solutions by majority rule; acting peacefully on the selected solutions to resolve the problem.

Mr. Juarez, a single parent, is searching for a developmentally appropriate kindergarten for his daughter. He wants her to be stimulated, challenged to be a risk taker and motivated to allow her creative self to grow. He wants a well-organized and structured day so that his daughter will have predictability. Above all, he wants his daughter to learn self-discipline and responsibility. He values play, active learning, and divergent challenging tasks that meet the individual needs of his daughter.

Mr. Juarez, a third generation Hispanic American, is searching for a classroom that values the democratic principles on which he was raised. His mother understood that for her son to have an equal chance to succeed in the United States she must model how to have freedom and responsibility at the same time. She knew that teaching him responsibility through allowing choices, listening to his concerns, and holding him responsible for his behavior would be the best approach. Mr. Juarez, growing up in this type of environment, now searches for a classroom that mirrors his values.

Responsibility Guidance System

Goal: creative, caring, responsible
people

Strategies: problem solving; consequences

Justice: fully fuctioning, connected
people

Society: one class based on equality

Feelings: love, acceptance

Morality: connectedness

Ms. Thomas starts the school year by reading a book called *Little Monster Goes To School* . In the book Little Monster sticks his arm out of the bus window, trips other children and even gets into other kid's lunches. Ms. Thomas' second-grade class is horrified by such behavior. The story provides a good start for a discussion about rules, why they are important and why they are needed. Ms. Thomas assists the children in combining their ideas into a few main points. She also helps them phrase their suggested rules in positive terms as opposed to negative terms. *Don't run in the classroom or halls* becomes *Walk inside the building.* Ms. Thomas writes down the rules for the class as they emerge from the brainstorming session. The children then decorate the bulletin board with monster picture rules as visual reminders.

Ms. Thomas values responsibility over obedience. She realizes that if she is to have a voice in the classroom (i.e., children listen to her), she needs to provide a structure that allows the children a voice also.

Making Internal Structure Come Alive

Watch children interacting on the playground to see the type of internal structure they are developing. Some children raised in a punitive guidance system will only be content as long as they are in control. Other children must do what they say, when they say it, or they will be punished (i.e., left out of the group, called names, or hurt physically). The children are developing a Power Over internal structure core. Some children will gladly do what others say, whether it is wise or not, to get the approval of the in-group. Some children may want things their way and when it doesn't go their way, they result to manipulation, whining and telling the teacher.

Being raised in a permissive environment, the children believe the teacher's role is to remove all of their discomfort. The children are developing a Power Under internal structure core. Still other children can play successfully with a wide range of children, resolve conflicts, and remove themselves and others from dangerous situations and choices. Personal Power is the core of these children.

The children are showing us not only the internal structure they are developing but the external structure they are receiving from the significant adults in their lives. If the children grow up to be teachers, they are also showing us what type of classroom they will create for their future students. Therefore, the structure we provide children will ultimately shape the lens by which they see the world.

• •

The structure we provide children will ultimately shape the lens by which they see the world.

• •

Remember Malcolm? His mom told me he should hit others, defend himself and not act like a sissy. That day both of us lost control, but two years later I had another opportunity.

This time I had understanding instead of judgment on my side when Mrs. Peters stormed into my room. She announced that if anyone touched her boy, he was to hit back and hit hard. A sense of terror fell over the entire classroom. Every child became quiet and motionless. I announced to the class that Mrs. Peters had come to talk about keeping the classroom safe. The children were instructed to continue playing. I then addressed Mrs. Peters.

"Mrs. Peters, it is good to see you, I hear major concerns in your voice. Come have a seat so we can talk, and I can keep an eye on the children at the same time."

She barreled right into why she had shown up. "Jerome came home and said you would not allow him to defend himself and that Steven was beating up on him and you did nothing. I teach my boy to defend himself and stand up for his rights. I won't have you messing with his mind. The other day I told him to shut his mouth and he said, "I don't like it when you talk to me like that' I told him not to talk back and slapped his face. He said you told him to say that. What's going on at this school?"

"Mrs. Peters, you sound really upset with me and have every right to be. I had no idea Steven was picking on Jerome. I am so glad you came in and brought this to my attention. I agree with you that school must be a safe place and that my job is to keep it safe."

"Well then, don't be telling my boy not to hit. His father and I work hard to get the boy to stand up for himself."

"I understand we all need to learn how to stand up for ourselves, but what I tell the children is - - it's not safe to hit in school. In school when you hit, you get in trouble. It does not solve a problem, but it makes a new one for you. What I would like to do is work together so Jerome has two sets of skills— hitting, if necessary, and problem solving. If we work together, we can give Jerome a bunch of skills to use in a variety of situations. I'm sure your husband would agree hitting sometimes can really cook your goose."

"That's the truth! Luckily that man can talk himself out of anything," she said. "Now, what about that ' I don't like it' stuff?"

"Until Jerome can get as smooth talking as your husband, I needed to give him some words to use instead of hitting. Words like,' I don't like it when you hit me. It hurts.' I guess Jerome, being such an eager learner, tried it out on you. You guys must be pretty close."

"Oh yeah! He's my firstborn. Now that I know what is going on here, maybe I could help him with his ' I don't like it' words."

"That would be helpful. We still need to help the children learn when is the right time to use words and when is the right time to use physical action. Can you stay with us and have lunch? I could use your help with an activity we are going to do this afternoon."

Mrs. Peters not only stayed that Friday, but she came back every Friday until her next child was born. In fact, we set up a hospital and maternity ward center in honor of the upcoming birth. I still remember that last Friday before Mrs. Peters gave birth; Alicia tried to put a doll up Mrs. Peters dress so she could play doctor. Mrs. Peters said, "Alicia, I don't like you sticking things up my dress. You can put the baby on top of my stomach and pretend!" Mrs. Peters had learned when it was a more effective time to use words, too. Her philosophy had begun to change.

Summary

Mrs. Peters and Malcolm's mom both taught me that one philosophy is not better than another. The punitive, permissive and responsibility guidance systems each present a different philosophy and worldview. Each guidance system was learned within a family and cultural context. Mrs. Peters learned from watching her mother and father interact with their world. Her child Jerome was internalizing the system from Mr. and Mrs. Peters. Malcolm was learning from his family and cultural system. I also learned that philosophy and guidance systems change. After modeling for Mrs. Peters, instead of judging her, we both grew.

Our view of our own power becomes projected outward in behaviors associated with three guidance systems.
Personal Power becomes a philosophy of responsibility.
Power Over is manifested in a punitive system and Power
Under allows a permissive guidance system. Each system
has an impact on children and their esteem of themselves
and their world. Each system has and will continue to shape
our society.

Personal Power
Responsibility

Power Under
Permissive

Power Over
Punitive

Chapter 4

**Sometimes I think I'm not cut out for this:
Self-esteem and Its Reflection of Your Philosophy**

Healthy and Unhealthy Self-esteem

One of the most profound discoveries of recent decades is the awareness that how we treat young children affects how they behave as adults. This may sound like common sense to you; however, many people still believe they can treat children any way they want without any ramifications for the children or society. I love the saying, " If you treated your friends like you treat your children, how many friends would you have?"

How we discipline children and structure our classrooms and homes creates the internal structure system of the next generation. If the internal structure core is based on safety or Personal Power and the child's behavior has been guided by responsible adults, healthy self-esteem will be evident. If the internal structure system is based on Power Over or Power Under and the child's behavior has been guided by punitive or permissive adults, self-esteem will be unhealthy. Discipline and self-esteem are two sides of the same coin; each affects the other. Children who are disciplined poorly develop unhealthy self-esteem. Children with unhealthy self-esteem act out and become discipline problems.

Many people refer to self-esteem as either being high or low. I prefer the concept of healthy or unhealthy self-esteem. This awareness of mine was sparked from my interactions with Angel, a leader of a tough urban gang. Angel had been abused as a youngster and expelled repeatedly from school. He had found a belonging in his gang. When we spoke, it was clear that having members of his gang look up to him created a sense of esteem. Now, would you say Angel had a low or high self-esteem?

I could explain Angel only in terms of healthy and unhealthy self-esteem. Healthy self-esteem comes from within. It is an inner knowing of worth; regardless of what others may think or do, our basic worth remains stable to us.

Healthy self-esteem is supported by the way we think about ourselves and others. A general state of peace is present, with harmonious thoughts prevailing. Unhealthy self-esteem comes from without. It is dependent on the thoughts, feelings and actions of others.

When the outside world shines upon us, we feel special, important, capable and loved. When the focus shifts to someone else, we may feel lonely, rejected and not good enough. H. Stephen Glen (1989) in his work, *Developing Capable People*, equates self-esteem to a hot-air balloon. If unhealthy esteem is a hot-air balloon without a fuel source, we would constantly be looking to get "filled up" by others. Once the balloon was full, we would sail a bit but ultimately deflate, leaving us desperately seeking ways to get pumped up again.

In a hot-air balloon of healthy self-esteem, we have our own fuel source in the gondola. When we need a boost, we pull our own cord and maintain the balloon's altitude.

So it is with the guidance system we use with our children: we either send messages that develop healthy or unhealthy self-esteem.

Discipline Means to Teach

Discipline is much more than just telling children to shut up and sit down. Discipline, which means to teach, comes from the word disciple. Discipline comes into play when a conflict of needs arise. This conflict can be between parents and children,, such as when a parent has a need for her child to go to bed and the child has a need to stay up. Conflict of needs can be between teachers and children. The teacher has a need for the children to listen while the children might have a need to share some life experience with the class. The conflict of needs could easily be between two or more children. A child may have a need to be first in line while another child may have the same need. Discipline is how we teach a resolution to the conflict of needs.

Since many adults have Power Over or Power Under internal structures and punitive or permissive guidance systems, they would use a form of force and fear to demand children give up their needs for the needs of the adult. For example, when children talk while a teacher is reading out loud, the children would be threatened to stop their need to talk so the adult's need to talk could be met. In the case where the two children are fighting over who will be first, the punitive system might send them both to the principal's office, having them give up their need to be first in favor of the teacher's need for peace and quiet.

In the Power Over punitive guidance system of discipline, what is viewed as successful is that which works. "Works" means that the child gave up his or her needs willingly, allowing the all- important adult needs to prevail. For the Power Over system to work there must be people willing to be Power Under victims. If the children willingly give up their needs, we call the children good or we say the technique worked. Children who persist in demanding that their needs have equal value as those of adults are labeled as discipline problems.

Punitive Guidance System and Self-esteem

The side effects of the Power Over punitive guidance system are the underlying messages being sent to the children. The underlying messages are simply, "Your needs are not important and therefore, ultimately, you are not important." The children may hear the following messages as they develop their understanding of themselves: *You are not important. Don't think. Don't be. You will be abandoned if you make a mistake. Don't trust your own competence. Don't be who you are. Don't be successful. Don't be capable. You are not lovable. You are not supposed to have any needs. Be perfect.* Some common feelings by children to these underlying messages are: feeling oppressed, power-less, distanced, angry, rejected, hurt, humiliated, inadequate, unimportant, scared, mistrusted, hopeless, imperfect, discounted and just plain no-good.

From these messages and the concurrent feelings the children experience, the children will tend to make decisions regarding their own self-esteem and internal structure. Possible thoughts could be: *I am not wanted. My parents or teachers don't care about me. Rules are more important than my needs. I will let others think for me. I will comply, rebel, or withdraw. I will blame myself or others. I will try harder, I will be strong, I will be perfect. If I don't do things right, I am a bad person. I can't be good enough. It's hope-*

less. Why bother? (Clarke & Dawson, 1989).

The type of structure provided in the classroom or home has a profound effect upon children's development for a lifetime. Choosing a Power Over punitive-oriented system of discipline as a structural base is developmentally inappropriate. Negating the needs of children through the use of punishment or the bribery of rewards ultimately sends the same message: Your needs are not important—mine are.

Certainly in the Power Over punitive system, one person or group of people must be the powerful and one person or group of people must be the powerless. The hope, of course, is that the adults are the powerful ones. This is not always the case.

Bad Day

Good Day

Really Good Day

Mrs. Clark was determined to control the children. After all, it was her job. She had punishments for those who broke the rules and rewards for those who obeyed them. She was ready for everything, except Robert. Robert seemed unaffected by her punishments. She knew he had a hard life but felt it truly was no excuse. He would have to leave his emotional baggage from home outside the classroom. Mrs. Clark was continually trying to find some painful experience to get Robert to shape up. After all, it was plain that rewards were not working. He just didn't seem to care. Nothing was working. Mrs. Clark was using a Power Over punitive guidance system in working with Robert. As she lay awake at night obsessing about how to control Robert, little did she know her obsession meant Robert was controlling her. Robert had the Power Over and Mrs. Clark was the Power Under victim.

In classrooms in which teachers are utilizing a Power Over punitive guidance system, a good day is when the teacher is powerful and a bad day is when the power flips and the children become powerful. This roller coaster continues until a holiday provides the teacher with the much needed break!

• •

Discipline is how we teach a resolution to the conflict of needs.

• •

Permissive Guidance System and Self-esteem

Many adults unconsciously choose to use the permissive type of discipline in which the child is declared the powerful one and the adult is powerless. This occurs through overindulgent techniques or through neglect and abandonment. This type of system grants freedom without responsibility. It discounts the child's ability and gives the child permission to be irresponsible and to fail. It tells the child that the adult is not available (either physically or emotionally) to him or her. This message is delivered by the lack of rules or lack of supervision and, therefore, the lack of protection.

Utilizing a Power Under permissive form of discipline may send the following messages to children: *Don't be competent or responsible. Don't be who you are. Don't grow up. You can have your way and be obnoxious and get by with it. I need to continue taking care of you and giving you anything you want, therefore my needs (the adult) are more important than your needs. I am not willing to care for you. I don't want you. Your needs are not important; mine are. No one is here for you. You don't exist.*

With these messages being sent over and over on a daily basis, the child may feel patronized and may remain incompetent in order to please the parent. The child may feel undermined, crazy, manipulated, discounted, unloved, unsatisfied, and angry. Furthermore the child may feel rageful, scared, terrified, hurt, upset, like a nonbeing, perhaps suicidal or homicidal. From these feelings children may make the following conclusions regarding their own self-esteem or internal structure: *I must take care of other people's feelings and needs, or I don't need to care about anyone but me. I am not capable of learning how to value and take care of myself. If help is offered, mistrust it or at least expect to pay a price for it but don't expect helpful structure from others. Don't ask for or expect help. No one cares. If I am to survive, I will have to do it myself* (Clarke & Dawson, 1989). Here's an example with Ms. Thomas and her children.

Ms. Thomas loved children. She hated to see them angry or sad. She wanted her classroom to be a special place for her little children. If the children were having a really fun time with an activity, she would continue the activity as long as they wanted. If this put her off schedule, she would just change the schedule to accommodate the desires of the children. Every time a child would show signs of frustration, Ms. Thomas prided herself in knowing she was there to fix it. Sometimes the children would get wild, and Ms. Thomas would cry and explain to the children, "I work hard to make this a fun place for each and every one of you. I don't understand why you take advantage of this." Can you discern the underlying messages Ms. Thomas is sending to the children?

Responsibility Guidance System and Self-esteem

The Personal Power responsibility system of structure and discipline may send the following messages: *Your welfare and safety are important. The adults in your world are willing and able to be responsible and enforce the rules. You can think, negotiate and initiate. Your needs are important and other's needs are important. You must deal with how things really are. You are expected to be powerful in positive ways for yourself and others. You can act. You can keep yourself and others safe.* In response to these messages, a child may experience the following feelings: safe, cared for, powerful, supported, responsible, as well as frustrated, irritated, and resistant at times. A child learns to evaluate rules, participate in the making of rules and develop the skills needed to follow rules. A child feels respected, listened to, important, loved, capable and intelligent. From these feelings the children may make the following decisions about who they are and about the world around them: *There are some rules I have to follow. I can learn from my mistakes. I am a good person and nothing I do will change that. I am lovable and capable. Others care about me and will take care of me. It's okay for me to grow up and still be dependent at times. I can think things through and get help doing that. I continually expand my ability to be responsible and competent (*Clarke & Dawson, 1989*).* Here's a glimpse into just such a structure.

Mrs. Constantine, a first-grade teacher, ran her classroom around nonnegotiable and negotiable rules. Her nonnegotiable rules dealt with safety issues. Her negotiable rules dealt with school issues. One day during the weekly class meeting, the children put the bathroom rule on the agenda. The children wanted to discuss why going to the bathroom one at a time was so important. In essence, they were ready to negotiate a rule change that would allow one or two people to leave the room at a time. As the class meeting began, the children presented their concerns. They ranged from being scared of going alone, to being more fun having company. Mrs. Constantine pointed out her concern, which was using the bathroom as an excuse to leave the class. After considerable discussion the rule was changed on a trial basis, so that it allowed two children to go to the bathroom together. Criteria for evaluating the success of the change were set , and the subject would be addressed at next week's class meeting.

Self-esteem Messages

The type of structure we provide young children will have a profound impact on them. It will structure how they view themselves, how they perceive others, and the type of world they see. It will train them to see the negative or the positive, to operate from fear or from love, and to see the world as a safe or dangerous place. The following exercise will give you an opportunity to explore and possibly uncover some of the underlying messages you may have received growing up.

Exercise: Read each of the following sentences. Ask yourself, "Have I ever thought this?" Then write a number after the statement that best represents your response.

0 = You never have this thought.
1 = You have this thought sometimes.
2 = You have this thought often.
3 = You have this thought almost always.

1.   If I don't do things right, I am a bad person. Others won't love me. _____
2   I must take care of other people's feelings. _____
3.   I can think, negotiate, initiate, make wise decisions and choices. _____
4.   I can't be good enough._____
5.   I don't know how to value or nurture myself. _____
6.   I think in terms of should, have to, ought to. _____
7.   I will let others think for me (I could be wrong). _____

---

8. If people offer help, they generally want something in return. _____
9. I can take action to get my needs met. _____
10. I tend to blame myself. _____
11. I don't need to take care of anybody but myself. _____
12. I can learn from my mistakes without feeling guilty. _____
13. I tend to blame others. _____
14. If I am to survive, I must do things myself. _____
15. I am lovable and capable._____
16. I feel hopeless. _____
17. Everyone else's needs are more important than mine. _____
18. I can think things through and get help doing that if I need to. _____
19. I will try harder, I must try harder. _____
20. I need someone to take care of me._____
21. I am a good person and nothing I do will change that. _____
22. I try to be perfect. _____
23. No one appreciates me. _____
24. I feel I help make the rules in society; I feel empowered. _____
25. No one really cares about me. _____
26. I am responsible for my thoughts, feelings and actions._____
27. I feel inadequate. _____
28. I feel crazy. _____
29. I feel supported. _____

Self-esteem Messages
Scoring Sheet

Instructions: Record your number scores from the exercise in the appropriate columns on this page. Note that number 25 is recorded in both columns A and B.

A	B	C
1._____	2._____	3._____
4._____	5._____	6._____
7._____	8._____	9._____
10._____	11._____	12._____
13._____	14._____	15._____
16._____	17._____	18._____
19._____	20._____	21._____
22._____	23._____	24._____
25._____	25._____	26._____
27._____	28._____	29._____
Total A_____	Total B _____	Total C _____

Add Column A + Column B = _____

Total Column C = _____

Column A represents messages you received from being raised in a Power Over punitive system. Column B represents those messages you received from a Power Under permissive parent.

Curious as to how you received both Power Over and Power Under messages? All systems seek balance, and family systems are no exception. An extreme punitive person is balanced by an extreme permissive person.

Power Over people tend to attract and marry Power Under people. You more than likely received many messages from column A and B. The total of these messages represents your unhealthy self-esteem score.

Your total column C represents your healthy self-esteem. These were messages of safety and empowerment. For a human being to be relatively happy and successful, messages from column C are required. The higher the score, the happier, more peaceful and more effective you are.

Summary

This chapter ends a personal journey to understanding who we are and how we got to be that way. It asked you to reflect upon the structure you received growing up in order to challenge you to make more conscious decisions about the structure you provide for the next generation. Discipline is a system: punitive, permissive, or responsible. This chapter focused on the impact of each discipline system on the self-esteem of a child. Blindly utilizing discipline techniques because they are familiar or comfortable may have lasting effects on society. As professionals in the area of education and human development or as parents, we must move beyond "it works" to a deeper understanding of discipline and self- esteem.

With a better understanding of our internal structure of power and how it manifests into a philosophy that guides our day-to-day interactions, it is time to gain some insight into the children themselves. The journey now turns to the world of children.

Before continuing on your journey, take a few moments to reflect upon what you have learned and/or discovered about yourself or others.

Reflections:_____

 What I learned about myself:_____

_____

_____

_____

 What I learned about others:_____

_____

_____

_____

What I have decided to change:_____

_____

_____

_____

• •

Discipline means to teach.

• •

Part Two

"I know they know better!"

Understanding Our Children

Love is the ability and willingness to allow those that you care for to be what they choose for themselves without any insistence that they satisfy you.

—Wayne Dyer

Chapter 5

**His brother never did anything like that:
The Good Child Myth**

The Good Child Myth

How often do we use the terms "good" and "bad" to describe children's behavior? My guess is nearly all the time! "Now you be good, Megan," a mom cautions her three-year-old in the grocery store. "If you are good, I'll let you pick one candy bar when we check out." Later in line, when Megan wants everything, mom angrily lists off a number of Megan's obnoxious and irritating behaviors while at the same time reassuring the cashier, "She really is a good kid."

We all want our children to make appropriate moral choices when they are older. We want them to be kind to others, socially responsible, respectful and honest. We want them to have clear moral principles and even, perhaps, certain religious beliefs to guide their behavior. These are all very desirable goals we want in response to our parenting and teaching efforts. Now what has goodness got to do with any of these goals? Nothing.

Children do not learn to become responsible because of their judged goodness. They are taught to behave in certain ways in order to get their needs met. Children don't learn kindness, respect and responsibility intuitively; they learn through demonstration and trial and error—a lot of trial and error! That is why childhood lasts eighteen years or so.

Many adults act as if children are naturally supposed to be good. They are shocked and angered when their children misbehave. They believe children should be endowed with a quality of inner goodness, and if the parent or teacher brings out this inner goodness, then this is a reflection of their own goodness as a person. This type of thinking creates many beliefs that prevent children from developing into their fullest potential. These beliefs are as follows: children should be good; children are motivated by this inner goodness; a good child is a reflection of a good parent or good teacher.

Children Should Be Good

Every school district has a classroom that appears perfect. Every neighborhood has a family that seems perfect. You can picture them in your head moving through the day with total organization and ease. The children are obedient and seem to be happy. All children cooperate and follow the rules explicitly.

This is pure fantasy! It is a fantasy we create that both provides inspiration in terms of something to strive for and despair when our goals are not met. We create this fantasy as a yardstick by which we measure ourselves, judge others, and compare classrooms, children, parents and teachers. Remember, all unhappiness comes from comparing. This belief in the perfect, all good classroom or family continually allows us to choose to be unhappy. We may repeatedly choose to be aware of our own shortcomings and do not believe we could ever achieve this fantasized perfection we attribute to others.

Why Be Upset About Typical Child Behavior?

Can families and classrooms be as perfect as some may seem? Absolutely not. Is it possible or even desirable to strive for this fantasized perfection? In reality, what happens is that there are such strong prohibitions against so many behaviors within a seemingly perfect classroom or family that inappropriate behavior never comes to light. Does this mean they are not there? No! The people in these families and classrooms have the same wants, wishes, needs, drives and conflicts as we do. What they do is put an enormous amount of energy into avoiding conflict. This translates into placing an enormous amount of energy into avoiding making mistakes or taking risk.

In order to avoid conflict, you must also avoid certain thoughts, feelings and behaviors associated with conflict. You have to live as a clone of authority. You can only do this by repressing and denying those aspects of yourself that may lead you into conflict with another person. This means you have to close off a lot of yourself to others and to yourself. You allow yourself to live only a fraction of life. Think of the price you pay in the loss of intimacy. In part you might be able to offset the stress and emptiness by compulsively working, eating, exercising and/or worrying. Families and classrooms that do not know how to deal with conflict are also unable to cope when things start to unravel.

I teach a discipline class at the University of Central Florida once a year. In this class I ask my students to share a discipline experience they can remember when they were children. I ask them for a home example and a school example. A significant number of my adult female students have no discipline experience to share because they were the "perfect" child. They never broke the rules.

What price do children and, ultimately, society pay in order to be good? First of all, they cannot behave as normal children do and learn appropriate behavior through trial and error. The result of this is reduced initiative and lack of exploratory behavior. Mistakes become something to be feared; pleasing others becomes the goal. Some "good" children react to stress with bodily symptoms such as headaches or chronic stomachaches. Others may act out with shocking, inappropriate behaviors during adolescence. Still others who do not succumb in this way report a pervading sense of emptiness. When adults place the emphasis on being "good," the child is forced to extinguish any form of perceived bad behavior.

• •

There is no such thing as a bad person or a bad child, just a hurting one.

• •

The second consequence of this faulty belief system is that a child has to act as if she does not have this "bad" side. The child cannot be accepted or loved as a whole human being but only as a "good" one. In order to carry out this lie in day-to-day living, the child has to pretend in front of her parents or her teacher that she does not exist. These children grow up with an ever-present feeling of being not-good-enough. These perfect children, now perfect adults, find themselves in a difficult situation. They are unable to acknowledge their anger and despair. After all, they are perfect and cannot admit to less-than-perfect feelings. Therefore the adult does not feel anger or despair, only a pervading emptiness.

Should children be good? No! There is nothing really desirable about a child learning to be good. In fact, when children do not learn to cope with conflict, the results can be quite destructive. Viewed in this way, misbehavior can be viewed as reassuring.

Children Are Motivated by Inner Goodness

There is a sentimental belief that children are sweet, kind, loving, respectful, and in all ways good. This inner core of goodness is supposed to transform into an obedient child as the child grows to maturity, regardless of what type of parenting has transpired. This, of course, is a myth. Yet many teachers and parents expect the children to know how to behave without first teaching them.

Children are motivated to be connected to others. They seek to belong, to be loved. As infants, they seek to have their needs met. As those needs are met, the motivation to be connected increases, and they seek to behave in ways that maintain and sustain that connectedness. If their needs are not met, they learn to behave in ways that attempt to control others.

It is both ineffective and illogical for parents and teachers to base their teaching practices on some assumptions about a child's basic nature. It forces them to see children not as they are but in some idealized form. This places a burden on the children, since they cannot live up to the ideal. It also sets up adults for disappointment. Children can learn to use manners when eating, to complete their chores, solve conflicts without resorting to physical strategies and share. But it is very hard for them to "be good." There is a clear difference.

A Good Child Is a Reflection of a Good Adult

This belief focuses on the competence of the adult: If you knew the right things, you would do the right things, so you would have perfect children. All those obnoxious temper tantrums, refusals to comply, crying scenes, and other embarrassing scenes are avoidable if only you would ....

This deep-seated belief holds the adults, not the child, responsible for the child's behavior. Adults who have exhausted all their own resources in dealing with a child generally seek help for the following underlying question, "What have I done wrong?" The problem is not that the child has had some trouble learning or has not been effectively taught appropriate social conduct, but that the adults, through their incompetence, have created a monster capable of great evil. Generally the problem is not that the adults have done something but that they have missed opportunities to discipline and thus teach their children.

Children are not a reflection of our basic worth as an adult. The idea that we must behave in certain ways or we are "not good enough" is tremendously destructive. Judging ourselves and each other does not motivate us to change; it just produces guilt that prevents change.

If People Are Not Good or Bad, What Are They?

Instead of viewing people as being good or bad, it is possible to view children as well as ourselves in different terms. The two states of being we all fluctuate between are extending love or calling for love.

When we are extending love, we feel whole, complete and peaceful. We feel worthy of giving and receiving love. When we are calling for love, we feel separate, alone, isolated and rejected. Think of how you behave when you have had a really stressful day. If you are a schoolteacher, you may have had a day where the children were out of control and not one single plan you made was successful. Upon arriving at your own home after work, you are tired and definitely in the calling-for-love state. You may walk into your house and start immediately shouting, "Why are these dishes still in the sink? Who left their clothes all over the living room? Why do you wait till I come home? Do you think I am supposed to do everything?" What you really needed was a hug, back rub and someone to wait on you hand and foot to recover from your day. You were calling for love but hid that need under angry questioning. Children will do the same thing. Their behavior may appear obnoxious but underneath this behavior is a call for love.

I personally believe there is no such thing as a bad person or a bad child, just hurting ones. In my own life when I feel poorly about myself or something is really bothering me, I may be a little more grumpy and uncooperative. **It is insanity to believe that if we get children to feel bad, they will behave better.**

This persistent need of many people to justify the "goodness" in children indicates two major areas that need clarifying. First, if we need to justify "goodness" in children, we must believe in "badness" in children. Second, if we believe in "badness," we must believe that children are born with socially appropriate skills and they just choose not to use them. In other words, they are just trying to make our lives miserable, generating from a genetic, innate need to be "bad." These unrealistic attitudes and expectations must be replaced with more realistic expectations for children. The first step in developing realistic expectations is to understand normal child development.

What Is Good Child Behavior?

Exercise: Read each statement carefully. Consider whether the behavior described is "typical child behavior for that developmental time" or whether it is "bad or inappropriate behavior." After making your choice, place a T for Typical or I for Inappropriate in the space provided.

_____ 1. A three-year-old child cries when another child takes his toy bear then proceeds to hit the child to get it back.

_____ 2. A five-year-old responds to a conflict with a classmate with, "I hate you, you are not my friend."

_____ 3. While listening to a story about a firefighter at circle time, a six-year-old blurts out, "We had a fire once!" and another yells, "We made popcorn."

_____ 4. A four-year-old, in response to being denied the opportunity to sit next to the teacher, throws a temper tantrum.

_____ 5. A first grader interrupts the teacher to ask a question.

_____ 6. A three-year-old wants to ride on the tricycle. The child pushes the rider off and drives off.

_____ 7. A two-year-old takes another toddler's doll.

_____ 8. Three kindergarten children race to the door to be first in line.

_____ 9. A four-year-old says "Damn" when he falls down.

_____ 10. A three-year-old watching others build a tower with the blocks, rushes over and knocks them over.

So, how did you do? All behaviors mentioned above were typical except for number 4. This behavior is inappropriate for that developmental time span and indicates a big call for love. It signals the child is under a great deal of stress. As you can see, most of the behaviors adults tend to label good or bad are neither. They are simply typical behaviors children demonstrate as they learn to make sense of the world, people and objects. More information on child development is presented in Chapters 6 and 7.

When Children Misbehave

When children misbehave, they are carrying out some of the healthiest activities of childhood. It is the way in which children learn to regulate themselves and understand others. By misbehaving they are able to test the continuity of their boundaries. It is the nature of young children to oppose the limits set by parents and teachers. Set a rule before children in the clearest black and white, and usually it isn't too long before they find a gray area to wedge themselves firmly into. This is very irritating for adults, yet very important for children.

One afternoon, Caroline walked into the living room with a large scrape on her elbow.

"Oh, Caroline," said her mother, "you have scraped your arm something terrible. I'm going to put some cream on it."

"I don't want any cream," declared Caroline. "I hate it."

"But your elbow is raw and you need cream. Now stop picking at that sore and let me put cream on it," replied her mom.

"Look, Mom," said Caroline, "This is my elbow, right?"

"Right."

"I am a different person from you. I'm not the same, right?"

"So?"

"So your elbow may be raw and need cream because you are a different person. This is my elbow and not the same as yours. My elbow is not raw and does not want cream on it."

What intelligence and creativity are coming forth from this seven-year-old child! Yet, too often we cannot appreciate the ingenuity in this form of learning. We tend to see this type of behavior in terms of its goodness or badness.

In other words, we see it on some type of moral scale.

It is not uncommon for teachers and parents to view each temper tantrum, power struggle or limit-testing behavior of children as some rebellion against the world order.

The misbehavior of the toddler, preschooler or young school-aged child is seen as a foreshadowing of things to come in adolescence. Many teachers and parents can be heard saying, "If he is like this now, what will he be like at sixteen?" We use our fear of future behaviors such as drug and alcohol abuse, uninhibited sexual behavior, gang membership, and violence toward others as justification to judge the behavior of young children. The judgments allow us to moralize all behavior into right and wrong, assign blame and punish children through threats, lectures, guilt or shame. We tend to view normal child developmental processes as sins that not only need punishing but deserve it.

● ●

The key to happiness is forgiveness.

● ●

Summary

The goal of this chapter was to begin to weed out the belief in the good child myth, with the ultimate goal of paving the way for planting new seeds in the chapters that follow. Three specific beliefs fostered by the good child myth were targeted. The beliefs that children should be good, that they are motivated by this inner goodness, and that a good child is a reflection of a good adult were all explored to provide for increased awareness of the damaging effects of such thoughts.

How much of your own potential do you think was lost in the never-ending search to be good? How many times has fear of taking a risk, expressing an idea or making a mistake stopped you from acting? The cost of being good is actually a loss of the real self. A significant number of adults are pretending to be something they aren't.

The goal is to shift our perception from judgment to acceptance. Instead of perceiving children as good or bad or their behavior as good or bad, we can perceive children as extending love or calling for love.

Jennifer was having a hard time cleaning up after center time before lining up to go to lunch. She had been working on creating a riverboat at the carpentry center and had waited patiently for the handsaw to become available. As soon as it was her turn, the lights in the classroom blinked, signaling the end of center time. As children were busy around her, singing the cleanup song and putting toys away, Jennifer worked diligently to finish her boat. Mrs. Mardell, the teacher, spotted Jennifer still working.

"Jennifer, do you know what time it is?" asked Mrs. Mardell.

Jennifer did not reply. She continued with her construction.

"Jennifer, it's cleanup time," Mrs. Mardell stated clearly.

Jennifer still did not reply, kept her head down and continued working.

Mrs. Mardell moved close to Jennifer, got on her knees so she was at eye level with her and in a questioning soft voice stated, "You didn't have enough time to finish your project and it's hard to stop when it is not completed?"

Jennifer looked up and made eye contact with Mrs. Mardell and nodded her head in agreement.

Mrs. Mardell asked, "Jennifer, where could you put your boat to keep it safe so you could finish it tomorrow? It is so hard to wait, and I know you can solve this problem."

Jennifer grumbled, "In my stupid cubbie!"

Mrs. Mardell responded, "You're pretty angry about choosing to stop. The cubbie just might work. Do you want to carry your boat to the cubbie or put the saw away first?"

Jennifer decided to put the boat in the cubbie first, then clean up.

In this example Mrs. Mardell heard Jennifer's call for love in several incidences. She heard the call when Jennifer refused to respond and when Jennifer called her cubbie stupid. Mrs. Mardell could have judged Jennifer's behavior in both instances as disrespectful of authority, noncompliance or as bad behavior. Mrs. Mardell, by choosing to accept instead of judge, was able to teach and guide Jennifer in a way that both she and Jennifer had their needs met.

When you are about to let a child push your buttons and you feel on the verge of losing control of yourself, remember these important points:

1. Your children are not **bad** for making mistakes. All children make mistakes. It is part of being a child, and this is why it takes twenty years to grow up—and then some.

2. You are not **bad** because your children make mistakes. Misbehavior is the way children learn. They are presenting you with the opportunity to teach.

3. The people around you do not think you are **bad** because your child is making mistakes. If they are teachers or parents, they will probably be quietly sympathizing with you—if they are paying attention to you at all. A person at my office once told me that at twenty years of age you worry about what people are thinking about you, at forty you decide, "I don't care what they think!" and at sixty you realize they weren't even thinking about you at all.

Misbehavior can be viewed as a healthy aspect of childhood. Not only is it healthy, but children tend to misbehave in very predictable ways depending on their age.

Chapter 6

Why are you doing this:
The Development of Misbehavior

Infancy: The Fussing
Toddlers: The Temper Tantrums
Preschoolers: "I hate you."
Kindergartners: "I'm the strongest."
School Age: "It's just not fair."

The Development of Misbehavior

Children develop particular abilities according to a rather orderly schedule. They also misbehave in fairly predictable ways. Their misbehavior coincides with their mental, emotional, social and physical development. The function of misbehavior from the children's point of view is 1) to provide the children with an avenue of learning self-control, and 2) to acquire the ability to predict how other people and the environment will respond to their behavior.

Infancy: The First Year of Life

As children begin their developmental journey, the first kind of upsetting behavior that adults must cope with is bouts of crying. The infant has certain developmental tasks that must be performed to help ensure survival. Among these are calling out for care, crying or otherwise signaling to get needs met (Clarke & Dawson, 1989). So as the infant goes about signaling the world, adults can interpret this in many different ways. Such things as, "She's just crying because she knows I am a pushover," "He always fusses when I get on the phone, because he thinks he should be the center of my attention," or "She is only crying because she is mad at me" are often heard. Sadly, as these adults project intentional behavior onto a developmental task, they may then seek to punish the infant for crying or for simply doing what babies do. Many protective service workers deal with parents who begin shaking, hitting and spanking babies in the first year of life in the mistaken belief they are helping their babies learn to be good.

Regardless of the many misconceptions about infants, in the first months of life they have no capacity for conscious intentional behavior. Until they have object permanence (the mental ability to envision objects, persons or events that are not in their sight), they cannot know that any action will bring about a desired result (Miller, 1990). Infants can only react unconsciously to internal feelings such as pain or hunger, and to external sensations such as things the infant sees, feels, hears, tastes or smells (Piaget, 1963).

So for infants, their developmental tasks involve signaling the world, accepting touch and nurturing, bonding emotionally to a consistent, predictable adult, expecting the world to respond and developing a sense of trust. In short they fuss, cry, cuddle, make lots of sounds, imitate, and look at and respond to faces, especially eyes. It is common to hear parents say, "He was such a good baby." In essence what this means is that the child was easy to soothe when uncomfortable, gave clear signals the adult could understand, and slept enough so the parents were not tired and overwhelmed.

The Perfect Child

One day while I was eating out, at a table nearby was a family of five—mom and dad and three girls. The oldest girl looked nine, the second child looked about five, and the baby appeared to be about six months of age.

Mom and the older daughters were up and down from the table. Dad and his infant daughter were left at the table the majority of the time. The infant at first made noises directed toward Dad. He ignored them. She began to fuss a little. Dad became irritated and shouted "No" in response to her fuss. The fussing turned to crying, and Dad commanded her to stop by increasing the intensity of his tone of voice saying, "No! Be quiet!" and "Stop that right now!" This father had managed to get into a power struggle with a six-month-old baby. He perceived her crying as a test of his authority. The baby continued to scream. Finally Mom and the sisters arrived on the scene. Mom joined in with Dad in their failed attempts to "shut the baby up." The oldest daughter handed the child a piece of bread, touched her head and kissed her gently. The baby was soothed. She had been hungry.

Most misbehavior in infancy is failed communication. The infant signals that a need is not met. If that signal is not heard, the infant increases the intensity of the signal. As infants get older, that intense signal is perceived as anger. How do we help infants in the first year of life cope with their anger? The infant learns by seeing a calm adult providing soothing behaviors and hearing calm, comforting words and songs as the discomfort is removed.

Infants may get angry when:
1. physically uncomfortable
2. physically restrained from moving or crawling
3. prevented from exploring
4. not provided with comfort and safety responses
5. scolded for behavior.

Toddlers: The Second Year of Life

It has been said that toddlers are "a force to be reckoned with." Those who have toddlers or work with toddlers certainly can relate. Toddlers make a huge cognitive leap from infancy in their ability to remember things and, in a very crude way, manipulate ideas mentally. Cause-and-effect relationships become the focal point for their learning. They love light switches, opening and shutting doors, the TV remote control, the stereo and other objects they can manipulate. Their boundless curiosity and need to explore can test the patience and planning of every adult. A toddler cannot look at a situation, think about it and then plan for potential consequences of his behavior. A toddler acts on impulse.

Toddlers also explore cause and effect in regard to social relationships. A toddler who has been told a hundred times not to touch the stereo will stick out her little pointed index finder as if to touch the stereo one more time and look back to the face of the parent or caregiver to test out the situation. A patient adult would say, "No, no. The stereo is not for touching." A wise adult would move the stereo. Toddlers are preoccupied with connecting the cause-and-effect relationships between their actions and the adult's reactions.

What happens when we put toddlers in group settings? They step on each other to get what they want, take toys from each other, scramble to grab food and proclaim most things *mine*. They develop a sense of themselves through their possessions, so comments such as "mine," "my mommie" and "my daddy" are common. Initially toddlers consider another child no more than another object with whom they have to compete for attention. Toddlers' ability to see the world from another's perspective is not well developed, if at all. Some toddlers who have observed and experienced a great deal of kindness, empathy and understanding may show concern for others, but their way of showing concern is egocentric.

I've worked with toddlers for many years. I find them absolutely the most fascinating of all children. They never cease to amaze me. Even though they have no ability to share whatsoever, they have a certain egocentric compassion. I never once saw a toddler take another child's blanket, binky, teddy or other transition object. They seemed to be able to relate to that need for security. I have also seen many toddlers try to soothe another child in distress by going to get the security object from its cubby and bringing it to the child.

One day years ago, I arrived at the day care where I was working, exhausted and on the verge of getting sick. I immediately plopped down in a beanbag chair and told the children, "I do not feel good," and of course my face and body language conveyed the message in a language they better understood. Melissa and Scotty both came over to me dragging their blankets and gently climbed in my lap. Scotty just laid his head on my chest quietly, and Melissa, while holding her blanket in the hand with which she also was sucking her thumb, handed me the other end of her blanket. Touched by the moment, I took the piece of blanket in my hand and put my thumb in my mouth. I never did get sick!

Developing Autonomy

After the infant has developed a sense of trust or mistrust in the world, the toddler developmentally begins his or her quest for independence. Adults can help toddlers on their road to autonomy by being very supportive of the child's need to "me do." In order to facilitate autonomy, the general rule is never do anything for toddlers that they can do for themselves.

Toddlers are interested in being involved in grown-up activities. They love to vacuum, wash dishes, wash the car and so forth. Toddlers are thrilled with the process and really have no understanding or concern about the end product or goal. They are more interested in soaping the rag while losing themselves in the dipping, pouring, rinsing and splashing of washing dishes rather than focusing on getting clean dishes for the next meal. Sensitive adults will provide opportunities for toddlers to be involved, yet wait until they are older to expect any type of quality end result.

Toddlers discover that the baby in the mirror is "me." This dawning sense of self-awareness manifests in toddlers becoming "full of themselves." If a teacher were to gather a small group of two-year-old children around to read them a book, she may soon discover that the children are more entertained by each other than the book. They may giggle and poke each other as well as start silly movements that to them are humorous. So as one toddler begins shaking her head and laughing, moments later the whole group is imitating the movement. In the meantime, the teacher sits book in hand watching the antics and joys of the delightful toddlers.

Toddlers have developmental tasks or jobs to perform just as infants do. Of these they must explore the world, test reality and push against boundaries and other people in order to begin learning about cause and effect, to express anger and other feelings, to separate from parents and begin developing autonomy and start to follow simple commands. In short, they say no, get into everything repeatedly, get very frustrated trying to do things for themselves, and perhaps throw temper tantrums.

The Delightful Toddlers

Temper Tantrums

Tantrums seem truly to intimidate adults, yet toddlers having temper tantrums are considered developmentally typical. Tantrums are usually related to power struggles, emanating from the toddlers' need to control their body and, when possible, their own world journey toward independence.

Many toddlers have temper tantrums. Some last 20 to 30 minutes and are often dramatic, involving screaming, head banging, breath holding and aggression. These tantrums reflect the child's final step in negotiations in getting its needs met. What these tantrums accomplish for the child is largely dependent upon how the parent or teacher reacts to their occurrences. The effective teacher or parent is able to act to contain the child's rage, recognizing and accepting it while protecting themselves and the child from its potential damaging effects. Then the teacher or parent is capable of helping the child identify ways to get needs met in spite of, not because of, the temper outburst (O'Conner, 1991).

Maria arrived at day care in what could easily be termed a bad mood. Her mom reported that Maria, as a result of a family celebration, had spent the night with grandma. Due to the celebration, Maria did not go to bed until almost two o'clock in the morning and had to get up at five thirty so mom could make it to work on time. Maria's beautiful, full of life, two-year-old face was sullen and her eyes were swollen when she arrived at school. Upon entering the classroom, two children smiled and looked at her. Her reply was to grab her mother's leg and announce, "My mommie." Separating from Mom was more difficult than usual; Maria began to scream and cry, "My mommie, my mommie!" Maria's mom, almost in tears herself, turned and walked out the door. Maria threw herself to the floor, screaming, crying and kicking. Sheryl, the teacher, went to pick up Maria, who kicked her, then bit her on the arm. Sheryl called to Brenda, a more experienced teacher.

• •

Anger signals a change is needed and therefore facilitates development.

• •

As Brenda approached Maria and knelt down next to her, she commented, "Maria, you seem so very, very angry and so very, very tired. You wish your mother had stayed with you. You wish your mommie would come back and make it better."

Maria continued to scream and kick shouting, "NO! NO! NO!"

Brenda's voice was warm and accepting as she continued, "You are just so tired you don't know how to get help. You really are angry. I am going to help you and keep you safe." Brenda leaned down and carefully picked Maria up off the floor.

Maria struggled in her arms and Brenda swaddled Maria snugly as Maria physically protested. "You seem so tired and angry. It's hard to relax and let me care for you. You wish you felt better so you could get down and play. I will hold you until you feel safe and are calm."

Maria kicked and screamed in response to Brenda's calm soothing voice. Within seconds of a final push to get away, Maria began to relax in Brenda's arms. As Brenda felt her let go of the struggle, she began singing, "Twinkle, Twinkle, Little Star. What a beautiful girl you are. Big blue eyes and gorgeous hair. A lovely girl for whom I care. Twinkle, Twinkle, Little Star. What a wonderful girl you are."

Maria stopped fighting and began sobbing. As she cried, Brenda sang. Within three or four minutes, Maria was asleep and taking the nap she so desperately needed.

In dealing with temper tantrums, adults must first offer boundaries as they contain the child, and second, the adult must validate the feelings of the child in an empathetic, understanding, compassionate voice. The rule is for the child to catch the adult's calm as opposed to the adult catching the child's panic.

But won't this spoil the child? Won't this reinforce bad behavior? Won't I be giving in to tyrannical behaviors? These are thoughts that may creep into your consciousness. A temper tantrum is simply a person (a small one in this case) who is out of control calling for love. Have you ever been out of control? Have you ever done and said things that you regret even to this day?

Being out of control is a frightening state of being. It is terrifying for the child also. An out-of-control person needs containment, protection and acceptance. An out-of-control person does not need another out-of-control person. When a person is facilitated in regaining control, then and only then are consequences possible. If Maria's tantrum had been over her refusal to pick up her toys after she played with them, then once she was assisted by an adult in regaining control of herself, her next task would be to pick up the toys.

Toddlers are moving from a state of total dependency in infancy to a less dependent state. This journey is riddled with frustrating situations and anger. Helping toddlers move through and cope with their anger is our job. We can help toddlers manage their anger and frustration by using a number of strategies:

1. Offer distraction and redirection. For example, when a toddler starts to become frustrated, tell a story, show a toy and try to focus the anger energy into skill mastery.

2. Let the child experience the consequences of his actions when possible.

3. Verbalize the child's wish in a fantasy. "You wish you could stay up and play all night long. It is hard to go to bed when you are having so much fun."

4. Offer choices. "You may go to bed with a piggy back ride or a horsey ride. Which one do you want?"

5. Rearrange the environment. If you don't want it touched, move it.

6. Change the routines to provide for enough sleep, reduction of stimuli and consistency.

7. Increase supervision to protect toddlers from older and younger children and each other.

Toddlers will get frustrated and angry as they strive to become more independent. We must facilitate their ability to express and cope with their own frustrations. Our biggest mistake is trying to prevent our children from expressing their anger, and our next biggest mistake is punishing them for being angry. Appropriately channeled anger is the energy of change. Anger in children that is not channeled by adults becomes inappropriately expressed or repressed.

Toddlers may get angry when they are:
1. restrained from independent movement, play or exploration;
2. restrained from demanding everything as "mine" ;
3. frustrated by their own physical or cognitive limits while trying to do something;
4. hearing repeated "no" and "stop that" commands;
5. making a bid for attention that is ignored or misunderstood.

Each angry moment for a toddler is a teaching opportunity for an adult. Anger *must* be labeled ("You seem really mad") and then redirected ("You can play with the blocks or the dolls. Which one do you pick?").

Anger Must Be Labeled

Then Redirection Is Possible

Preschoolers: 3-5 Years

While toddlers function primarily by impulse, playing
with whatever catches their eye for the moment, preschoolers

are more inclined to select an activity very carefully and then stay with it longer, sometimes even coming back to play the same thing over and over. One of the developmental accomplishments demarcating toddlers from preschoolers is the development of language. Preschoolers are able to use language to categorize experience. Toddlers were only able to conceive of objects in terms of how they looked, sounded, felt and related to each other. Preschoolers can conceive of objects both perceptually and symbolically. In other words, they can perceive a block as a physical object to stack, throw and bang together, as well as a "pretend" car to zoom around the room. The block becomes representative of a car and the development of symbolism is off and running.

With these new cognitive and language abilities, the developmental task of the preschooler is to acquire identity and power. The preschooler focuses on activities that help him or her establish an individual identity, learn skills and figure out role and power relationships with others. Specifically, preschoolers continue to assert an identity separate from others; acquire information about their world, themselves, their body and their gender; learn that behaviors have consequences; discover their effect on others and their place in groups; learn to exert power to affect relationships, practice socially appropriate behavior, separate fantasy from reality and learn what they have power over and what they do not have power over (Clarke & Dawson, 1989). What developmental tasks these children are charged with! Just the one task of learning that behaviors have consequences could wear an adult down. Think about it—how do you think the child goes about learning these concepts? You got it! Repeated trial and error.

They must repeatedly create behaviors that have an effect on us and observe the consequence. And as you might imagine, they must do it a number of times to process the information and ultimately internalize the knowledge. How many times do they actually need to test out certain behaviors? The answer to the age-old question of "How many times do I have to tell you?" is 2000 times in context. Research indicates that for a concept to be formed in young children, they must experience it a couple of thousand times in context. We, as adults, have no problem with this idea when we think of cognitive concepts such as the color red, addition or the concept of justice. Yet when it comes to "Do not hit your friends," we expect them to understand this concept after several warnings. It is indeed strange that we expect a three-, four- or five-year-old to acquire nonviolent conflict resolution techniques, when many adults and nations are not yet able to practice such skills. Maybe we just need to tell governments that "it is not nice to shoot people."

Learning to Be Friends

Preschoolers begin to be interested in their relationships with other children. Between three and five years of age, children begin to learn how to be friends, a very important kind of learning for the child's long-term social and emotional adjustment (Gorsaro, 1981). This is a very trying time for adults. Children are elated when they feel they are liked by their peers and have friends, and then crushed when they imagine they have none. This emotional roller coaster is a fast one and is related to how preschoolers experience emotions.

Young children experience one emotion at a time and experience it totally. Adults, given a certain situation, can feel happy, sad and a bit angry all at the same time. This is not true for young children. They experience one emotion with their total being and experience it intensely. Just as suddenly as one disappears, another one replaces it. Comments such as "just stop that crying right this minute" or "I will give you something to cry about unless you stop" are commonly heard. Emotions cannot be demanded or commanded away from another person. Emotions never die; they are just buried alive. Handling children's emotions requires validation and comfort on our part.

• •
How many times do children need to test out certain behaviors? 2000 times in context!
• •

Since preschoolers are learning how to be a friend and how to have a friend, it is our job to guide the process. The following example demonstrates this process.

Rick and Kevin were painting at the easel having a wonderful time. "I am drawing this spaceship that has twenty hundred people on it to save the good guys," commented Rick as he painted.

"Mine has thirty trillion people on it, so it will save all the good guys in the whole world," responded Kevin.

At about this time Gary approached the painting area. He saw Rick and Kevin painting, laughing and talking and was drawn over to the easels.

Rick immediately turned to Gary and said, "Go away. You can't play with us." Gary kept approaching the easel area and Rick then said, "You can't be our friend because you don't have a football shirt on. We don't play with stupid kids."

At this point Ms. Esposito intervened and responded to the pain felt by Gary at being rejected. "Gary, Rick just called you stupid. That might have hurt your feelings. Did it?"

Head down, lips quivering, Gary answered, "Yes."

"Tell Rick, 'I don't like it when you call me names.' " facilitated Ms. Esposito. She then turned to Rick and Kevin and said, "Can you tell Gary, 'I like you but I don't want to play with you right now?' " Both boys tried out the new language. Gary went to garden center to plant some seeds, and Rick and Kevin continued with their pictures.

As children learn the ins and outs of friendship, the issue of exclusion becomes a major issue for teachers and parents. Children have the right to choose their own friends, but they also have an obligation to avoid being cruel in expressing those choices. We must teach them how.

Exerting Power

Because preschoolers are striving for personal power and to gain control over their world, they try out all kinds of tactics. Teachers hear such things as "My mommie said I could" or "My daddy always lets me do what I want to." Conversely, parents hear "My teacher never makes me take a nap." These are not conscious lies, but rather embellished wishful thinking. As the children try to discern power, what it is, how it is used and who has it, many of them resort to a higher power such as, "My mommie says." Listen as Casandra and Maggie try to figure out how to influence each other's behavior.

Casandra and Maggie play together every day. Casandra is bigger and more domineering than Maggie and loves to exercise her power over Maggie. Maggie is a bit shy and sensitive; yet today, she has had enough.

"You be the baby and I will be the mommie and get you ready for school. Lie down in the bed, and I will tell you to get up when it is time for school," stated Casandra to Maggie.

Maggie laid down on the floor and pretended to be asleep.

"Wake up, baby, wake up, baby, it is time for Mommy to go to work. You have to go to school. Now you get up and sit in this chair so I can feed you breakfast," dictated Casandra.

Maggie got up and sat at the table and began to shout, "I want my food, I want my food, I want it now."

"You can't talk. You are a little baby," rebuffed Casandra.

"I don't want to be a little baby. I want to be a big girl," said Maggie as she got out of the chair and set the table.

"You have to be the baby. If you'll be the baby, I will be your friend," bargained Casandra.

Maggie continued to set the table.

"The teacher said you have to be the baby so get back in your chair," Casandra demanded with her hands placed firmly on her hips.

Maggie looked intimidated, yet she said, "I'm telling."

Casandra responded, "Then you are not my friend and can't come to my birthday party."

Maggie, with tears in her eyes, said, "So, I have a new Barbie."

Casandra hit Maggie and went to tell the teacher, "Maggie is not playing nice."

Maggie went to the teacher crying, "She hit me."

Can you imagine trying to solve this problem? Yet

this is a typical day in the lives of many four- and five-year-old children. In the example, can you see how the children were trying to influence and coerce each other's behaviors? They were not immediately hitting, grabbing or throwing a temper tantrum as a toddler would because they truly desire to play with each other. Yet the skills of influencing each other's behaviors are not yet well defined. The sad part is that the skills Casandra and Maggie are using are those they are learning from the adults in their lives, at home and at school.

Primary Children: 4 - 7 Years of Age

As children become cognitively capable of classifying objects and events in their world and of using language to express those classifications, they begin to become aware of themselves in relationships and in comparison with others. The outcome of this synergy (embedded in the culture of the United States) is competitiveness through comparison. As children are describing themselves as bigger, better, faster or smarter, they are moving from nominal categorizing (for example, naming fruits, vegetables and colors) to categories based on some order of elements.

As children begin this comparative process, several things happen. First, children begin interacting in peer groups; they begin to establish relationships based on perceived similarity. This is why boys play with boys and girls play with girls. They perceive each other as being similar. This also explains why little boys emulate their fathers and little girls emulate their mothers. As they engage in this process, they identify themselves not only as boys and girls, but work to match the stereotype associated with their gender. Boys will learn not to cry and girls will learn not to be aggressive.

Second, children begin to realize they have more in common with other children than adults. The relative value placed on peer relationships will rise accordingly. If one places a three-year- old in a peer group setting, the child's tendency is to ignore his peers unless they have something he wants. The young preschooler is too preoccupied with his own needs and strategies. By the time the child is five or six, however, he will have developed a very strong pattern of attending to peers and even of viewing them as potential sources of both material and emotional supplies.

Finally, children will become competitive and will frequently make such comments as "I'm the prettiest," "My picture is the best," "I can run the fastest," and "I'm the tallest." As children seek out the teacher or the parent to agree with their discovery, adults find themselves in tough situations. One way to handle this is to reflect the child's accomplishment back to them. For example, if a child comes to you and says, "My picture is the prettiest, huh?" you could respond with, "You seem really proud of your picture." If a child comes to you and says, "My building is the tallest," you could respond by saying, "Wow, you stacked these blocks higher than you ever have."

Teachers and parents can be tempted to exploit the tendency to be first and best by motivating young children with competitions such as "Whoever can be the quietest during nap time will get a treat" or "The table that cleans up fastest will get to line up first" or "See if you can get dressed faster than your sister." These challenges with young children will indeed "work," yet the long-term outcomes of using these types of motivating statements are more competition and more friction. Additionally, whenever there are winners, there are losers. Winners may feel stressed and compulsive about the need to keep winning, and losers may feel more and more inadequate.

Understanding and Reducing Egocentrism

Egocentrism is the inability to see the world from another's perspective. The process of becoming less egocentric, I have decided, is a lifelong process. Much of my work with teachers and parents is teaching adults to see the world from the child's point of view. So in essence, effective discipline is based on the ability of adults to be less egocentric.

What is required to reduce egocentrism? First would be a standard of living above the survival level. Living with poverty, alcoholism, violence, emotionally abusive environments or any kind of chronic stress situation will retard the

reduction of egocentrism. Think about this in regard to your own life. When you are in a very stressful situation, you may find yourself focusing on yourself. Such thoughts as "Nobody loves me, nobody cares whether I live or die," or "Look at all I do for everyone else" may begin to creep inside your head. These thoughts are all focused on us and what we need, what we want and, most important, what we are not getting in comparison to others. We become very egocentric. We lose the perspective of the other person. Many stressed parents called in for parent-teacher conferences come in very egocentric; yet we as teachers try to convince them they need to focus more on their child. If you have tried this throughout the years, you may have discovered it is very ineffective. To get through adult egocentrism, you must use compassion, listening and validation of the adults' experiences; then and only then can the other adults begin to focus outside themselves.

• •

Effective discipline is based on the ability of adults to be less egocentric.

• •

The second thing necessary to reduce egocentrism is the cognitive ability to role-play. A child must be able to transform him- or herself into another person in pretend play in order to begin taking the perspective of another person.

Tracy and Mckensie were playing in the housekeeping area. As they began to set the table for dinner, Albert stormed through, announcing he was a Power Ranger. Mckensie immediately transformed himself into Tommy, and they both announced that Tracy was the "bad guy." Tracy, insulted with her dictated role, turned herself into a "princess."

These children practiced seeing the world from another perspective. They picked the perspective they wanted to experience, becoming less egocentric. Albert was able to see the world as Albert and as a Power Ranger. Mckensie was a bit more skilled than Albert and was able to be a specific Power Ranger, in this case, Tommy. Tracy indicated she understood the perspective of being a "bad guy" and decided to be a more pleasing princess.

Lastly, to reduce egocentrism children need conflict. They need to interact with other children who have a different perspective from themselves. In role-playing, children practice viewing the world differently; however, they are in charge of the view they see. Conflict with other children demands each child negotiate a perception. This is best illustrated with an "I had it" example.

Juan was walking through the classroom unsure of what he was going to do next. As he passed Landon, who was drawing, he got an idea. He wanted to draw. Focused totally on his desire to draw, Juan grabbed the marker from Landon. Landon, shocked at first, looked up and hit Juan on the arm and shouted, "I had it!" Juan, shocked that Landon had hit him, screamed back in return, "I had it!" At this point, both boys were holding a piece of the same marker and screaming at each other. The teacher arrived on the scene to help them negotiate the problem.

The teacher has many options available to her in this situation. She can view the children as being "bad," remove the marker from their hands and put it away until they can learn to share. She can view the children as being "mean" and put them both in time out until they can "be nice." She could view them as being "helpless" and solve the problem for them by saying, "Juan, you can have the marker for five minutes and then it is Landon's turn. Landon, you set the timer." She could view one boy as the "good guy" (Landon) and one boy as the "bad guy" (Juan) and say something like this: "Who had it first? Whose marker is it? Juan you know better than to take things from someone. What is our class rule? Now give Landon his marker and turn your "happy face' to a ' sad face.' You have lost five minutes of recess time." And last but not least, she could have viewed the situation developmentally and proceeded as follows:

"Stop! What happened?" asked the teacher.

Both boys began shouting and talking at the same time. The teacher calmly said, "Landon you tell me first." As she did this, she stood next to Juan with her arm around him, verbally and nonverbally assuring him he will get a chance to tell his side.

Landon began, "I was making a picture and Juan grabbed my marker and now my picture is ruined."

Juan jumped in and said, "He hit me."

The teacher reflected back Landon's perspective to him. "So, Landon, you were coloring, Juan came and grabbed the marker, and you hit him to get him to let go so you could finish your very important picture."

"Juan, you tell me what happened now," the teacher said as she shifted to put her arm around Landon.

"I wanted to draw a picture, too. So I got a marker. Then he hit me."

"So you wanted to color and saw Landon with a marker. You took it from him, and he got angry and hit you for taking his marker," reflected the teacher.

"So the problem is you both want to make a picture with a marker and you don't know how to use your words to make that happen," clarified the teacher. "Juan, Landon had the marker. You may not grab things from other children. What else could you do to get a marker besides taking Landon's?"

Juan had a blank look on his face. Landon's brows were furrowed, and all of a sudden Landon said, "He could get one out of the box on the art shelf." Juan's face lit up, and Landon appeared pleased he had come up with such a brilliant idea.

"Landon, when someone grabs things from you, you may not hit in this classroom. What else could you do to let the other child know you don't like what he is doing?" asked the teacher.

Landon, with head down said, "Use my words."

"What does that mean?" asked the teacher. As she had guessed, Landon had not a clue; he had learned that phrase in day care. The teacher instructed Landon to tell Juan, "Stop! I don't like it. Get one from the art box."

As the teacher used problem solving and negotiation to help the boys solve their current problem, she did a number of things simultaneously. First, she used a process that allowed each child to hear the other child's perspective. Landon learned that Juan wasn't just out to get him but to find a marker and make a picture. Juan learned that Landon gets upset when he grabs things. This process reduces egocentrism. Second, she sent a message to the boys: you can solve your own problems. Finally, she facilitated a problem-solving process the boys will ultimately learn to do by themselves, freeing the teacher to do other learning tasks.

The Growing Ability to Use Logic

As children become six and seven years of age they become more adept at understanding and using logic. A very common phrase heard from adults now is "because I said so." With advancements in language and cognition, the children are more apt to argue, analyze rules and see situations as not fair. They are extremely motivated by a need to belong to a peer group. They sometimes make up their own clubs and cliques with some semblance of rules and rituals with actual clothing requirements (Miller, 1990). The overall developmental task of school-age children is to develop those skills they perceive as necessary to become an adult. As you can well imagine, children from certain environments may perceive those skills as reading, writing and math. Other children, from different environments, may perceive those skills as stealing, lying and fighting.

Because of a shift to language-dominated information storage, processing and memory, the school-age child will gradually lose direct access to many of the memories and experiences acquired during the toddler and preschool years. This does not mean the experiences in the early years will not impact later choices and events. Just as in our own lives, the very early years definitely will have impact on our adult choices, perceptions and abilities; however, specific memories under the age of five are rare. Many of our earliest memories are very emotional events or experiences that have been retold with family pictures over and over again, so we have claimed them as our own. When young school-age children recall memories, it is often haphazard. These children still tend to retrieve information according to emotional priority (O'Conner, 1991).

For example, ask a couple of fighting seven-year-old boys who started the fight. Both will answer the other one did. And more important, both believe they are telling the truth. If Patrick wanted Matt's book and took it from him, which resulted in Matt hitting Patrick, then Patrick would reason that the fight started when Matt hit him. Patrick would say this because the hitting was the point at which he became aware of his pain and subsequent anger. During the school-age years, children reason that a problem begins when they feel pain.

The ability to understand the true sequence that leads up to a fight or conflict does not occur until around the age of eleven (O'Conner, 1991).

Helping preschool and primary children move through their anger requires a great deal of understanding of child development. A preschool or primary child may get angry when he

1. is required to think of others;
2. is in competition with others or is jealous of siblings;
3. does not receive enough attention and approval;
4. is forced to follow rules;
5. is hit or yelled at;
6. has things damaged or taken away;
7. is hurried or rushed;

8. feels others have more;
9. is frustrated by not mastering a skill;
10. feels the situation is not fair.

As you can see, the young child may experience many frustrating situations. Our job is not to avoid these situations nor punish the child for experiencing them. Our job is to allow the child emotions and teach socially acceptable ways of expressing them, while at the same time teaching the skills needed to meet our expectations of appropriate behavior.

Summary

First and foremost, it is important to understand that *all* irritating, oppositional and noncompliance behaviors have a healthy purpose and are ***crucial*** to child development (Williamson, 1990). These behaviors may be typical in the developmental sequence (as are temper tantrums for toddlers) or they may signal to us a child with problems. Whether the behavior is typical or not is an assessment process. With information from this chapter, you will be able to discern developmentally troubling behavior from that of troubled children.

Children from infancy through early school years are limited in their intentional behavior by their level of cognitive development. In other words, there is a developmental sequence of misbehaving. Infants cry and fuss, toddlers say "no" and throw tantrums, preschoolers hit each other or call each other names to get the toy they want, and school-age children argue about fairness.

Most young children are not able to regulate their behavior on the basis of abstract rules. We have all fallen into the trap of moralizing to young children. Towering over a four-year-old and lecturing the Golden Rule until we are blue in the face is unfortunately a common occurrence. I'm not advocating "having no values"; we must model values for them and give them the information of the value's impact on other people. With these experiences, the formulation of values is a seed planted within them as opposed to a rule held over them. The next chapter explains how children develop the concept of rules.

Chapter 7

There is no excuse for this behavior:
Children's Understanding of Rules

How Children Perceive Rules
Learning About Rules
Rules: Current Dilemmas

"What is a rule? What happens when you break a rule? Who made up rules? Why are rules made?" When early childhood teachers were asked these questions, similar answers were given. They generally defined a rule as something that governs behavior. Breaking a rule yields some consequences. The rules are made by those in charge for the safety of the citizens. These adult answers were a far cry from the answers given by three-, four-, five- and six-year-old children asked the same set of questions.

Three-year-old children attending day care responded to the question, "What is a rule?" with such answers as "an arrow, an alligator, a monkey" and "I don't know." Obviously these young children were not familiar with the word or simply had no idea of a rule. To further explore the issue with these young children, they were asked, "Can you hit your friends?" The children responded with "yes" or "I don't know." When they were asked, "Are you supposed to hit your friends?" they responded "no." This indicates that some type of understanding is forming in their minds. To discern their understanding of consequences, they were asked, "What happens if you don't clean up your toys?" Answers to this varied from "I don't know" to "The bugs will come." Communicating with three-year-old children is a challenging and exciting adventure. It probably is safe to say they may have some vague general understanding of the world of rules. Precisely what they do understand still remains a mystery.

• •

Rules alone do not teach young children.

• •

Four-year-old children were able to communicate their ideas more effectively. When asked, "What is a rule?" these children responded with examples. Such comments as "You have to listen, you must put your backpacks up, you pick up toys" were made. In response to "What happens when you break a rule?", the chidren generally answered, "You get in trouble." When asked, "What does get in trouble mean?", the usual answer was time out or a spanking. When the classroom teachers were asked if they used "time out" or "spankings" in their school, the answer was no. These children had generalized from home to school. To further tap the wisdom of the four-year-old mind, the children were asked, "Who made up the rules and why are the rules made?"

The answer to who made up the rules was consistent. The children responded, "I did." Why the rules were made yielded a variety of answers from "I don't know" to "My teacher says so." The four-year-old children are gaining a sense that there are some things you are supposed to do and if you don't do them, something bad happens to you.

The belief being formulated in the minds of these young children is that to make a mistake equals being bad. Separating the action from the doer in the minds of young children is impossible. A consequence simply equals getting in trouble, and it appears that the consequences given by the parents are generalized to their world at large. For example, for Tasha "getting in trouble" at home means a spanking. She then believes that the same consequences will apply at school. Four-year-old children seem to have a better understanding of rules, or at least better communication skills in relaying their knowledge about the world of rules, than three-year-old children. They know for sure that rules exist, they believe that they themselves made them up for some unknown reason, they know that if you break a rule something bad will happen to you, and they equate something bad happening to you with being bad.

The five-year-old children were much clearer and more precise in their answers. The question "What is a rule?" produced many examples from the boys such as "no hitting, no pushing, no pinching, no biting, no kicking" and "you can't bring a dog to school." The girls responded that a rule is "something you have to do" or "what mother says, what father says." When asked, "What happens when you break a rule?", the same response as the four-year-old children—"you get in trouble" — was given. The five-year-old children did have a more exhaustive list of what getting in trouble means. Their list included "spanking, a talking to, going to your bedroom and crying, being grounded and the time-out chair." None of these procedures except "talking to" were used in the school.

The children again generalized from the home to the school. Surprisingly, the five-year-old children responded to "Who made the rules?" with the same answer as the four-year-old children: "I did." "Why were the rules made?" yielded the following types of answers: "Because you can be bad," "Sometimes you don't believe God," and "Because that way everyone does not get hurt." The five-year-old children are demonstrating greater cognition and classification skills. They understand rules exist for a reason generally related to safety and that a consequence follows the breaking of the rule. Their understanding of consequences has broadened to include a variety of discipline techniques including "reason" or "being talked to." Surprisingly, the children still believe that they make up the rules. Sadly, the children now believe they are bad persons when they break the rules.

Recently, I was walking through a public school cafeteria. I spotted, at an isolated table, a young kindergarten student that I had been working with. Linda had been part of a play-therapy program I was conducting to help children with self-esteem problems. As I approached Linda, she lowered her eyes and withdrew her body from me. I could tell by her facial expression she was on the verge of tears. Sitting next to her, I began validating her feelings. "Hi, Linda. You seem very sad." She withdrew further from me with her body, and her lower lip protruded in a pout formation. I responded to her nonverbal communication with, "You seem very upset and maybe even scared." At this point three kindergarten girls sitting at a nearby table begin to tell me the whole story.

"She is sitting at the bad table. The bad kids sit at the table, and they don't know what is going to happen to them." My heart went out to the children who were just trying to make sense out of their world. Later I asked the kindergarten teacher if the table was referred to as the "bad table." She said no and asked me where I got such a silly idea. I answered her honestly, saying that her students told me. She looked at me and replied, "That is ridiculous, those children know the rules." As I walked off, I wondered if children are truly any more egocentric than adults.

Six-year-old children seem to have developed the concept of rules. When asked "What is a rule?", the children asked in return, "A rule at school or a rule at home?" They have differentiated home and school rules from each other, a skill not clearly seen until this age. Their response to the question, "What is a rule at school?", yielded examples of classroom rules such as "No toys from home at school," "Tires are not allowed on the playground ramp" and "You may not hurt your friends." When asked "What happens when you break the rule?", they responded as their younger classmates, "You get in trouble." When asked to elaborate, they said getting in trouble means "being scolded," "yelled at" and "being told to use your words." Their responses to who made up the rules were "the principal and vice principal of the school, the police, the President of the United States" or "mom and dad." It was surprising to note these 30 or more six-year-old children did not perceive the teacher as a rule maker. The reason for the rules was so that no one gets hurt or into trouble. It appears that by six years of age the children have pulled together the concept of rules and many of the ramifications of this very abstract notion.

Rules: A Developmental Process

For people to follow the rules or be able to govern their own behavior, Hughes (1991) believes they must possess the following skills:
1. sensitivity to the viewpoints of others
2. ability for mutual understandings
3. willingness to delay gratification
4. high degree of cooperation.

How many two-, three-, four-, five-, or six-year-old children possess these skills? For that matter how many twenty-five-, thirty-five-, or fifty-five-year-old adults possess them?

Take, for example, the weight problem in the United States. People may decide to exercise or stop eating dessert. Then they make up a rule for themselves such as "I will exercise for 30 minutes three times a week." This rule may last for two to three weeks until ultimately the rule is changed, and the adults feel "bad about themselves," as if they once again have failed.

How many rules about your own behavior do you make? What types of rules do you make? Have you made a rule not to lose control and yell at the children under your care? Have you made a rule to build a relationship with the children by playing with them daily? Have you made a rule that you will not let the pressure of the school or work get to you? Have you made a rule that you are going to stop taking work home with you at night and during the weekend and "get a life"? Our ability for self-discipline in this society is low, yet almost every school and home professes this as an educational goal. Who is modeling this skill for the children? Not television. It models immediate gratification, displays lack of mutual understanding and prevents a sensitivity to others through stereotypical programs.

In many classrooms, competition is the norm and cooperation is rarely encouraged. Family systems may or may not model these skills; however, just living in a racist, sexist, capitalist society would prevent children from acquiring all the skills needed for self-discipline.

All social interactions are rule governed. Every time children interact with each other or with adults , they build the skills necessary for self-discipline or they build the skills of "other discipline." "Other discipline" is a way of governing ourselves with the goal of meeting the needs and expectations of other people.

Who Makes the Rules?

Since it is impossible to meet all the needs and expectations of others, it is a way of getting children to feel not good enough. For example, a child spills his or her milk at the child care center, and the child care provider says to the child, "Look what you have done now; you always manage to spill something at snack. Look at Sarah. She pays attention and holds her glass carefully. Why can't you pay attention to what you are doing?" How sensitive was this child care provider to the child? Using the following list of self-discipline skills as a checklist, check off the skills that the above child care provider modeled for the child.

Self-discipline Checklist

1. The teacher was able to view the situation from the child's point of view (sensitivity to the viewpoints of others).
yes ___ no ___
2. The teacher was able to add language to the experience so that each person involved understood the position of the other (ability for mutual understanding).
yes ___ no ___
3. The teacher was willing to delay his or her own impulses for long-term gains of skill building in children (willingness to delay gratification).
yes ___ no ___
4. The teacher modeled cooperation by NOT comparing one child to another (high degree of cooperation).
yes ___ no ___

As you can see, this child care provider modeled egocentric, impulsive, competitive behavior for this child. How many of us complain about children who are egocentric, impulsive and overly competitive? Using the same evaluative procedure above, assess the difference in how Mrs. Tate handles the same situation. "Sarah, you were reaching over to get Joshua'a attention and knocked over your milk. What do you need to get to clean up the milk?" "A rag," responds Sarah. "Exactly," says the teacher. "Where can you find one?" "I don't know," Sarah says quietly. "I will show you

where you can find a rag and you can clean up this milk. Better hurry. It is running all over the table." Looking at the self-discipline checklist form, this teacher was sensitive to the child's perspective, modeling impulse control and cooperation, as well as using language to describe the situation from both a child and adult perspective.

Learning About Rules: The First Year of Life

For young children, the ability to adhere to a set of rules is a developmental process. This process begins during the first year of life with the interactions between the parent and infant. The framework for understanding rules is laid as the child interacts with his or her parents in parent-infant play. It generally is a joyful time in parents' lives when their infants begin to play with them. Many parents love to play with their babies, but they may not realize that such play is more than simply enjoyable; it is extremely beneficial to the child. The parents, as the first social partners of the infant, provide the "structuring role" that will ultimately be the foundational pattern for rule-governed behavior.

During the first year of life, early social games between parents and their infants provide the child with many of the basic building blocks of rule-governed social interactions. One basic building block is taking turns. An example of this parent-infant taking turns is as follows: the parent builds a tower of three blocks, the baby waits until the tower is complete and then knocks over the tower; the baby in turn, through nonverbal cues and gestures, signals the parent to repeat the process and waits for the tower to be rebuilt. In essence, the parent engages in an action, then stops and waits for the baby to act; this nonverbal pause and facial expression signals "it is your turn." The baby then responds to the action and acts in a prescribed manner, thus signaling to the parent to repeat the process. The baby then waits for the parent's turn (Ross & Lollis, 1987). This same procedure can be seen in the game of peek-a-boo. The parent initiates the game with the verbal action of "Where's Kaitlin?" and the nonverbal action of covering the eyes. Then the parent signals to the child "it is your turn" by pausing and waiting for the infant's response. The baby responds by laughing and giggling, which signals nonverbally to the parent "do it again." The cyclical game continues until one of the partners becomes tired, and the partner to tire first is generally the parent.

The benefits of parent-infant games are readily apparent. The baby learns how to wait for his or her turn (beginnings of delay of gratification) and how to adapt to the schedule of another person (beginnings of sensitivity to the viewpoints of other people). Both skills are prerequisites for the child's establishment and adherence to a set of rules. Awareness of others is reinforced in such early parent-infant social games because careful attention to a partner's actions is a necessity. Parent-infant play is often so delightful an experience for both parties that it can facilitate the process of attachment between parent and child. And finally, since these early social games involve a considerable amount of verbalization, it has been suggested that such play encourages the development of language in children.

Parent-infant games appear much earlier than games with peers, indicating the importance of the adult's role. Children spend a year playing peek-a-boo, patty cake, and "this little piggy" before they ever have interest in playing with other children. The adult provides the structure in these early social games. The adult provides the scaffold upon which the game is built, and as the infant matures, the adult can become less and less involved in this structuring process (Hodapp, Goldfield, & Boyatzis, 1984).

This structuring process established by the parents becomes internalized by the child and is then utilized by the child in his or her social interactions with peers. Infants missing these early social games become "at-risk" for establishing a functioning rule- governing system of their own and/or for being able to control their own impulsivity long enough to adhere to the rules set by others. The children who miss these early parent-infant games become ineffective in their social interactions with their peers. With 25 percent of all young children growing up in poverty, the chances of more and more of our young children missing these experiences are increasing exponentially.

Children who receive parent-infant social play in the first year of life acquire two major building blocks for self-discipline. One is the ability to follow the rule of taking turns. The second is the beginning of the ability to delay gratification (impulse control). These two skills set the infants on a social competence course as they begin their second year of life.

Learning About Rules: The Fantasy Years

Beginning in the second year of life children start engaging in symbolic or pretend play. Symbolic play, just like parent-infant play, is an essential ingredient for children to learn self-control. In symbolic play children use rules to organize their play. The purpose of rules in this type of play is to assign roles and engage in complex negotiations about designated roles (e.g., "You can be the bus driver next time if you will be a passenger this time"). These negotiations naturally involve a measure of give-and-take, and this give-and-take provides the beginnings of cooperation and mutual understanding, both of which are necessary for the development of and adherence to a set of rules.

Maria is running across the yard, her arms outstretched, shouting to her friends, "Ah! Let's chase the monsters! C'mon, let's turn into Wonder Women!" Three girls form a circle in the sandbox and turn around in place three times as Maria directs the action. As they complete their spins, Maria holds her arms above her head triumphantly. "Wonder Women to the rescue!" she screams, and leaps out of the sandbox. Tashika announces she is a Power Ranger and she must work with Wonder Women to catch the bad guys. The play changes from chasing a monster to catching bad guys instantaneously, and the girls continue saving the day.

In pretend play children alter reality. The roles and themes of the make-believe play change continually. As reality changes, so do the rules of the social order. In essence, children are forming pretend rules and adhering to them. If the pretend rule interferes with the child's goals or desires, the rule is quickly changed. In the above example Maria constructs a play episode and just as the girls turn into Wonder Women to chase a monster, Tashika alters the direction of the play. She changes the rules and turns herself into a Power Ranger and the monsters into bad guys. As the children change reality, they concurrently change the rules.

This can be easily seen with young four- or five-year-old children when they attempt to play a rule-bound game such as Candy Land with their parents or teacher. As soon as the child perceives him- or herself in an awkward predicament (going to lose), they change the rules of the game (i.e., "Let's say the person who gets here first wins"). These young children five years of age and under are not cheating; they are showing you their understanding of the concept of rules. Rules, according to the child, are something that serve the immediate need for order and safety, yet can be changed unilaterally upon request from the child. Remember at the beginning of the chapter when young children were asked "Who made up the rules?" they responded, "I did." Developmentally they indeed believe this and live by these beliefs.

During the fantasy years young children also learn a great deal of language. They progress rapidly from two-word utterances at two years of age to complete sentences by age three. Language is critical for self-control. Adults are constantly talking in their heads to organize their day, rehearsing a confrontation that may be on the horizon, solving everyday problems or, in essence, governing their behavior. Children typically do not obtain the ability to use this internal speech (talking to oneself in one's head) until around the age of six or seven. Therefore to govern their own behavior, they must talk out loud. Listen to Micha as she plays in the following scenario:

"Hi, baby! I am going to take you for a ride. Uh oh, I need a wagon! Here it is. I put you in here. You are safe. Ride, baby, ride. Mommy is driving. Got to stop, we can crash. This way. Good baby. I push the wagon for my baby. I'm driving."

Micha uses language in similar ways as adults do in their heads, but she must talk out loud to achieve the same results. She uses her language to express her play theme, organize her play, determine problems and solve them. Without language to structure her behavior, her play would have looked very different. She probably would have filled the wagon full of toys and pulled it around the room, dumped the toys out of the wagon, filled it up again and repeated the routine tenaciously. Language organizes thought and thought controls behavior. Children with language delays probably have difficulty in impulse control (delaying gratification), organizing themselves, and following the classroom rules or limits. For these children we must use our language to reflect their experiences by using a skill called "tracking."

Tracking

Tracking is a wonderful way to give children attention, notice them and provide language for their experience. The role of the teacher or parent is to describe what they see the child doing. This descriptive process provides children an awareness of themselves. Tracking is critical if we want children to become self-reflective as they grow. Tracking of behaviors involves simply stating what you see the child doing. For example, if a child is hopping across the room, you may comment "You are hopping around the room." If a child is placing a block on top of another block, you might comment, "You are stacking one block on the other. You are checking the sides to make sure it won't fall."

This may seem silly to you. In fact you may be thinking, *why on earth would I be reflecting back to children what they are doing, don't they know what they are doing?* The answer is, not necessarily. Remember tracking is a method of giving positive attention to children. It is much like sportscasting. The actions are described from the child's point of view, rather than the adult attributing his or her own meanings to the child's behavior. Notice in the examples provided I did not judge the child. I never said good, great or wonderful. As teachers and parents, we have heard over and over again "catch them being good." Many of us who work with young children occasionally fall into the trap of thinking, "How can I catch a child being good when it never happens." Of course, in these moments of desperation we need to change our thoughts about the child, and then we can begin using tracking skills. Tracking provides positive attention to a child who is skilled at eliciting negative attention from the adults in his or her world.

Tracking

Learning the complexities of social interaction takes at least a lifetime. No wonder young children with egocentric ideas and very little experience often have problems and find themselves in conflict with each other and the adults who care for them. To make matters worse, society thrusts young children into preschool, child care or kindergarten programs with such expectations that the children "get along" by "sharing" and being "nice." When children are unable to rise to these unrealistic expectations, adults generally consider the conflict a discipline problem. Those who choose conflict as an opportunity to teach **responsibility** respond in one way to conflict, while those who view conflict as something that needs to be controlled and **punished** respond in another way.

Conflict and Punishment (Punitive Power Over System)

Two children are playing at the same table with a set of miniature people and vehicles. They have been playing together for over ten minutes when suddenly one says, "Teacher, Courtney won't let me have any little people." When the teacher arrives, Courtney is hoarding all the small figurines in her play space. Mr. Brookes, the teacher, immediately comes to the rescue. "Courtney, you must share the people with Etta. All the toys in the school belong to everyone. What is our rule at school? We all must share is our rule," responds the teacher, answering his own question. Courtney still will not part with her pile of figurines, so Mr. Brookes becomes more firm. "Courtney, if you can't share, you must go to the time-out chair and think about being kind." Courtney knows she has to give up some of the people or she will lose out all together. Sullenly, she sorts out some of the "ugly" people and shoves them at Etta.

Mr. Brookes is operating on several beliefs about children and discipline to respond in such a manner. First, he believes that punishment is effective; second, he thinks that making rules are enough to govern the behavior of young children; and finally, he believes that young children understand such complex concepts as sharing, being kind, and reflecting silently upon one's behavior. As you can imagine, Mr. Brookes is in for a long year.

Conflict and Responsibility (Personal Power System)

Kelsey and Corey pulled the zoo box out to begin designing their zoo. Kelsey busied herself putting the cages together, while Corey sorted the animals to go in the cages. There were two sets of animals all mixed up. One of the animal sets was notably newer than the other. By the time Kelsey got the cages ready, Corey had decided he didn't want to play with her after all and was building his own cages with Legos. He had all the shiny new animals hoarded away in a tub next to him. Kelsey noticed that the only animals left were the scuffed-up ones with broken legs.

Kelsey protested, "You can't have all the good animals!"

Corey retorted, "I got 'em first!"

Kelsey, sullen and disappointed, whined, "But I was building the cages for them."

"Well, I got my own cages!" snapped Corey.

"You can't have all the good ones," said Kelsey as she grabbed the tub of animals. Corey held on to the tub for dear life and Kelsey continued to pull. Martha, the teacher, overheard the disagreement and intervened to assist when it got out of hand.

"You both want the same animals," she began.

Kelsey clarified, "He's got ALL of the good ones! All that is left are the broken old animals that won't even stand up."

Martha continued, "You don't want to play with the older animals?"

"They don't even stand up," responded Kelsey as she demonstrated by trying to stand a few animals on their broken legs.

Martha acknowledged her demonstration by saying, "The ones with broken legs won't stand up."

Addressing both children, Martha encouraged them to brainstorm solutions. "What could you do with the old animals?"

"Throw them away!" snapped Kelsey. Remembering

that if they were thrown away she would not have any, she then added, "But I want half of the new ones."

Martha invited Corey's input, "What do you think we could do with these animals?"

"Fix 'em," replied Corey.

"How would you fix them?" asked Martha.

Corey said proudly, "You fix them at the animal veterannarium!" (His dog had been run over and he knew about fixing animals.)

Martha asked, "Could you have an animal hospital here?" Eager to show off his knowledge about animal hospitals, Corey quickly transformed the zoo into a hospital.

Kelsey, not sure about this new direction asked, "But can I have some of the new animals?"

"O.K., but I want all of yours with the broken legs," insisted Corey.

When all the children involved agree upon the unspoken rules in play, all goes well. Many times during the play of young children, one child will be playing by one set of rules and another child will be playing by a different set of rules. Then conflict arises! How the teacher responds to the children at that time impacts their concept of rules and their present and future ability to adhere to them. Martha, the teacher, demonstrated her beliefs about children and discipline in how she handled the situation. First, she believes that children, with guidance, have the ability to resolve conflict; second, she believes children can be responsible for their own problems; and finally, she believes that children can be taught skills of negotiation and problem solving.

Many classrooms for young children operate like the classroom Mr. Brookes portrayed. The teacher at the beginning of the year had made a list of rules for the children. He further decided on consequences for those rules. When the child broke the rule, the predetermined consequences were applied. This is an example of a rule-governed system. The teacher believes that rules will maintain order. Many classrooms that use the punitive Power Over philosophy of disciplining children rely heavily on rules to do the job of maintaining order. Children who are asked to function in social rule-governed systems before their concept of rules is fully developed are unconsciously being asked by adults to develop alternative strategies for dealing with rules, as opposed to developing skills necessary to adhere to them. For example, children might learn to cope with rules through negotiation (i.e., "Just one more turn on the swing and then I'll be ready to go. Please, just one more"), domination (i.e., threats like "You are not my friend" or "I'm telling my mommy on you") or withdrawal from the social situation.

Rules for the young child are created by the child to sustain his or her goals and changed by the child as the goals of the interaction may change. Teachers perceive rules and their functions differently than the children. For teachers working with children in kindergarten or preschool (or parents at home), it will be no surprise for you to hear that the children are simply pretending to go by the rules. It is actually amazing how well young children do, pretending to go by the rules in order to be a part of a class or family and be in relationship with adults.

Learning About Rules: The Primary Years

Some time in the fifth, sixth, or seventh year of life, pretend or symbolic play evolves into games with rules. When children begin playing games with rules, they truly have acquired the basic understanding of rules and have the capacity to adhere to them. Children approximately six years of age are entering a new stage of developmental thinking, what Piaget (1963) referred to as the stage of concrete operations. The result is that thinking takes a more logical and orderly appearance. The emergence of a logical system to govern one's thinking allows children to perceive the universe as an orderly place. Therefore, the school-aged child at play will be more realistic and more rule-oriented than the preschooler. Play will reflect a developing need for order, a need to belong and a need for industry.

"If you step on a crack, you'll break your mother's back." Children's play during the elementary school years is replete with such chants and rituals, and they reflect both the orderliness of the children's thinking and the extent to which ritual is involved in the socialization process. Counting rules like "one potato, two potato" or "eeny meeny miny mo" are not to be taken lightly. If a child attempts to cheat or refuses to accept the role determined by the count, that child will be harshly criticized by peers. Learning the rituals puts the child "in the know"; learning to abide by them teaches the child how to obey rules and follow moral and social order.

**Don't Step on a Crack -
You'll Break Your Mother's Back!**

Games with rules are governed by a set of regulations agreed to in advance by all players. These rules may not be changed in the middle of the game unless the players have previously determined that modifications will be acceptable. The rules themselves may be handed down by code, as in the game of chess, or may exist in the form of a temporary agreement between players. In other words, children may either learn the rules from their older peers or establish their own rules at the onset of a particular game. Games with rules represent a democratic system of rule governance. Rules are predetermined by the group and voluntary adherence to the rules is agreed upon. This democratic system took at least six years for the child to formulate and is dependent on how well the child was provided with the necessary adult structuring and nurturing. Children who are not provided the necessary prerequisite adult structuring and nurturing could easily develop a punitive system within themselves to guide their own behavior and the behavior of others.

Rules: Current Dilemmas

Young children are in the process of developing the skills necessary to adhere to external rules as well as the internal process of understanding the concept of rules. The concept of rules does not completely form until approximately age six. The dilemma becomes how to have young children in rule-governed classrooms when they do not comprehend the concept of rules. Historically, we are in a new era. Never before in the history of the world have we attempted to put 15 to 20 three-year-old children in a classroom social setting. Never have we put 20 four-year-old children together to learn in a cooperative setting. We are placing children five years old and younger, who do not have a concept of rule-governed behavior, in age specific group settings, and demanding that they adhere to the rules of the social system. To compound the problem, we are putting 15 to 20 children in a classroom setting with one adult, placing both the children and the teacher in very difficult situations.

Using the same classroom structure of rules and consequences employed with older elementary, middle school and high school students is inappropriate for young children. Day care providers historically have not focused on rules per se. However, today more and more states are mandating kindergarten and offering prekindergarten classrooms in the public school settings. As more early childhood programs enter into the public school system, many are being forced to create and maintain rule-governed classrooms.

Limit-setting Systems

When working with children five and younger, the most effective classroom management technique to utilize is that of limits instead of rules. Rules are based upon the belief that students know the rules, understand them and are aware of the consequences if they choose to break them. Young children do not comprehend rules or the concept of rules as do older children who are more logical. Young children are in the process of discovering the principles of cause and effect, and therefore are incapable to some degree of predicting the effect of a particular cause before taking action. For example, young children will not really be able to answer the question "What would happen if you broke the rule of hitting?" They may be able to recite a rehearsed response given to them by teachers or simply state "get in trouble," but they will not be able to use the information to control their own behavior.

●●●●●●●●●●●●●●●●●●●●●●●●●

Young children need limit-setting classrooms.

●●●●●●●●●●●●●●●●●●●●●●●●

Young children, with little understanding of rules, will repeatedly reason "I am bad" when rules are broken and enforced. The rules become a hindrance to the building of self-esteem as well as ineffective in facilitating classroom management. Using a rule-governed system with young children impedes the development of problem solving. For example, if the classroom rule is "do not hit" and a child in frustration hits another child to obtain a toy, the child may lose the privilege of playing with the toys or be removed to time out. The problem with this procedure is twofold: 1) the child reasons he or she is "bad," which lowers self- esteem, and 2) the child does not learn an alternative socially acceptable way of possibly getting the toy or a toy substitute the next time this same situation arises.

Young children need to be in limit-setting classrooms. Limits are the way children build boundaries. Boundaries are the safety zones in which children feel secure and cared for, free to explore what they and others are and are not permitted to do (Clarke & Dawson, 1989). Rules say, *You may not break the rule, do not even try, or something will happen to you.* Limits say, *I am here to keep you safe, you may test the limits, and I will redirect you so you may learn that the territory outside the boundaries lacks the protection that lies within the boundaries.*

Limits assist the children in developing self-boundaries based on safety, respect and responsibility. Through the use of limits, children are facilitated in their development of the rule concept process. Rather than receiving a dictate from a rule, children participate in a learning experience.

Rule-governed Classrooms

In a traditional rule-governed classroom the expectation is that the rule will teach the child right from wrong, appropriate from inappropriate behavior. For example, "Jessica, the rule is *Keep you hands and feet to yourself, fighting is not allowed.* I will put your name on the board as a reminder. If you get two checks by your name, you will not have popcorn on Friday." Jessica learns from this that if you break the rule, you "get in trouble," and possibly she learns not to fight to get her space in line. However, she has not learned any skills of what to do when someone pushes her or butts in front of her in line. What will she do tomorrow when Kathia does this?

Limit-setting Classroom

In a limit-setting classroom the teacher would facilitate the resolution of the conflict by teaching socially acceptable skills to the children involved. The following steps could be used to assist in the situation where one child, Jessica, hits Carlos to secure a toy.

"Carlos, that must have hurt! You were playing with the toy and Jessica hit you and took the toy. Did you like it when Jessica hit you and took your toy? Tell her, ' I don't like it when you hit me.'"

"Jessica, when you are frustrated, you may not hit. This is a safe classroom; hitting hurts. Give Carlos the toy back.

When you want a toy that another child has, what could you do besides hit?"

By using limits in the above classroom, the teacher has the flexibility to teach both the victim and the aggressor socially acceptable behaviors as the need arises. In the rule-governed classroom, the teacher is bound to predetermined consequences that may or may not teach the child anything except that "the teacher doesn't like me" or "I am bad." Limits not only benefit the child but also liberate the teacher, allowing him or her to join the child in the processes of thinking, questioning, wondering and, of course, problem solving (Reynolds, 1990).

There is only one limit in working with young children. That limit is safety. It is the teacher's responsibility to establish and maintain an environment in which children are physically and psychologically safe. Any situation that threatens the body or esteem of a child must be dealt with immediately by the teacher. In this manner, consistency and predictability are assured in the classroom.

You may be thinking that setting limits is a time-consuming task and teaching is a busy profession. I always get several questions from people when they are first exposed to limit setting. One is, "What are all the other children doing while you are carrying on this conversation?" My reply is, "The same thing they are doing when you are writing a name on the board: watching and learning." The second most common comment is , "I don't have all that time." My response is twofold: 1) The limit-setting skills are new and therefore seem time-consuming and cumbersome. For me they are as swift and easy as removing marbles, giving pink slips or writing names. 2) Once I teach the children ways of thinking and solving their own problems, they no longer need me to facilitate. If schools starts in August, by December I have in effect very few discipline problems because the children are capable for the most part of solving their own problems.

Summary

The development of the concept of rules is an ongoing process beginning from birth. During the first six years of life the child utilizes his or her pattern-detecting brain to discern the rules of social interactions, the rules of family systems, the rules of cause and effect and even the rules of language itself. During these first six years, adults can facilitate this process by being available for children by playing parent-infant games, facilitating pretend play and maintaining limits of safety. When children are capable of playing games with rules successfully, we then know they have developed a concept of rule-governed behavior.

Before rule-governed behavior is internalized, limits instead of rules are more effective in facilitating the development of the child. Limits help children learn from their behaviors, internalize responsibility for their actions and develop a scaffold on which the concept of rules can be placed. Limits help children learn the value of rules by the constant focus on safety. All children can relate to safety on some level. When we focus on the need to have and maintain a safe classroom, we are not as dependent on focusing on the logic inherent in rules. The need to rely on logic is not helpful in working with young children who have yet to develop the cognitive capabilities of understanding logic. Focusing on safety as opposed to logic creates a child-centered environment that is more meaningful to young children.

Limits also prepare the children for rules through the never- ending implementation of limit-setting strategies that teach children ways of functioning with socially acceptable behaviors. Children who understand the rationale and need for rules in a home, classroom and society are more likely to internalize a functional nurturing rule system and thus develop self-discipline based on self-esteem (Hoffman, 1970). Children five years of age and younger need a limit-setting system. Children six years of age and older can utilize a rule-governed system.

Part Three

"I'll give you something to complain about."

Creating an Environment Where Children Choose to Cooperate

True obedience is a matter of love, which makes it voluntary, not compelled by fear or force.
—Dorothy Day

Chapter 8

You better get control of yourself right now:
Creating a Safe Environment

Structure Versus Control
Self-control in Adults

Every new teacher or parent at one time or another is given the advice "get control of them and get it early." Adults fear that if they do not clearly "show them who is boss," the children will take over, grow up to be serial murderers or drive them absolutely into an early grave when they become teenagers. These fears then create anxiety as to how to handle certain situations. The anxiety produces adults with controlling, erratic behavior. Adults then justify these behaviors in an attempt not to spoil the child.

I have always thought deeply about this notion of spoiling children. The only thing I have to relate the concept to is food. I know I have seen meat spoil. It smells and we throw it away. It becomes "not fit for the dog." I have seen the same with vegetables that wilt and fruit that develops a fungus. In either case the food item is declared no good and discarded— left only to the prey of insects and other animals that ultimately eat it. So I think to myself *the price of spoiling children is very high.* They become no good, unwanted and discarded. To avoid this drastic fate, certainly all precautions on the part of adults must be taken to prevent this spoilage in children. Preventing spoilage is the rationalization given for coercing children, spanking children, manipulating children and other **control** techniques that have been declared useable because each supposedly "works."

• •

The ultimate goal is to structure situations for children and to control ourselves.

• •

This chapter will explore the difference between control and structure. Once the difference is defined, your journey from control to structure will become clearer and more focused. The ultimate goal is to structure situations for children and to control ourselves.

To be in **control** means we are consciously aware of our thoughts and feelings. When adults are unaware of their own thoughts and feelings, they are out of control and seek to alleviate the problem by getting control of children. The problem in this approach is that to get control of children, we must get control of what children think and feel. In order to do this we must tell children how to think and feel, which negates the children's own thoughts and feelings. The message becomes, "You don't have enough sense to think and feel for yourself. I'll let you know what is best." We then systematically train children not to listen to themselves, think for themselves or trust themselves. Controlling children is a costly loss of human potential.

Structure is defined as the process whereby the adult gives children the necessary information and skills to meet the adult's expectations and meet their own needs at the same time. Structure implies that I, as the adult, have a clear expectation of how I want children to behave in certain situations and at the same time have some sense of children and their unique needs at each developmental stage. With this combined knowledge, I will be able to teach and guide the child in such a way he is able to meet his needs and my expectations simultaneously. Read the following scenarios and see if you believe the adult involved was controlling or structuring:

❐ The block area was strewn with blocks, jumbled everywhere, littered with the many small cars and trucks that were used to highlight the play. Amidst the mess stood Janice and Careem looking hopeless. Mrs. Farmer, noticing the situation, walks over and starts picking up the blocks. She hands Janice the short rectangular ones and the round cylinders she hands to Careem. Mrs. Farmer makes sure the children are able to match the blocks with the outlines painted on the shelves. As the two children become involved in the clean-up process, Mrs. Farmer calls their attention to the different sizes and shapes. Shortly the task was completed. Did she use structure or control?

❏ The block area looked like a tornado had hit. The blocks were strewn all over the floor, scattered amidst many small cars and trucks. Two children, Melinda and Ida, were standing in the middle of the block center looking lost. Ms. Palmer approaches the girls saying, "Do you know what time it is? What do you need to be doing? Why are you just standing here? It is clean- up time. If I have to speak to you again, you will lose the chance to play in this center for one day. Do you understand me?" Did she use structure or control?

As you no doubt guessed, Mrs. Farmer structured the situation for Janice and Careem. She provided a framework from which they could succeed. Ms. Palmer, on the other hand, was controlling. She quizzed Melinda and Ida as if they had a framework inside them they were not utilizing. The only information she offered the girls was what they would lose if they did not meet her expectations.

• •

Controlling children is a costly loss of human potential.

• •

What You Need to Do to Provide Structure

Structuring is a way of providing young children with a safe environment. Sometimes when we think of safety, we only think of physical safety. One of our key roles as adults is to provide for our children's emotional safety. Structuring guarantees emotional safety. You only have to look at our prison system to see the price of not being raised in an emotionally safe environment. An enlightening book entitled *Men Are Not Cost Effective* states that crime costs $300 billion a year (Stephenson, 1991). The price of safety is staggering. Three years without crime would pay our national debt with cash to spare. To explain the components of structuring, I have used the acronym SAFETY PRICE to remind us that fearful people become destructive, and ultimately we all pay a high price when safety is not provided for young children.

To successfully structure children, we must do the following consistently :

State clearly what your goals and expectations are.
"When you get to the doorway, stop."
"When you enter the room, you will find a carpet square to sit on. "Sit quietly until we begin singing together."
"When Brooke talks, you are to listen to what she says."

Anticipate potential problems.
Ms. Slavik knew Taylor and knew her well. Every time the class would transition from one place to another, Taylor would get anxious and become disruptive. To help with her anxiety the teacher had a visual timer made out of two liter bottles full of sand just for Taylor. When a transition was about to occur she would say, "Taylor, we are going to change from small group time to outside time in a few minutes. Turn your timer on so you can prepare yourself to walk from your table to the door." In addition, Ms. Slavik stood next to Taylor during these transition times. She also had picture cards of the daily routine on Taylor's work space, so she could track the parts of the day by turning the cards over as the day progressed.

Forgive yourself when you lose control; regain control by soothing yourself.
Ms. Slavik was very good at anticipating "hard times" for Taylor. Yet some days she still found that no matter what she did to structure the world in a way that met Taylor's specific needs, Taylor would "go wild." One day Ms. Slavik had been to the end of her rope and tied twelve knots, and still Taylor was bouncing off the walls. Ms. Slavik began to think, "I really have had it with this child. I have gone out of my way to structure this classroom just for her. I don't make enough money to put up with this nonsense. That

child needs to be taught who is in charge, I will show her what for!" Ms. Slavik's thoughts became more and more negative, more and more out of control. Finally, she shouted, "Taylor, I have had enough of you today. I want you out of my sight and in time out. You should be ashamed of how you have treated your friends and me. I won't stand for it. You are being naughty, rude and ugly. Now get in time out and stay there until I come get you. Do you hear me? Now go— so I don't have to look at you!"

Well, within about twenty minutes, Ms. Slavik felt horrible. She knew she had lost control and handled the situation poorly. Instead of "beating herself up," which would have created more negative thoughts, she decided to take some deep breaths, ask for help from a colleague and forgive herself. She was ready and able to talk to Taylor about what had happened.

Look to the **E**nvironment for solutions.

Mr. Grace had been given the rare opportunity to buy some extra supplies for his classroom. He began excitedly ordering a variety of things from a catalog. Then it dawned on him, if he could buy two or more of everything, he could begin teaching problem solving this year. So he bought two of everything. When the school year began, he had plenty of opportunities to try out his new strategies.

On the second day of school Carla and Pattie were both holding the firefighter's hat screaming, "I had it! No, I had it! It's mine." Mr. Grace approached the girls calmly and began to try out the new problem-solving process he had learned in a workshop. He said, "Whoa, girls. Hold on. You both seem really upset and have a big problem." The girls responded by getting louder and pulling harder.

Mr. Grace almost decided just to put them in time out, but he continued with the process. "You girls have a prob-lem. You want to play with the same hat. When this hap-pens, the first thing to do is look around the room and see if there is another hat just like it. Can you find another hat just like this one?" Carla said, "I see it! I see it!" "Me, too. me, too," responded Pattie. The girls ran over and got the other hat and began playing mommies going to church. Mr.

Grace was still kneeling where the children used to be and was pleased that the strategy he used brought an unexpected resolution.

Teach the children the skills necessary to meet our expectations.

One of my favorite pastimes is to observe families in the grocery store or the mall. One day I was wandering through the mall and a mother pushing a stroller with two children passed me. In the stroller was a four-year-old child in the back with his ten-month-old brother sitting up front. The child in the back was using his brother as a wonderful play toy. He would pull his hair, hit him on the head and swing his arms outward in awkward positions. All the while, the younger baby brother was screaming. The mother, in response to the screams, was rocking the stroller saying, "Ssh now, now." The lid on the stroller kept the mother from seeing the boys, and she assumed her baby was just "fussy." The mother looked exhausted, and I approached this family, commenting to the mom about her beautiful children. She rolled her eyes. I asked if I could look at them. She proudly agreed.

As I leaned down and looked under the stroller lid, I said to the older brother, "When your brother screams, that means he does not like it when you hit him. He is saying stop, ' I don't like that, it hurts.'" The little boy gave me an indescribable look as if to say, "So that is why he is crying." The family moved down toward one end of the mall and I headed to the other. I'm not sure of the outcome of my intervention; however, I did see the family later, and both boys were peaceful and happy.

You are in charge.

I believe there are basically three types of people when it comes to being in charge. There are passive people, who fail to stand up for their rights or stand up in such a way their rights are easily violated. Mrs. Carmady below represents a passive person.

"Children, when you are quiet, I will begin. Now, Lee, listen up please, and see if you can try and find your seat, okay?"

There are aggressive people. These people stand up for their rights but do it in a way that violates the rights of others. Ms. Higgins demonstrates aggressive behavior:

"Children, I will not talk over all this noise. You are being rude and disrespectful. You should be ashamed of yourselves. One more peep and no recess."

There are assertive people, who are able to stand up for their rights and simultaneously respect the rights of others. This is truly being "in charge." Mr. Jennings in the scene below stays in charge.

"Children, when you talk when I am talking, I feel frustrated, and cannot remember what I wanted to say." Being in charge requires that the adult is conscious of his or her thoughts and feelings and knows ways to accurately express them.

Plan ahead.

It has been my experience that many discipline problems occur during transitions, when children are moving from one activity to another or from one place to another. Many of these problems happen because the adult unrealistically expects the children to wait patiently for too long while other children get ready to join them. Planning ahead during these times would eliminate these problems. In this example, Ms. Bronson demonstrates various ways to plan ahead.

When group time is over, Ms. Bronson avoids a stampede to the center areas by making a game out of sending a few children at a time. Sometimes she says, "Everyone wearing stripes today may go to the center of their choice." Next, it might be those with plaid or print designs on their clothing. Other days, Ms. Bronson will focus on eye color or hair color. Still other times, she will hold up name cards to excuse children one at a time; the children practice reading their own and their friends' names to determine whose turn it is. This year she has a suggestion box so children can suggest categories or attributes to use in dismissal from large group time.

Ms. Bronson also is aware that you should always

"pull children, not push them." This means some exciting activity must be attracting them during transitions. In this case, the centers are so appealing to children they naturally are excited, yet she still stands up and positions herself between the group of children sitting on the floor and the centers they will be going to. By positioning her body in the middle, she is planning ahead in case conflict erupts.

Rehearsing—practicing what to say and do.

The first eight weeks of school are critical for children as they make the transition from home to school or from day care to school. Rehearsal or practicing what to say and do can be used a great deal at the beginning of the year. Children can rehearse coming in the morning, putting their backpacks away, turning over their picture for roll call and placing a picture of themselves by the money, the paper bag or milk carton to let the teacher know if they are buying their lunch or not. Children can rehearse this sequence by role playing, drawing pictures, seeing sequenced pictures, retelling the morning routine and making a video of the morning sequence. The more creative ways you can think of to have children rehearse and practice behavioral expectations, the easier and safer the classroom is for children and teachers. The same is true for parents at home. The more rehearsal the better!

Visual Pictures Help with Rehearsing

"After you eat, then brush your teeth, then . . . ."

Information needs to be given to children about what is likely to happen.

"Children, we just finished with the morning message. It is now story time. Gather round so we can hear. Let's see who will be reading from the author's chair. Karissa, that's right. Go ahead, Karissa. Boys and girls, be helpful to your friends." The more information that can be given in visual form, the better. Sequence cards of a bedtime routine help young children meet the expectations of their parents. (See appendix for ordering information.)

Communicate procedures clearly.

"It is time for listening to the stories you have written. Come sit on a carpet square. Karissa has signed up to read from the author's chair. You will sit and listen to her story." These are clearly stated communications as opposed to the following. "Okay, children, let's see what time it is. Maybe we need to sit with our legs crossed. Perhaps you could move closer so you can hear. Let's see who will be reading from the author's chair. Karissa, was it you? Go ahead, Karissa."

Expect children to be successful and focus on their successes.

Kimberly had the hardest time coming to circle. She would dawdle and drag herself around the room. As the days went on, the teacher began to expect Kimberly to dawdle. The more she expected it to occur, the more the teacher would command, warn and nag Kimberly. It turned out that Kimberly was getting more one-on-one attention for dawdling than she was getting for doing anything else. As the teacher became aware she was focusing on Kimberly's failure to get to circle on time, she decided to change her attitude and her focus. To assist in this change of focus, she practiced what is called "positive pre-play." She would in her mind's eye imagine Kimberly coming successfully to circle. As she began focusing on Kimberly coming to circle on time, she noticed she was reinforcing Kimberly every time she headed toward the circle and basically ignored her when she was heading away. Lo and behold, Kimberly started coming to circle on time. Kimberly had, with the help of the teacher, learned how to get her attention during circle time, not in the process of getting there.

The price we pay for not structuring our environments is the loss of self-confidence in ourselves and the loss of self-esteem in children. Structuring ensures the safety net children need to free themselves intellectually and socially to meet their potential in our classrooms or in our families. Following is a summary of the components of structure.

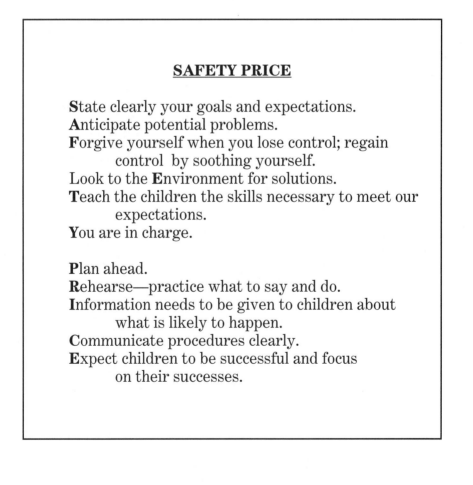

SAFETY PRICE

State clearly your goals and expectations.
Anticipate potential problems.
Forgive yourself when you lose control; regain
        control by soothing yourself.
Look to the **E**nvironment for solutions.
Teach the children the skills necessary to meet our
        expectations.
You are in charge.

Plan ahead.
Rehearse—practice what to say and do.
Information needs to be given to children about
        what is likely to happen.
Communicate procedures clearly.
Expect children to be successful and focus
        on their successes.

Beliefs That Prevent Successful Structuring

Three common beliefs are embedded in our socialization that prevent adults (especially women) from successfully structuring situations for themselves and children.

Clearly defining and stating what you expect from children is rude. Structuring requires you know what behaviors you want from children, communicate these expectations clearly and provide many creative opportunities for children to practice the expected skills. Therefore, you must know what you want and how to get it. If you have been socialized, as are millions of people, to be "people pleasers," you are not trained to think this way. You are trained to focus on what you think others want. To clearly have a desire, want or expectation is considered selfish. To give a command is rude for women. Watch how differently men and women communicate. At home you may hear a husband say, "Get me a sandwich out of the fridge, Hon." This is very clear and straightforward. A woman may approach the same task by saying, "Honey, while you are up would you mind getting me a little something out of the fridge, please?" He may respond, "Sure. What do you want?" The reply many times is, "I don't care. Whatever is fine with me." When we believe that being clear and asking for what we want is being controlling, rude and selfish, we then become paralyzed in our ability to structure.

"They should know by now" or "I know you know better." Many times as teachers we do a fine job of structuring situations at the beginning of the year. We clearly state our expectations, we teach children the necessary skills they need to meet them, we plan ahead, we anticipate problem areas, and so on. However, six weeks later we no longer continue to repeat the expectations and the skills we wish to see demonstrated. We fall into the trap of "they should know by now" or "I know they know the rules." We forget that we are dealing with very young children who learn through repetition. How often do we need to repeat ourselves for children to learn the rules or the skills they need to function successfully? Remember, the answer is **2000 times in context.** Just think how long it truly takes for a child to internalize just getting up in the morning, getting dressed, grooming oneself, feeding oneself and getting out the door. Some of you who are parents may have preadolescents who still haven't mastered this "morning routine." Yet with young children we tend to tell them a few times and expect them to retain the information, apply it and be happy about the whole process. When you find yourself talking to yourself in your head saying, "I know they know" or "They should know better than that by now," stop yourself because you are not helping the situation.

Giving commands is rude.
Since many people are socialized to believe that giving commands is rude, they fall into what could be called the "pitfalls of structuring."

✔ *Asking questions instead of giving information.* Instead of telling children to "stand up, push your chair in and walk quietly to the door to line up," we tend to say, "What time is it? What are you going to do with your chair? How are you going to walk? What are you going to do when you get there?" We quiz children as to the structure as opposed to providing the structure. You might ask, "Shouldn't they know by now?" If so, you have fallen into the unsuccessful belief I just discussed. You might ask, "How will I know if they know the procedures?" Well, you will know when they can successfully achieve them by their actions and behaviors.

✔ *Language that asks permission or gives away power.* Being socialized as people pleasers, we begin to develop a language system to support that socialization process. The system is based on the premise that to avoid hurting anyone's feelings and losing their approval, it is best always to get their permission before you act.

"When you are ready, I will begin."

"Let me finish this story, then you can tell me yours."
"Would you please be quiet when I am talking?"
"I'm going to talk to Kevin now, okay?"

The above comments ask the children's permission to do your job. You have then put the children in charge of the classroom or home. Children in control of adults is just as deadly as adults in control of children.

Self-control in Adults

If we are not supposed to control children, who do we control? The most important technique adults can learn in working with or raising children is self-control. All self-esteem problems in children are due to lack of self-control in adults. Adults, be it parents or teachers, who are enraged, depressed or guilt-ridden are less able to implement appropriate guidance techniques for children. Therefore, before adults can adequately structure children, environments and situations, they must first get better control of themselves. Face it, most of the time when you are in control of yourself, you do an excellent job of disciplining children. Until we learn how to maintain self-control, no books, no workshops and no wonderful guidance strategy will ever be effective. Self-control is especially important with our challenging children. Children who are severely troubled do not necessarily respond to social reinforcement (i.e., smiles, hugs, praise). So no matter how "nice" we are to these children or how loving we try to be, they persist in their behaviors, and we tend to feel rejected and ultimately resentful and maybe even revengeful toward them.

Understanding Behavior

The work of Albert Ellis (1962, 1969), Aaron Beck (1972), Maxie Maultsby (1975) and others has demonstrated that there is a relationship among what we *think* about a situation, how we *feel* about the situation and how we *behave*. Essentially they all suggest that our thoughts dictate emotions and behavior. Actually if you think about it, it does make sense. For example, at the count of three I want you to have a feeling, no thoughts, just a feeling. One - Two - Three! I dare say you were unable to do this unless you were pregnant or in some other high hormonal time. The following equation demonstrates what variables cause us to behave in certain ways.

Behavior = Choices = Feelings = Thoughts = Beliefs = Programming (2000 times in context)

What this equation says is that our behavior is governed by our choices. You chose to buy this book. What causes or affects our choices? Our feelings. You might have felt desperate in searching for a book to help you with a specific child. You may have felt inspired to learn new skills for the upcoming school year. Whatever your feelings, they influenced your choice to purchase this book. What causes certain feelings to arise within us? These are created by the thoughts we think. For instance, if we view an event or person in hostile terms, we are likely to express anger and aggression. Similarly, fearful thoughts often breed anxiety and withdrawal. On the other hand, thoughts that emphasize our ability to cope and remain composed engender a feeling of competence and support effective self-control. As you may have noticed by now in your life, many people have different thoughts about the same experience.

Let's listen in on a teacher and a teacher assistant reflecting on and discussing an event they both experienced in the classroom.

Assistant: Could you believe circle time today?

Teacher: I thought it went quite well.

Assistant: What on earth do you mean? Did you see Tyler? He wiggled. He hit. He even left the group twice.

Teacher: I saw that he left the group to get control of himself and the situation. I was actually excited he took charge like that.

Assistant: Well, I saw him take charge all right. He took control of the entire classroom and chaos prevailed.

As you can tell from the conversation, each adult perceived and interpreted the same situation in a different light. What causes us to have certain thoughts? It is our beliefs. Our beliefs are then created from our programming or that which we were told or saw over and over again. In the situation above, the teacher and the assistant have had different experiences and therefore reacted differently to the child.

Self-control Techniques

Calming Self-Talk: Using the above behavior formula, we can conceptualize any given situation in terms of the following sequence:

A = Something happens (A behavior gets your attention or taps into your belief structure.)

B = A person has thoughts about the situation, initially in the form of self-talk (i.e., you begin to talk to yourself in your head).

C = Based upon the particular thoughts chosen, a person begins to feel a particular way.

D = The person behaves consistently with those feelings (Fleischman, Horne & Arthur, 1983).

For example, a child is asked to clean up the toys. The child arrogantly refuses. This is step A. The parents or teacher may begin to think of the child as disobedient, disrespectful and uncaring and begin such self-talk as "She's a selfish brat. I hate that. She's just trying to show me who's boss." This is step B. As the adults think these thoughts, the adults themselves will become very angry. This represents step C. As a result, the adults (either parents or teachers) will more than likely deal with the child by yelling, possibly spanking or imposing harsh punishments they may later regret. They have arrived at step D.

It becomes critical for adults that we 1) become aware of how our thoughts and beliefs affect our behavior and 2) modify those thoughts to improve our self-control. The most direct method for modifying self-talk is to recognize the negative self-statements that generate within us anger, depression and/or guilt. We can then replace those thoughts with other equally valid but less upsetting self-statements.

Returning to the example of the child who refuses to clean up her toys, we can see that the adult in charge can choose upsetting thoughts such as the ones mentioned, or the adult could replace those thoughts with "This child is checking to see if I mean what I say." Every moment, we have the choice of choosing upsetting thoughts or calming thoughts.

• •

Each thought we choose to think impacts our behavior.

• •

Pushing Your Buttons!

Exercise: Children can only push our buttons if we let them. The two columns below provide examples of thoughts that can lead to a loss of self-control and alternative thoughts that can help adults remain calm and in control.

Upsetting Thoughts	Calm Thoughts
"That child is spoiled. How dare he talk back to me. He is just disrespectful. I'll teach him."	*"I am calm and safe. I can teach the child how to talk respectfully to get his needs met."*

In the space below list the three behaviors from children that push your buttons. Whining immediately sets me off. What are those behaviors for you? Write them down.

Behaviors That Push Your Buttons

1._____

2._____

3._____

Discerning Your Upsetting Thoughts

Now for each behavior mentioned above try to catch your immediately triggered upsetting thoughts. Replay scenes in your mind to assist you in discerning your upseting thoughts. These thoughts are like reflexes. They are programmed in from your past experiences. Write your immediate upsetting thoughts in the space provided below. Once you have written your upsetting thoughts, then write your new, calming replacement thoughts.

Behavior 1: Upsetting Thoughts_____

_____

Calming Thoughts _____

_____

Behavior 2: Upsetting Thoughts_____

_____

Calming Thoughts _____

_____

Behavior 3: Upsetting Thoughts_____

_____

Calming Thoughts_____

_____

Because the brain works somewhat like a computer, it becomes important that we take charge of our own programming. Some of you may have trouble catching the original trigger thought that sends you on a loss-of-control tailspin. Others may have identified the upsetting trigger thought but had difficulty in coming up with a calming replacement thought. We have not been socialized to be responsible for our thoughts. We have grown up with, "Look what you *made* me do" or "See how you *made* your sister feel." These statements put other people in charge of our thoughts and feelings. This is an extremely important and beneficial exercise. Now for those of you who copped out—back up and give it a try!

As soon as a child starts whining, my trigger-upsetting thought is initiated. I say to myself, "I can't take this. I don't have to take this. I'm not going to put up with this all day." Of course once I get that resentful ("How dare they do this to me!") frame of mind, my upsetting thoughts increase until I lash out, release and temporarily feel better. Sometimes this temporary release feels powerful; however, it is really hurtful. Once this process kicks in, I now recognize the trigger and take control of myself by inserting a calming thought. I usually recognize I am losing control. I then take a deep breath and say, "I am calm. I am safe. I can help this child with the problem."

Goal-Oriented Questioning

For some people, substituting thoughts is extremely difficult. Some of you might like an alternative technique that focuses on questioning yourself during moments of conflict. Specifically, this technique involves having the adults learn four basic questions that they ask and attempt to answer during those challenging times. Try these questions:

- What is my goal?
- What am I doing now?
- Is what I am doing helping me to achieve my goal?
- If it isn't, what do I need to do differently?

For example, a teacher is trying to read a story to the class and is interrupted repeatedly by a child talking to his friends. Irritated and on the verge of losing control, the teacher begins the goal-oriented questioning.

What is my goal? *My goal is to finish reading the story without interruptions.*

What am I doing now? *Stopping the story to remind Kevin of the rules and get him to stop talking.*

Is what I am doing helping me to achieve my goal? *No, I am continually stopping the story and getting angrier each time. If I continue to get angry, I will probably say something to Kevin I will regret.*

What can I do differently? *First, I will relax myself a little. Then I will offer Kevin a choice to sit quietly or leave the group. Then I will relax some more. After the story I will talk to Kevin and develop a strategy that will work for each of us.*

The following chart is a list of the subskills of self-control. Pick a child with whom you have had difficulty. Next to the sub-skill provided, put a check if the child demonstrated that skill. Next to that in the following column, place a check if YOU demonstrated that skill in relation to that child.

Self-control Subskills Include the Ability to

SKILL	CHILD	ADULT
1. Select and attend to relevant stimuli. (Focus on problem or behavior at hand to avoid focus on blame or personality.)	_____	_____
2. Remember those stimuli. (Continue to focus on here-and-now problem without focusing on past or other conflicts.)	_____	_____
3. Sequence stimuli or events as well as the ability to predict a logical sequence. (Understand what led up to the event.)	_____	_____
4. Anticipate the consequence of one's own or another's action.	_____	_____
5. Appreciate one's own or another's feelings.	_____	_____
6. Manage one's frustration regardless of perceived origin.	_____	_____
7. Inhibit one's tendency toward action, especially to delay one's initial (gut level) response for at least a few seconds.	_____	_____
8. Relax with only a minimum of external assistance. (Can calm oneself once excited.) (O'Conner, 1991)	_____	_____

Summary

There is a difference between control and structure. Being in control is when you get in touch with your own thoughts and feelings so as to maintain self-control of yourself. Structure involves clearly and assertively stating to children our expectations in regard to their behavior and then teaching them through providing the skills and information they need to know to be successful in the structure we provide. To ensure our classrooms and our homes are indeed providing children with emotionally and physically safe environments, we must structure children, situations and environments and then control ourselves. If we do not, there is a **safety price** we pay by loss of self-esteem and human potential in ourselves and in our children.

Behavior is created by the interplay of our beliefs, emotions and thoughts. Emotions are very healthy because emotions (energy in motion) serve to motivate us to take some action. Fear, for example, motivates us to leave a dangerous situation. In families and in classrooms, feeling annoyed or disappointed by something a child has done helps motivate the adult to remedy the problem. However, when adults allow themselves to become so upset or overwhelmed that they overreact (become out of control of the thoughts they are thinking), the consequences can be unfortunate. Adults at this time may say or do something they soon regret (strike a child, humiliate or say hurtful things, impose punishments they cannot enforce). Often after we calm down, we feel guilty about our actions and hesitate to deal with the child for fear of repeating the last episode. For the child, seeing a parent or teacher lose control is frightening and anxiety provoking. In addition, we then are modeling for the child the exact behaviors we are trying to eliminate. The cycle of overreaction and avoidance means that the adult cannot deal with the child in a way that will achieve lasting changes in behaviors.

Our self-talk, that which we tell ourselves in our head, is directly related to our behavior. There truly is no such thing as an "idle thought." Each thought we choose to think will impact our behavior. We can choose to talk to ourselves in a way that creates fear, anger and hopelessness, or we can choose to talk to ourselves in a way that creates love, desire and hope. The choice is up to us.

The ultimate goal of structure is safety. Once safety is achieved, trust is easily established. Both trust and safety are facilitated by environments that are structured to provide consistency and predictability.

Chapter 9

Why do I always have to tell you what to do:
Providing Predictability Through Routines

Providing Predictability

"Good morning, boys and girls. Who can tell me what today is?" "Monday, Wednesday, Saturday, Sunday," shouted the children. "Let's look at the calendar. Yesterday was Monday, so today is _____." "Monday, Wednesday, Saturday, Sunday," shouted the children. "Let's say the days of the week together," said the teacher. "Monday, Tuesday, Wednesday, Thursday, Friday, Saturday, Sunday," the children responded in unison. Feeling somewhat frustrated at this point, the teacher tried again. "If yesterday was Monday, then today is _____." "Saturday, Monday, Wednesday, Tuesday," shouted the children once again. "Yes," exclaimed the teacher with a sigh of relief, " today is Tuesday." Thus begins another day in the life of children and teachers throughout the United States.

Children do not understand the concept of time until the first or second grade. Until this point they live in the now or the moment. They develop concepts of before and after, later and next as they experience life in the first six years. For children, time and space are the same thing. That is why we schedule their day in segments called rest time, lunch time, center time, story time and bedtime. As we provide children with a consistent schedule and a consistent routine of the day, the environment becomes predictable. The more predictable the environment is for children, the more in control they feel and the safer they feel. Children who feel safe are less likely to feel a need to defend themselves or attack others.

Daily routines are the mechanism by which teachers and parents establish and regulate activities and, as such, increase the predictabilty of the environment (Savage, 1991). Routines are used by teachers and parents to move activities along and structure the day. Routines are socially shared procedures of sequenced behavior in the classroom. Although routines help to regulate behavior by improving predictabilty in the classroom, they are not rules. You can think of routines in regard to gymnastics. In gymnastics each participant, whether on the bars, horse or in the floor exercise, devises sequences of movements called routines.

This is very similar in the classroom. There are morning routines, lunch routines, tardy routines and many more. The same is true in homes. There are morning routines, pick up-from-school routines, homework routines, bedtime routines, etc. Each routine is a social script of sequenced behavior. Although rehearsal is necessary to establish routines, they commonly evolve. For example, a classroom morning routine usually emerges during the first several days of school.

In Ms. Lee's classroom the children arrive on the bus and enter the classroom, where each child is greeted by Ms. Lee with a warm and inviting welcome. The children immediately take their backpacks and belongings and put them away in their cubbies. The children are then able to choose to engage in activities set out by the teacher on certain tabletops.

Routines are essential for young children. To reduce the complexity of the classroom or home environment for the children and increase the predictability of the environment, the adult must:

☛ Establish a daily schedule and visibly post the schedule in a manner in which the children can "read" it frequently (i.e., with picture cards).

☛ Write down all the routines for the day, so that the adult is clear about what she is expecting children to do.

☛ Teach the schedule to the children in as many ways as possible over an extended period of time until all children know what will happen next.

☛ Teach all routines to children, repeatedly utilizing a variety of different strategies.

There are management routines in the classroom that include the "housekeeping" tasks such as attendance, collecting lunch money, permission slips and moving the class to different parts of the building. There are routines in regard to eating (snack, lunch), personal belongings, toileting and washing. There are activity and transitional routines for children to follow to select an activity center. And the same is true for knowing what to do when a task is completed and it's time to clean up. The day is basically a socially scripted event of routines for the children. The more the children are familiar with the routines, the more in charge of their lives they feel. Many young children take 3-5 months to learn the routines for the day. If each day varies because of special pullout programs (e.g., art, music, speech therapy), it may take longer or at worst never occur. Teachers can facilitate this process of learning the routine by taking conscious control of the process.

Step One: Developing the Daily Schedule and Writing Down the Routines

The first step is to write out the routines, being sure to include the following:

- Arrival routines
- Management routines (i.e., attendance, lunch money, lunch count, permission slips, notes from home)
- Transition routines (i.e., clean up, center time, small group time)
- Lining-up routines (moving groups of children throughout the building)
- Hygiene routines (toilets, hand washing, teeth brushing)
- Circle time routines
- Eating routines
- Center routines
- Departure routines

Routines for the home vary slightly from school routines. The school arrival routine becomes a "getting up" routine. School clean-up routines become household chores. Transition routines involve getting the child to redirect focus from his own world (playing outside) to focusing on the needs of the parent (coming in and getting ready for dinner). A school lining-up routine becomes getting ready to leave the house. What is effective for teachers is also effective for parents.

By writing down the routines, the adult becomes aware of how much sequencing the child is asked to learn and retain. The second step is to decide which routines will be taught first and what varied strategies will be utilized.

Step Two: Teaching the Schedule and the Routines

The following ideas will help you teach the schedule and the routine to young children.

☞ Provide a visual display of the daily schedule. For teachers, this would consist of the total daily routine from arrival time to dismissal. For parents, these schedules would be only parts of the day. Parents would have displayed the morning routine (eating breakfast, brushing teeth, etc.) and the evening routine (bathe, go to bed). In addition, parents can create errand cards. With the child, cut or draw pictures of the bank, grocery store, post office, etc. Sequence these and let the child take them in the car. If the child says, "Where are we going?" say, "We just finished at the bank. Look at your cards and see what is next." Have the children practice sequencing the day. Put a set of cards in a center and have the children act out the daily routine. Place the cards face down and have a child pick a card. Then have them tell you what happens before and after the card is selected.

Brushing Teeth

Eating Breakfast

Routine and ResponsibilityCards
for Parents

Daily Routine Cards for Teachers
(Ordering information for these cards is in the appendix.)

☞ Take sequenced pictures of children engaging in a specific classroom routine (e.g., morning routine). Provide sequence cards visually depicting a routine (e.g., pictures of a child doing the morning routine when entering the classroom). Have the children play with the cards at a center. Children can sequence the day with the cards and then act them out in order.

☞ Parents can take pictures of certain routines to post in the house. This is especially helpful for the bedtime routine.

☞ Cue the children repeatedly as to what is happening next, what they are presently doing and what they have just completed doing. "Children, center time will be over in five minutes, then it will be clean-up time." "Children, you have just finished story time. Lunch time is next. Those children with velcro on their shoes may go to the door." "We have just finished breakfast. It is time for you to brush your teeth and comb your hair."

☞ Have a puppet corner where children can act out routines. "Hi, I am Theresa the turtle and I just got to my classroom after getting off the bus." "Hello," said the frog teacher, "I am soooo glad to see you. Put your backpack in your cubby, turn your popsicle stick so that I know you are here to stay and choose what area you want to play in while all the other children arrive." "Hmmm," said Theresa, "I like it when the teacher smiles and says hello to me. I am going to put my things away and play. Oh boy! The water table is out. Oops, I almost forgot to put my backpack up and turn the popsicle stick so everyone knows I am here. There now, I am ready to play." Frog teacher saw Theresa and said, "Oh, I see you picked the water table to begin your day of learning at school."

☞ In small groups, role play various daily routines. This cooperative activity would have as its goal to assist all group members in remembering and reenacting various daily routines. Likewise, parents can have young children put on a play. The title could be *The Breakfast Routine.*

☞ Discuss with children in small groups what it feels like to "know" what will happen at school and "not to know." Parents can do this also!

☞ Write a class or family book about the "morning or arrival routine."

☞ Sing songs to assist children in memorizing the routines (e.g., "This is the way we get ready for snack").

☞ Have children write songs, chants or raps to represent a routine sequence.

☞ Create poems to go with routines and transitions, like the one that follows:

When the Lights Blink I Know What to Do!

When the lights blink I know just what to do.
I clean up my toys and look for you.
You're always sitting in the circle with a smile,
Greeting everyone "come sit awhile."

I go sit down at circle in the place of my choice.
The singing has started and I add my voice.
We sing two songs and a finger play,
Then listen to hear what we will do today!

☞ Have the children make a video of a routine and set up a center so children can play and discuss the sequence. Parents and children can have a delightful time together creating a morning routine video. Children love to watch themselves being successful.

Children must be taught the daily routines. The more creative the teacher or the parent, the better. Remember, for children to obtain a concept, they must be exposed to the ideas 2000 times in context. Young children encode information visually. The more we ask them to manipulate visual images representing what we want them to do, the more successful they will be.

• •

Children do not understand time until the first or second grade.

• •

The Final Step: Evaluating the Classroom or Home Routines for Predictability

The final step is to evaluate your environment to ensure the educational goals you want for your children are being modeled in your daily routine. Many adults state they want self-disciplined, independent-thinking children with the capacity to get along with others and problem solve. Yet their routine may indicate otherwise. To evaluate routines, use the following scale:

Routine Evaluation Form

Structure   Control

1   2   3   4   5   6   7   8   9   10

To what degree does the adult use control of the children to sequence the day as opposed to providing structure for the children? A score of 1 would indicate the adult structures the day for the children. The adult provides the boundaries. Within those boundaries the children are free to make their own choices. A score of 10 would indicate the adult controls all the decisions in the classroom. The children are coerced into thinking, feeling and behaving as the adult demands. A score of 5 would indicate the environment has a 50/50 combination of structure and control.

Clarity   Ambiguity

1   2   3   4   5   6   7   8   9   10

To what degree is the adult clear about the behavior she or he wants from the children? Do the children know exactly what is expected of them? Do they know where each one is supposed to be located during circle, after circle or at rest time? Or does the adult assume the children know? Does the adult use clear terms like "put your toys on the shelf in your room, instead of " put your toys away"? A score of 1 would indicate the adult is very clear in his or her routines. A score of 10 means the environment is full of ambiguity, assumptions and confusion. A score of 5 would mean a 50/50 combination exists.

Sociable						Unsociable			
1	2	3	4	5	6	7	8	9	10

To what degree does the adult model socialization skills? Are the children encouraged to talk to each other, practice language skills, use each other to solve their problems and acquire social competence? A score of 1 would indicate the adult structures a very sociable classroom or home, encouraging the children to communicate with each other and the adult. A score of 10 would indicate that most of the talking in the environment is done by the adult. A score of 5 would be a 50/50 combination of child and adult communication.

Independent						Dependent			
1	2	3	4	5	6	7	8	9	10

To what degree does the adult value and promote child independence, child initiative and child autonomy as opposed to adult dependency? The same scoring system applies as explained above.

The following is a teacher's list of routines utilized in her classroom. In italics are questions to help you analyze this teacher's routine, so you may score the teacher's classroom on the Routine Evaluation Form presented at the end of the exercise.

Kindergarten Classroom Routine

Coming inside in the morning - Children come in and put their backpacks in their cubbies. Children with lunch money put envelopes in the container marked lunch money box. Children with notes put them on the teacher's rocking chair. Children may go to the bathroom, get a drink and sit on the floor to listen to records until eight o'clock.

Morning exercise - pledge, anthem, calendar, caterpillar, weather.

Does the teacher model greeting children? Does the teacher encourage (mentor) language development by facilitating child/child interactions?

Tardy students - Children who come in late must obtain a tardy slip from the office.

Are these children welcomed into the room upon arrival?

Bathroom - Children may use the bathroom at any time the sign is on green. The children need to ask to use the bathroom only if they are on the floor during an activity. During quiet time all children will have a chance to use the bathroom.

Does the teacher encourage independence?

Finished activity - If children finish early, they may get a book from the classroom library corner to read.

Snack - Children go outside and sit along the wall to receive snack.

If you were in this class, would you know where you eat and what you do upon completing your snack?

Recess - Children are to walk to the playground. They may play on the equipment, jump rope on the cement or use the balls on the grass. When children see the teacher raise her hand and begin to walk toward the building, they are to come inside.

Lunch - As a child's table is called, they are to use the restroom, wash hands and get what they need for lunch. When called to line up, children have assigned spots.

Does the teacher encourage independence in this sequence?

Quiet time and rest time - Children get their towels and lie in their area. They are called to select a book to look at or

read. The children are called individually to use the bathroom. When quiet time is over, children return their book and towel to the proper place.
What do you think "proper place" means? Could that mean different things to different children?

Centers - Children are called to assigned centers (unless it is a free center day). They may play with the items that have been discussed. Five minutes before centers are over, a bell is rung to begin pick up.
Does the teacher encourage independence, decision making, problem solving and trust in the child to choose?

Getting ready to leave - Tables are called so children can get their belongings to go home. Bus rides are called and dismissed. When the extended day teacher comes, extended day students are dismissed.
Is saying good-bye to people modeled?

Fire drill - Children are to line up at the door and go quietly out to the fence.

Lights - Any time the lights are flashed, the children are expected to stop talking and direct their attention to the teacher.

This is one teacher's representation of the daily routines. If you had these directions for a day in a classroom, would you have any questions? Are you sure you would know where to go after certain routines occur? For example, after centers are cleaned up, where would you go?

Kindergarten Classroom Routine Evaluation: Circle the score you would give the above classroom on the form that follows:

Structure   Control
1   2   3   4   5   6   7   8   9   10

Clarity							Ambiguity		
1	2	3	4	5	6	7	8	9	10

Sociable							Unsociable		
1	2	3	4	5	6	7	8	9	10

Independence							Dependence		
1	2	3	4	5	6	7	8	9	10

Summary

Writing down the daily routines that children are expected to learn through osmosis will demonstrate the complexity of the school or home environment. These same procedures can be done by parents in home situations. It also will help the adult become aware of what he or she is assuming children will understand. Many children do adjust and learn the routines of the day, but many others have trouble with the complexity and possibly have never experienced environments with predictabilty. Children with limited or no experience with predictable environments have difficulty in discerning patterns, and therefore cannot pick up the daily routines as easily as other children. Their minds have been trained to expect the unexpected, not grasp similarities. The more successful the teacher or parent is in clarifying and teaching his or her routines, the more successful the children will be in functioning in the classroom or the family. Routines are also an excellent way to assess whether the teacher is conducting a developmentally appropriate, child-centered classroom.

The classroom is a culture, and students entering the classroom must learn the culture. Our job as teachers and parents is to be aware of the cultural expectations of the classrooms or homes. Imagine entering a different culture and discerning the embedded "rules" of that culture, both without a guide who is conscious of the culture and with a guide who is aware of the culture. Having an adult who is aware of the routines of the day and the evolving nature of those routines will aid children in their ability to function.

Remember, a routine is basically a sequence of movements or behaviors that increase the predictabilty of the environment. You can learn a lot about an adult's beliefs about children, learning and development through viewing the routine. Reviewing your routines will help you discover inconsistencies between your philosophy (what you hope you are doing) and your practices (what you are actually doing).

The first eight weeks of school, the curriculum needs to focus on teaching children the routines of the day, the rules and limits of the classroom and problem-solving skills to get needs met. Also it is important to establish a relationship with each child and his or her family.

The first eight years at home, parents will repeatedly need to teach their children the routines, the rules and the communication and problem skills they will need to get their needs met. Once this safe, predictable and consistent environment is developed, both the children and the adult are free to grow.

• •

A routine is a sequence of behaviors that increase the predictability of the home or classroom.

• •

Chapter 10

Why can't you just be nice:
Providing Consistency Through
Rules and Limits

Providing Consistency Through Rules and Limits

Before reading any further, write five rules you might have in a prekindergarten, kindergarten, first- or second-grade classroom. For parents of young children, write five house rules.

1.

2.

3.

4.

5.

Rules vs. Principles

Mrs. Thomas posted her rules for her kindergarten class in the room as required by the school. Since she had kindergarten children, she kept the number of rules small and the wording simple. Her rules were: 1) Please keep your hands to yourself; 2) Be a good listener; 3) Show kindness to others; and 4) Raise your hands when you have something to say. She knew the children were young, yet she wanted them to be able to sit quietly and listen during show and tell. So, she would adapt her good listening rule to the situation. Actually what she realized was that her definition of a good listener was different during circle time than during small group time and during center time. She actually came to realize that her definition of a good listener depended on how patient she felt on any given day.

Beth, a meticulous mother, didn't actually write down the house rules of her young children, but she knew she had gone over them many, many times. Her rules were: 1) Ask before you take; 2) Be nice to your brother and sister; 3) Listen to adults; 4) You may not go out of the fence; and 5) Once in bed, stay there.

What Mrs. Thomas and Beth have done is a common

mistake many adults make. They have confused principles and rules and therefore unknowingly created a very inconsistent environment for their children. Working with young children requires an understanding of the differences between rules and principles. Rules are predetermined laws that are enforced each and every time they are broken. When a child breaks a rule, some consequence will occur; the teacher is drawn to action. Rules are to be enforced consistently with specified consequences. Principles are based on values and provide guidelines for behavior. Principles are to be taught each and every day. The adult teaches principles by her or his actions; they are modeled. The adult also nurtures the development of the values within the children; they are encouraged. A relationship between rules and principles does exist. Rules are enforced, principles are taught, and they both come from the values the adult wants to instill within the children.

Historically, rules and principles have been confused. Many adults have written principles thinking they are rules, such as "Respect other people" or "Show kindness to others." When it comes time to enforce the rule, ambiguity exists. What is respect, defined by whom, and how is it consistently enforced? If the parent or teacher is in a good mood, does his or her definition of respect change? In some cultures, to look into the eyes of an adult is disrespectful, while in another culture, looking into the eyes is a sign of respect.

Exercise: Read the phrases below and decide which is a rule and which is a principle by writing R or P in the space provided.
1. Sleep or rest on your mat at rest time. _____
2. Respect your friends. _____
3. Listen when others are talking. _____
4. Keep the room a safe place. _____
5. Clean up your toys when finished. _____

Statements 1 and 5 are behavioral expressions that can be enforced consistently without ambiguity. If a child is off his or her mat, it is a clear indication that the rule has been broken. If the toys are on the ground while the child is walking away from the area, there is no question as to whether the rule was broken or not. Statements 2, 3, and 4 are principles. Respect your friends is a cultural value, with many definitions of respect available depending on a student's family, culture and past experiences. Item number 3, listen when others are talking, may have confused some of you in this activity. How can you know if someone is truly listening? You cannot. You can only conclude they are listening after viewing some behavioral indicators. This alone would clue you to the fact that this is a principle because rules are the behavioral expressions of principles.

●●●●●●●●●●●●●●●●●●●●●●●

The difference between rules and principles is what to enforce and what to teach.

●●●●●●●●●●●●●●●●●●●●●●

You could possibly assume someone was listening if he was looking at the person speaking, remaining quiet or refraining from excess movements, but these are still culturally specific indicators of what you believe listening to be. A young kindergarten student was asked to take a note home to his parents from the teacher. The teacher had written that Steve was having trouble listening in class. The child looked at his mother and said, "How does she know what my ears are doing?" Finally, statement number 4 is also a principle. What is safe? Many families or teachers who hit children on a regular basis consider their home or school to be a safe place. Children then come to school with many definitions of safety. Only those children who hold the same definition of safety as the teacher will function successfully in that classroom.

By understanding the difference between rules and principles, the teacher is able to discern what he or she is to enforce and what she or he is to teach. Imagine driving down the road and the posted speed limit is NOT TOO FAST. What would you feel if you were stopped for a ticket? Confusing rules and principles create inconsistency in the classroom and unconsciously penalize all children who have had cultural experiences different from the teacher. Principles are expressions of values, and rules are behavioral expressions of principles. It all begins with what you value.

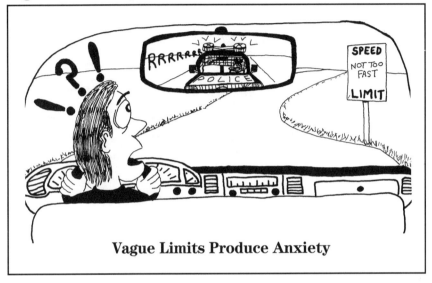

Vague Limits Produce Anxiety

Figuring Out Your Principles from Your Values

To determine your principles ask yourself, "What is it that I value?" It is critical that teachers and parents discern their values, to understand the principles they want to teach their children. Ask yourself, " Do I value respect for one another?" If so, what does respect mean? If I respect someone, what actions are required of me? Many adults have grown up with a one-sided view of respect that includes, listen to what I say and don't talk back, interrupt me, or be rude. However, in practice we may find ourselves not respecting children, yet demanding they respect us. By discovering the principles you wish to teach each and every day, and the way in which you plan to mentor and model these for young children, the chances of creating an environment of "do what I say, not what I do" is greatly reduced.

List some of your values below. List the first ones that come to mind.

1. _____

2. _____

3. _____

4. _____

5. _____

Some classroom values from middle-class teachers and parents from the United States are listed below:
- ♥ Respect one another and the environment.
- ♥ Be honest.
- ♥ Be responsible for one's thoughts, feelings, and actions.
- ♥ Use manners such as saying "Please" and "Thank you."
- ♥ Listen when others are talking.
- ♥ Keep the room safe for everyone.
- ♥ Always try your best.
- ♥ Share.
- ♥ Treat others as you want to be treated.

What were the similarities and differences between the values and principles you hold in esteem and the ones stated above?

It is important to understand that the values we hold dear and true to ourselves are taught within a cultural context. The principles one adult aspires to teach may not be the same for other adults. Just as important as this awareness is the fact that children attending school come from many cultural perspectives.

> *Exercise:* In your class you have the following students: 7 European Americans, 2 Native Americans, 2 Vietnamese Americans, 6 African Americans and 3 Hispanic Americans. Four of the above children are from low-income households; 1 child is from protective services. List two strategies you could utilize to find out the differences, if any, between your value system, which you would like to instill within the children, and the value systems of the families from which the children originate.
>
> 1._____
>
> _____
>
> _____
>
> 2._____
>
> _____

This activity may have felt difficult to you. The United States' educational system has historically not encouraged students to think of other people's value systems for comparison's sake. Therefore, you may have felt anxious about the activity and done one or more of the following: 1) skipped the activity; 2) attempted the activity with a focus on trying to get the answer "right" (i.e., "What does she want me to say?"); 3) focused on the question for just a moment and kept reading, dismissing the importance of the exercise; or 4) risked answering the question with whatever popped into your mind. However you dealt with this anxiety-producing situation will give you a clue to how you will unconsciously model for your children ways to deal with anxiety-producing situations. Every action you take in the classroom, whether consciously or unconsciously, is a teaching moment. Now back to the value activity!

Several options are available to discern if your values

differ from the values of the children and families you serve. First, become familiar with other cultures through readings, research, friendships and acquaintances, and through cooperative endeavors. Second, communicate with the families in your classroom. Ask for input, and be open with the families from different cultures. Ask them for help in becoming aware of the values of their culture. Here are some sample questions you may ask parents to help you better understand the values and concurrent principles they would like taught and/or reinforced with their child:

1. What is your cultural heritage? Do you identify with it?
2. What languages are spoken in your home? What is the predominant language?
3. How comfortable are you speaking and reading English?
4. What traditions, objects or foods symbolize your culture?
5. Why are these things important? What values or history do they represent?
6. What is your church affiliation or religious background?
7. What values do you want us to teach to your children?
8. In what way can we at school support and encourage your cultural values?
9. What heroes, celebrations, music, stories and games could we include that would represent and support your cultural traditions?
10. Does your family celebrate birthdays? If so, how?
11. Would you be willing to come and share your family's ways of celebrating holidays with your child's class?

These questions can be asked directly of parents or solicited through a letter. (The same questions, written in Spanish and English, are provided in letter format at the end of the book.)

By taking time to determine your own values and principles and those of your students, you will be modeling respect for others. Respect for others means accepting their thoughts and feelings as valid. It does not mean you must agree with them, just that you will not devalue their existence and expression.

Once you have a complete and comprehensive understanding of the principles you wish to teach the children, it then becomes imperative that you list the modeling skills you will be utilizing to teach these principles and the techniques you will use to nurture them. This process makes the invisible curriculum more conscious and reduces the double standard of "You treat me this way, and I'll treat you any way I want depending on my mood and my perception of your worthiness."

The following are examples showing two different teachers' principles and their mentoring and modeling techniques.

Mrs. Carter's Classroom

Principles
1. Show respect for all people.
2. Practice self-control.
3. Cooperate and share with others.
4. Listen when others speak.

Mentoring and Modeling

I , Mrs. Carter, will model and mentor my principles first and foremost by showing respect for my students. I will let them know that my goal is to create a safe environment for them. I will not allow anyone to hurt others by words or actions. I will develop a relationship with each student in which that child will feel comfortable and safe; a relationship in which he or she can tell me something and know I will listen with empathy and understanding, without criticism or judgments.

Showing respect, my number one principle, really includes the other three I've added. Self-control, cooperation and listening are all ways of showing respect for another person. Through individual, small group and large group activities, the students will have opportunities to develop these principles. I will model self-control in all dealings with my students, cooperation with my colleagues and listening skills with all the people who want to share their world with me.

Mr. Armstrong's Classroom

Principles

In my classroom the teacher and children will care for themselves, others and the environment.

1. Care for the environment—toys, property, plants, animals.

I will mentor and model
- playing with toys respectfully with children.
- taking care of my things, keeping my desk orderly and returning all items I use to their place.
- supervising the care of all pets and plants in the classroom.

2. Care for others—respect feelings, curiosity and problem solving.

I will mentor and model
- mirroring the child's feelings.
- providing puppet demonstrations of problem-solving techniques.
- patience as I wait for children.
- giving time and encouragement to each child.
- listening to children without interrupting.
- expressing my anger without hurting others.
- showing empathy for others.
- showing enthusiasm for learning.
- explaining and discussing personal body space.

3. Care for yourself—respect myself by getting enough rest, eating proper food and exercising.

I will mentor and model
- avoiding negative self-talk.
- eating my lunch with manners.
- expressing my feelings to the children.

- providing myself with options on days when I begin to lose control of myself.
- overlaying child talk that is self-destructive.
- not coming to work sick or overly tired, using the excuse the "children need me."

Teachers will be unique in how they write their principles and what principles they choose to include. Mrs. Carter and Mr. Armstrong varied in their approach to writing how they were going to actually model and mentor their principles in their classrooms. The more you can become aware of your principles, the more honest your classroom or home becomes, the less ambiguity exists, and the more consistency is provided for the children. After identifying your principles, you must then clearly discern how you are going to teach and nurture these principles in your classroom. The "do as I say, not as I do" principle is a myth; children learn through action and by our actions. It is time to stop asking children to walk in the halls as teachers run to answer a phone call in the office. It is time to stop asking children to sit in their seats as the teacher sits on the desk. It is time teachers quit screaming to children for them to use their inside voices. The same is true for parents.

Posting Your Principles

Once you determine your principles, then post them in the classroom and relate them to parents. Posting the principles can be done in many creative ways. The following suggestions may get you thinking of the million and one ways to involve parents and children in developing the classroom culture of values:

♥ Discuss the principles with the children. Have the children write or dictate stories that demonstrate a certain value and principle being shown.

♥ Use storytelling as a way to model principles. After the adult makes up a story, conclude with, "The moral of the story was . . . ." Then ask the children to add morals to their stories.

♥ Have children draw pictures representing each one of the class principles. Assign the pictures as homework in which parents or guardians and the child draw a picture together, showing the class principle operating at home.

♥ Have the children create a bulletin board entitled "Beliefs we value" or "We all are responsible to . . . . "

♥ Place one classroom principle (for example, Sharing or Listening) on a big sheet of paper and have a group of children create a collage. Cut pictures from magazines and/or articles (if working with second- and third-grade children) that demonstrate that particular principle.

♥ Have the children write songs that focus on the principles. You could, if they needed more structure in the task, give them the tune (i.e., Old MacDonald) and give them the principle (i.e., Be kind) and let a small group of children begin composing. For young children the teaching team could make up the songs and sing them with the children.

♥ The children could create "play scenes" or dramatic plays to act out a story involving a principle. The same thing can be done with puppets. The stories will vary in complexity depending on the age and developmental level of the child. Christian chose to act out his story on "Try your best." He began by jumping on the floor eight times, then he jumped off the ladder on the loft.   He then said, "The end." When the teacher prompted him with, "Christian, what was the moral of your story?" Christian responded, "Always try your best."

The most significant point is that adults structure the environment in which values and principles come alive.

Limits vs. Rules

Limits are boundaries utilized with young children who have yet to develop the concept of rules. Limits teach children that boundaries exist on their behavior, as well as teaching them socially acceptable ways of getting their needs met. Rules are laws on behavior that when broken yield consequences for the child, generally arranged by the teacher. Prelogical children who have not fully conceptualized the concept of rules learn little from a rule-governed system to promote self-discipline. Limits must be used as a prerequisite for rules with children five-and-a-half years of age and younger.

Limits are the boundaries defined by the global principle of safety. When a child steps over the line, breaking the limit, she is guided back into functioning within the boundaries through limit-setting techniques that teach socially acceptable strategies to young children. For example, a child at the sand table begins throwing sand. A limit is necessary. The teacher may say to the child, "Sarah, you really feel like throwing. You may not throw the sand. It could hurt others if it got in their eyes. If you want to throw, you may go outside and throw the beanbags or the balls. What is your choice?" Both limits and rules are behavioral expressions of principles and, therefore, share similarities and differences. Rules, however, are enforced through penalties of consequences when broken, while limits teach acceptable behaviors through problem-solving strategies. Using the above example of sand throwing, a rule would be "keep the sand in the sand box" and the concurrent consequence would be loss of privilege to play with the sand. The goal of rules is to stop behavior, while the goal of limits is to facilitate the child's expression of him- or herself in a socially acceptable manner. Rules teach children there are negative consequences to inappropriate behavior and positive consequences to appropriate behavior, while limits teach children what is appropriate behavior.

• •

Respect for others means accepting their thoughts and feelings as valid.

• •

Limits and Rules		
	Limits	Rules
Goal:	Learn alternative behavior	Stop unacceptable behavior
Strategy Used:	Problem solving and logical consequences	Rewards and punishment are natural consequences
Assumption:	Strong need on behalf of child to belong will elicit acceptable behavior	Consequences can coerce "good" behavior
Motivator:	Love, desire	Fear
Methodology:	Taught— Ages 0-5 years	Enforced— 6 years and older

Limits are utilized with children in kindergarten and younger. Rules are utilized with children who are in kindergarten and in the older grades. The overlap that occurs in kindergarten is an important learning time. Children may start the year with limits and, with the assistance of the teacher, turn the limits into rules around the middle of the year.

Using rules with the very young child is ineffective. Many adults may have a rule for cleaning up and a concurrent consequence of loss of opportunity to play with the toys, yet when a child "forgets" about cleaning up, the adult is more likely to remind the child than enforce the consequence. This type of sometimes-I-will-enforce-and-sometimes-I-will-teach method creates inconsistency, which inhibits the development of the children to their optimal potential. Environments that are consistent are safer, and safer environments are more effective.

Summary

Review the rules you wrote at the very beginning of the section. Did you write rules or principles? Managing classrooms to ensure that consistent, developmentally appropriate structure is established requires a certain set of skills for primary and preschool teachers. Preschool teachers and parents of very young children must set up environments based on limits to assist children in learning that all behavioral choices have consequences. Primary teachers and parents of older children must set up environments based on rules to assist children in choosing appropriate behavior that yields desired outcomes and positive consequences.

All adults need to provide an anti-biased classroom that reflects the cultural values of the teacher and all the children. The "invisible curriculum" of principles and values must be made alive and visible for young children. This can be done by the adult providing the opportunity for children to express their values through art, music and drama. Rule-governed systems require that adults have skills in writing appropriate rules and enforcing them. Limit-setting systems require that adults have skills in problem-solving discipline techniques. Both systems require precise routines and well-managed and designed environments so the classroom and home are both predictable and consistent.

Part Four

"How many times do I have to tell you?"

The Basic Discipline Techniques and Skills of Discipline Every Adult Must Know

I want you to get excited about who you are, what you are, what you have, and what you can still be. I want to inspire you to see that you can go far beyond where you are right now.
—Virginia Satir

Chapter 11

But I want them to like me:
Setting Limits That Are Safe

Using Limits in the Preschool Years

Pretend you just had a fight with your spouse or best friend. It was a knockdown, drag-out fight. Things were said by both parties that were hurtful. The fight is over, but you are still not ready to let go of the anger. You continue the fight in your head by using your inner speech to find more and more reasons why you were right and he or she was wrong.

The relationship you have enjoyed with that person has now suffered a blow and is presently severed. Now pretend the other person is ready to heal the relationship, or "forgive and forget" as the saying goes. You, on the other hand, are not ready to let go of the anger. How do you think you would respond to that person? Would you be open to his or her soothing apologetic approaches? Would you be willing to do what they say or follow their suggestions? Probably not! When a relationship is not functioning between two people, cooperation and pleasantness are difficult to come by. The same is true with young children. If we do not establish and maintain a healthy functioning relationship with young children, our ability to get them to comply with our wishes is minimal. Therefore, limit setting with young children is intricately tied to our relationship with them.

Exercise: Complete the following sentences with the first thought that comes to mind. Do not judge your thought to be good or bad, right or wrong. Just answer automatically.

1. When I ask children to do something they do not want to do, I feel_____.
2. Bending the rules a little bit every now and then is_____.
3. When a child refuses to do something I have asked him or her to do, I feel_____.
4. When a child screams at me "I hate you! You are mean!" I feel_____.
5. I feel best about setting limits and "holding the line" with children when they_____

_____.

6. After you set a limit, the child screams, "You are not fair; it is not fair." Your response to this child would be
_____.

7. When children do what I say, when I say, and are happy about it, I feel _____.

8. When children do what I say, when I say, yet are grumpy and complaining, I feel like saying_____
_____.

The answers you automatically gave to the above questions will give you insight as to how attuned you are with children. Questions number 1, 3, 4 and 7 dealt with your feelings. Questions 2, 5, 6 and 8 asked for your thoughts. On the feeling questions do you tend to become unhappy if the child is unhappy? Do you become angry when the child becomes angry? When the child obeys you happily, as in question number seven, are you then happy?

If in the feeling questions your feelings matched the underlying feeling of the child, you are in tune with the child. The child is capable of getting you to feel how he or she feels. However, if you judge the attunement to be "bad" or view it as an irritation ("the child is out to get me or make me feel miserable"), you, are no longer "tuned in" but "hooked in." Questions 2, 5, 6 and 8 will give you insight into how you think about feeling like the child. Question number eight will give you the most specific information about yourself.

If a child complies to your wishes and expresses some negativity while complying, do you feel negative toward the child, the situation or yourself? If the answer is yes, you are judging your attunement skills to be "bad," and therefore you may tend to judge the child "bad" for having feelings. You are allowing yourself to be "hooked in" to children as opposed to being "tuned in" with them. For example, when they are upset and you become upset about them being upset, you are very "hooked in." "Hooked in" means that your self-esteem is directly tied to the happiness and unhappiness of the children. Evidently you have been taught that when people around you are happy, you are lovable, and conversely, when people around you are angry, sad, scared or upset in any way, you are not lovable or worthy. To set limits with young children, this is the first belief that must be changed. Your worth does not depend on the moods of those around you. You will not be able consistently and successfully to set limits for young children if you feel responsible for *their* happiness to maintain *your* self-esteem.

Limit setting is one of the most important aspects of the preschool classroom and usually one of the most problematic for teachers. Limits provide structure for the development of the teacher-child relationship. Without limits, relationships would have little value, and without relationships, learning has no meaning. This can be dramatically demonstrated with autistic children. These children may have access to a lot of data or knowledge, yet the information they have is meaningless (i.e., it cannot be applied in context). Relationships are the cradle of all learning, and the relationship between the child and the adult is the driving motivator behind achieving maximum development and learning.

Limits provide a structure to the environment and the adult-child relationship so children can feel secure. Young children have difficulty in controlling their own impulsiveness and so they need the security of experiencing limit setting. Limit setting provides the children with an opportunity to gain control of their own behavior. Limits, therefore, help to assure the emotional safety of children. When children "act out" their anxiety in the classroom or home, the adult must think of this as an opportunity to assist the children to regain self-control. Repeatedly assisting children by setting limits provides the children with an opportunity to learn self-control; knowing they can make a choice; the experience of makng choices; and the responsibility that goes with it. Therefore, when limits should be set and they are not, children are deprived of an opportunity to learn something important about themselves as well as the prerequisite skills in the understanding of rules and a rule-governed system. Look back at the answer you gave to number two in the exercise. Did you respond by writing it was okay to bend the rules every now and then? If so, become more aware of this opportunity—especially when working with young children.

Relationships Are the Cradle of All Learning

Many beginning teachers or parents seek to "be friends" with children. They want the children to like them. With these beliefs motivating their behavior, the new teachers or parents tend to be inconsistent. They have been taught that "giving people what they want" will ensure being loved and likeable. Children grow up believing, "If I give in to Mom and Dad, then they will love me. If I do not do what they say, I am unlovable and a 'bad' person." Quite the opposite is true. Holding limits for young children is an act of love that teaches them they are capable of meeting their own needs in a socially acceptable way. Holding limits for young children keeps them safe from their own impulses. Holding the limits is essential. Sooner or later, all teachers and parents realize this.

Darious was running in the classroom again and again and again, and both Ms. Robinson and Ms. Kirby were exasperated! Listen to the inner speech of these two teachers and try to discern who is "hooked in" and who is "tuned in." Ms. Robinson has many thoughts rushing through her head this morning: *How many times already this morning have I reminded that child of the safety rule? I have had it! The classroom is crazy; the children are wild. Why did I ever want to teach? This child is driving me nuts. Others may let him get away with murder but not me.* "Darious, get over here and sit down and do not move from this seat until I say so. Do you hear me?"

Ms. Kirby has just as many thoughts as Ms. Robinson in her head: *How many times this morning have I reminded Darious of the safety rule? I feel so frustrated, my whole body is tense. I feel like screaming. I had better get control of myself or things are going to get real crazy in here.* "Darious, I want you to go and be quiet someplace away from me right now. I am feeling too angry to talk to you about running now. When I am feeling better, we'll talk about how to help you remember to walk in the classroom."

As you probably know, Ms. Robinson was hooked in and Ms. Kirby was tuned in. Ms. Kirby knows that holding limits is an act of love for herself and the children. Ms. Robinson believes control will help keep the "bad" from coming out of them both (the child and herself). Holding limits requires that adults be tuned into and consistent with children.

The Functions of Limits

Limits are critical in the developmental process. The following are the basic functions limits serve in the development of young children:

Limits help assure the physical and emotional security of children and the adult. The role of the adult is to establish and maintain safety in the child's environment. Any behavior that falls outside the boundary of that safety requires limit setting. All limits are based on safety.

Limits empower children. In limit setting children are always given a choice. This allows them to become responsible for themselves and their own well-being.

Limits facilitate a cooperative classroom or home.
Children are more likely to comply when they experience respect for themselves and acceptance for their feelings and behaviors (both positive and negative). Limits are based on the acceptance of the child's feelings and desires, creating a cooperative classroom or home atmosphere.

Limits facilitate the development of decision making, self-control and self-responsibility of children.
A child hears the teacher or parent say, "You seem to be enjoying throwing sand. Sand is NOT for throwing. You may throw the balls or the beanbags. What is your choice?" The child then must make a decision to go with the original impulse of throwing or to exercise self-control and choose an acceptable alternative. In this way limit setting allows children to learn self-control, decision making and responsibility.

Limits provide consistency in the classroom or home environment. Each time the classroom or home becomes unsafe or the relationship between the adult and child is being strained, the adult must take action. This guaranteed action provides the basis for the consistency and predictability.

Limits help the teacher in his or her own growth as a professional. An unequivocal belief by the adult that children will choose positive cooperative behavior given an empathetic and understanding environment is a prerequisite for limit setting. The teacher must hold strong in his or her faith in the child's desire to function within the classroom or family. This deep-seated belief will provide the teacher with the motivation to remain empathetic and accepting of children during the most trying of times. Teachers must hold children and the families from which they come in the highest esteem. It is a well-known psychological principle that we can only "see" our own thoughts. If I am thinking Jason is a "bad" child, I see a *bad* boy. If I am thinking Jason is "cute," I see a *cute* boy.

Children who challenge us the most are our best teachers. They demand that we grow, self-reflect, be positive longer, love harder and gain new skills. Perhaps a child with whom you are having difficulty setting limits inspired you to read this book.

Limits Are Based on Safety

The adult role in the preschool classroom is to establish and maintain safety within the environment. Limit setting is utilized to accomplish this goal. Any behavior that is damaging to the well-being of the children, the teacher, the toys and furniture within the school or the school building itself, is to be limited.

Many classrooms and homes will have the same limits; however, variations will exist based on the adult personality. The responsibility of the teacher is to maintain a warm, caring, accepting attitude toward all children. For the teacher to maintain this attitude while a child is hitting him or her on the knee with a hammer is virtually impossible. Teachers are not superhuman. They are subject to experiencing normal, sometimes uncontrollable, emotional reactions. As soon as a teacher experiences reactions of anger or rejection for a child, this will be sensed by the child. Therefore, appropriate limit setting is crucial to maintaining an attitude of acceptance and positive regard for all children. Activities that are likely to arouse feelings of anger or anxiety in the teacher must generally be limited to ensure children are safe from the teacher's own personality issues.

Some teachers may experience anxiety and anger over what might be described as "children just being children." For example, noise may bother some teachers; lots of movement may create anxiety for another teacher; messiness in the room may be irritating to some; or the constancy of children asking questions may push the buttons of another teacher. Adults who work with children but dislike who they are, must examine their own motivations for teaching young children and the limits they are setting. Are the limits being set to facilitate the teacher/child relationship or to accommodate some rigid need within the teacher to keep him- or herself safe and in charge of all interactions at the expense of the child? All limits must protect the physical well-being of the teacher and facilitate the acceptance of the child at the same time.

Most classrooms are not blessed with unlimited budgets for toys and materials. Allowing children to destroy toys becomes an expensive, if not irresponsible act on the part of the adult. When children attempt to destroy materials, opportunities for limit setting are created, and the children and teacher or parent all learn something valuable themselves. Setting limits usually involves providing the child with alternative methods of expressing a wish or need.

"Gary's building is not for smashing.
You may smash the egg cartons or tear the paper.
What is your choice?"

Thinking of alternative acceptable ways to destroy is sometimes difficult for teachers. Classrooms could have items supplied by parents (i.e., egg cartons) that can be stacked, kicked, jumped on, smashed, broken apart, thrown and painted. By having a place and some specific items that can be treated as mentioned above, adults then have an alternative behavior to recommend to children who want to destroy another child's building.

The adult might set the limit by saying, "You feel a need to destroy something to show your power. Gary's building is not for smashing. You may smash the egg cartons or tear the paper. What is your choice?" Teachers who have a number of children in their classroom who are learning to control their anger may find a smashing area useful.

Just as the teacher's role is to establish and maintain safety in the classroom, the role of the parent is to establish and maintain safety at home.

Limits Must Be Kept Minimal and Enforceable

A common question asked is when limits should be set. Should limits be part of a general introduction to the classroom, or should the teacher wait until situations arise and set limits at that time? The overall answer is a little of both. Teachers need to explain to children their role in the classroom the very first day. Teachers must tell children they are there to keep it safe for them. This cannot be overly stressed. Providing children a long list of limits at the beginning of the first day is not necessary. This tends to set a negative tone. Talking about safety in general and what things could be done to maintain a safe classroom is reassuring.

For some children, a listing of limits only serves to give them ideas. For shy and fearful children, the early introduction of limits only serves to inhibit them more. The best time to learn is when the limit issue arises. Self-control cannot be learned until an opportunity to exercise self-control occurs. A good rule of thumb is that **limits are not needed until they are needed.** Providing visual displays of choices children have within the safe environment will also assist them.

● ●

Self-control cannot be learned until an opportunity to exercise self-control occurs.

● ●

Unenforceable limits are limits imposed on children that prevent them from being children. For example, having a limit for a four-year-old child to wait until called upon to speak is unenforceable. It asks the child not to restrain impulses but to restrain from being a four-year-old. Almost any limit that is not developmentally appropriate is unenforceable. An example of some unenforceable limits for that child include:

- sitting still
- raising your hand before speaking
- waiting over 5 minutes without being active
- playing quietly without talking
- focusing on activities that are meaningless to the child.

At the beginning of the school year, the teacher must first focus on the schedule and daily routines. Teaching children the routines is the main priority; setting limits will evolve naturally as the children begin interacting. To begin the school year the teacher must:

✔ Tell the children that the teacher's role is to provide safety in the room.
✔ Discuss safety and what it means to children. Conduct a brainstorming session. Write down all answers. Remember not to judge a child's response.
✔ Ask the children, "What can I do to keep this classroom safe?"
✔ Then ask, "What can you do to help keep the room safe?"
✔ Role-play examples of each.
✔ Display the visual limits in the room to assist children in making choices that facilitate safety. (See order form in back of book.)
✔ Begin teaching the children the daily routine. (See order form in back of book.)

To begin this process, the teacher might choose to read a book that demonstrates being safe and not being safe, or going by the rules and breaking the rules. A list of children's books is included at the end of the book. Remember, no matter what book you choose, focus the conversation around the issue of safety.

Limits Facilitate the Development of Self-control

Before children can resist following through and expressing feelings in ways dictated by first impulses (e.g., anger = hit), they must have an awareness of their behavior, a feeling of responsibility and self-control. In the midst of intense emotions, children are often unaware of their behavior and therefore lack responsibility.

Limit setting addresses the immediate reality of the situation and indirectly calls attention to the child's behavior through statements such as "The wall is not for painting." How can children develop a feeling of responsibility if they are unaware of what they are doing? And how can they experience a feeling of self-control if they are too defensive to change their behavior?

● ●

Display the visual limits in the room to assist children in making choices that facilitate safety.

● ●

Limit setting does not stir up feelings of defensiveness, which often accompany rule-governed attempts to stop behavior. This can be clearly seen in the statement, "You would really like to paint. The wall is not for painting." In this way the child's need to paint or be messy is accepted and communicated. The child is presented with acceptable alternatives. "You can paint on the easel or on your paper. What is your choice?" Such a statement clearly indicates to the child a permissible way to express him- or herself. Now the child is confronted with a choice: to act on the original impulse or to express one's self through the alternative behavior.

The choice is the child's, and the adult must allow the child to choose. Responsibility accompanies decision making. If the child chooses to paint on the easel paper, it is because the child decided to exercise self-control, not because the adult made the child do so. Limit setting is critical in facilitating the development of self-control.

Limits Help Children Focus Reality

Some children become caught up in pretend play. As they spend time in the enactment of fantasy scenes, they effectively avoid any personal responsibility for actions or behaviors that may be socially unacceptable or destructive. When the adult verbalizes a limit, the experience is quickly changed from fantasy to the reality of a relationship with an adult where certain behaviors are unacceptable. When the adult states, "You would really like to run through the room to catch the bad guys. The inside space is not for running. The backyard is for running," the child is confronted with reality. The child has an opportunity to choose what will be done next and experiences the accompanying responsibility. The child can no longer live in the fantasy enactment. The child must now focus on the reality of making a decision.

Limits Provide for Consistency
in the Classroom and the Home

Many children may come from homes characterized by inconsistency in behavior on the part of the parents. Additionally, many parents, lacking any role models or educational assistance, have difficulty maintaining limits and rules. What was prohibited today may or may not be allowed tomorrow. What was an accepting attitude by the parent in the morning before the child went to school may or may not be evident in the afternoon when the child arrives home. Many children from very consistent homes find themselves in classrooms with inconsistent teachers. Children in such environments are never quite sure what to expect and often attempt to cope by being very cautious or by overtly acting out in an attempt to find out just where the boundaries are.

Children need to experience consistency in their lives if they are ever to achieve some degree of emotional balance. Consistency of attitude and behavior on the part of the teacher or parent helps children to feel secure, and this inner security enables children to move toward being the person they are capable of being. One way a teacher or parent establishes a consistent environment is through use of consistent limits. Limits are presented in a consistent and nonthreatening manner, and the adult is consistent in seeing that the limits are maintained. It is important that adults know they can be understanding and accepting of the child's wish or desire and still not accept the behavior. Limits, therefore, help to provide the structure for a consistent environment. What was unacceptable and unsafe yesterday is still prohibited today. The environment has predictability, thereby increasing the child's feeling of security and ability to be responsible.

Limit Setting Is Based on the Belief in Children

Consistency in limit setting is a function of the adult's attitude and is a tangible demonstration of the adult's commitment to the welfare and acceptance of the child. Teachers or parents who are unable to maintain a warm and empathetic environment for children are adults who do not believe in the inherent desire in all children to love and be loved. Once an adult begins to believe children are "out to ruin her day" or "out to get him" or "just trying to make everyone miserable," the adult is on an abusive course. One sign of abusive parenting is that type of talk. Abusive parents believe the child to be the devil out to destroy their day and their life; the same is true of an abusive teacher. Adults who treat children poorly by losing control and screaming, humiliating children, putting them down, punishing their attempts to understand the world or attempting to control them are in large part displaying their own insecurities about the world.

The Goals of Limit Setting

The process of limit setting involves a procedure designed to convey understanding, acceptance and responsibility to the child. The objective of the adult is not to stop the behavior but rather to facilitate the expression of the motivating feeling, want or need in a more acceptable manner. The adult in a limit-setting environment is a facilitator of expression rather than a prohibitor of action. The goal of the teacher is to facilitate the child's expression through actions and behaviors that are more socially acceptable.

Examining how an adult goes about setting limits will give insight into the personality of the adult. For example, an adult who repeatedly says, "Don't you do that," is an adult who is determined to stop the objectionable behavior. The message to the child is "your motives, needs, wishes are not important; just stop what you are doing." The child may then feel rejected or misunderstood. In any case, the relationship between the adult and child suffers.

If the adult lacks confidence in him- or herself, statements such as the following may occur: "I don't think you should do that" or "That probably is not a good thing to do." Many children persist in a certain behavior the adult seeks to limit because the uncertainty and insecurity of the adult is communicated to the child. Adults who use fear tactics to set limits display their own anxiety about being in relationship with people. When confronted with an "I've told you before you can't do that" attitude, children seem to feel they must protect themselves by persisting in their original behavior. The result is likely to be a power struggle between adult and child.

• •

We must be able to set limits for ourselves before we set limits for children.

• •

> *Exercise:* Listed below are common ways of communi-
> cating with children. Read each statement or question
> and decide whether the teacher is communicating uncer-
> tainty and insecurity (UI), anxiety and fear (AF) or
> responsibility and love (RL). After each teacher com-
> ment write UI, AF or RL.
> 1. Don't you think it would be better to build your blocks
>   over here, Melissa? _____
> 2. Couldn't you and Mark play nicely with the
>   truck?_____
> 3. I wouldn't try that if I were you. _____
> 4. I have told you twenty times to stop it. _____
> 5. You really want to test your jumping skills. Chairs are
>   not for jumping. You can jump over the ropes. _____
> 6. You wish Jason would let go of the toy. Children are
>   not for hitting. You can ask for the toy or wait for the
>   toy.____

In the above activity, the first two teacher comments
relay the message of uncertainty and insecurity to the child,
the second two comments send anxiety and fear outward and
the last two comments relay responsibility and love to the
child. Just as children get us to feel how they are feeling, we
too have the same impact on children. Our anger triggers
their anger, and our insecurity triggers their insecurities.

Rather than attempting to stop behaviors, the adult's
objective is to respond to the child in such a way that the
child is left with the responsibility for changing his/her
behavior. If the adult tells the child what to do, then the
adult is responsible. And there are certainly many times
throughout the day the adult needs to be responsible. However, there also are times when children must be responsible
for their own behavior and their own choices. In those
situations the adult trusts the child's capacity to respond
responsibly and communicates, "You would really like to
dump the water on the floor. The floor is not for pouring.
You may pour water in the sink or in the bathtub. What is
your choice?" The child is then free to decide what to do
next and is, therefore, responsible. Remember the role of

the adult in limit setting is different than the role of the adult in rule management systems. The adult's role is to state the limit in a manner in which the child's feelings, wishes and wants are acknowledged, the limit is communicated and acceptable alternatives are available. The goal is not for the adult to stop behavior but for the child to redirect his or her energies.

Summary

Limit setting is probably the most important skill an adult must master. The way we set limits for children provides the external building blocks for the next generation. Limit setting is intricately tied to our relationships with children and our relationship with ourselves. Realize that we must resolve our own struggles before we can guide anyone else. We must first be able to set safe limits on our own behavior before we can extend it to others. Meeting the needs of children and teaching them to meet their own inner needs through limit setting is our ultimate challenge.

Chapter 12

You have a choice:
Techniques for Limit Setting

The Basic Techniques of Limit Setting

There are several basic steps that can be used in the limit- setting process. One of the key factors in limit setting is the understanding of the child's intention and motivation. Limit setting works better when the adult acknowledges the child's feelings, wishes and wants, communicates the limits clearly, and targets acceptable behavior.

Step 1: Acknowledge the child's feelings, wishes and wants.

Verbalizing the understanding of the child's feeling or want conveys to children acceptance of their motivation. By understanding, we are saying that their inner self and their emotions are okay. Simply setting the limit without acknowl- edging the feelings might indicate to the child that emotions are not important. Verbalizing an empathic understanding of the feeling often helps to defuse the intensity of the feeling. This is especially true in the case of anger and is often all that is needed for the child to begin modifying personal behavior. Acceptance of the motivation seems to be satisfying to the child, and a need for the act no longer exists.

Acceptance of motivations can facilitate the child's self-control when the reflections occur before the physical act. Feelings should be reflected just as soon as they are recognized. Once a block of wood is being thrown across the room, acceptance of the feeling can no longer stop the child from throwing the block. Acknowledge feelings *before* the inappropriate behavior is activated by the child.

Examples of statements that acknowledge feelings are:
"You seem angry."
"You seem frustrated with the puzzles."
"Katie, what a surprise. Kenny knocked you over and you seem startled."
"It seems to me you are really sad today."
"Seems like you'd like to go to work with your mom and dad. It's disappointing to have them leave."

"You seem to be in a lovable and cuddly mood today."

"Carlos, seems like you are enjoying those blocks."

By acknowledging the child's feelings or intentions, the child is more likely to feel understood. As you begin with the process of understanding, the child is likely to perceive you as an ally, thus strengthening your relationship . This sets the stage for what follows. It is much easier to accept the limits imposed by others if you perceive them as supportive. This is true for adults as well as for children.

Step 2 : Communicate the limit.

Limits must be specific and clearly delineate what is being limited. No doubt should exist in the child's mind as to what is appropriate and what is inappropriate or what is acceptable and what is unacceptable behavior. "The sand is not for throwing" is a clearly stated limit. The statement, "It's probably not a good idea to paint on the wall," is a poorly stated limit. "We can't paint walls here" is also a poorly stated limit if the child is presently painting the wall. To state "we don't do something" when the child is presently doing that action is a contradiction to the child. From the child's perspective the answer to the limit is, "Yes we do; what do you think I am doing right this minute?" Also, limits that include the pronoun *we* must be used only when the teacher is limiting his or her behavior along with the child. In this case both the teacher and the child must be painting on the walls for the pronoun *we* to be appropriate.

Mrs. Harmon was preparing her class for lunch. Nick was not paying attention to the teacher. Mrs. Harmon walked over to Nick, stood over him in a dominating position and said, "Nick, it is time for us to put our lunchbox under our seat." From his expression, Nick seemed confused and looked around the room as if searching for something. This infuriated Mrs. Harmon, who assumed Nick was being disrespectful. This time with the veins in her neck bulging out, she yelled, "I said it is time to put our lunch box under our seat." Since I was in the classroom and the teacher was "calling for love," I asked if I could help her. She replied, "This child is impossible. There is nothing you can do but go ahead. I have had it!" I turned to Nick, positioned my body at eye level with his and calmly said, "Mrs. Harmon wants you to put your lunchbox under your seat." His face lit up as if to say "Oh, I get it," and he placed his lunchbox under his seat.

Mrs. Harmon had used incorrect pronouns and the child was confused. He knew where his lunchbox was but he could not locate "our" lunchbox.

In communicating the limit, the following phrases are to be avoided:

♥ "You need to . . . ." This is a common phrase used by adults as a way of giving orders to children. This disguised command is a form of manipulation that adults use, not to establish and maintain a healthy relationship with young children but to get more control of children. By using the word *need*, adults are conveying an urgency to the child that does not exist. The word *need* implies something you cannot live without such as water, air, love and attention. The correct word to use in most situations would be *want*. The adult would say, "I want you to pick up your toys" as opposed to "I need you to pick up your toys." When using *need*, the adult sets him- or herself up to be hooked into the child. Since a need implies a necessity for the adult, the adult feels threatened on some basic need level when the child does not choose to comply.

Think about your own life. If you were to say to your mate, "I need for you to mow the lawn," and the person chose not to, you would feel "not loved." The refusal to comply becomes further evidence of a relationship that is missing something. However, if you were to say, "I really want you to mow the grass," and your mate doesn't find the time, you would probably be frustrated or angry. One hooks you; the other just disappoints you.

♥ "I think . . . . " Instead of using a direct statement to communicate a limit or give a command, adults tend to use "I think" Instead of saying "I think it is time to eat," it is much clearer to say, "It's time to eat." The latter statement is clear, concise and direct. The ultimate problem stems from the adult's belief that giving direct statements is "rude" or "disrespectful" and teaches young children to be rude or disrespectful.

This belief comes from programming adults received in the family system in which they were raised. When they were growing up and spoke directly to their parents, such comments as "Don't you ever talk to me that way" or "It is rude to talk back to adults" were often heard. Of course, in those days children were to be seen and not heard, so any comments from a child to an adult could have been perceived as improper.

♥ Commands such as "Don't touch that," "No," "Keep your hands and feet to yourself," "Behave yourself" or "What do you think you are doing?" provide children with no usable information. Telling children what not to do is not brain compatible (Hart, 1983). The brain processes information in a positive form. Telling a child "Don't fold your paper that way" requires that the child process information and transform the command into acceptable behavior.

For young children who are more comfortable thinking in actions rather than thinking in representations, giving them commands in the negative form is asking them to repeat the behavior. Saying "Don't throw" to a small child is in essence saying "Throw—Throw." This is the reason why when you tell two-year- olds not to touch something, they will inevitably touch the object and most likely smile and look to you for approval. They did not hear "Don't touch the lamp"; they heard "Touch the lamp." Unfortunately, they believe they are complying with the adult request. As they look to the adult for approval, they generally hear "I said don't touch that." The child's perceived compliance is met with disapproval from adults. This is very confusing for young children who are trying to discern what is acceptable and what is not acceptable.

♥ Phrases like "You are a bad girl," "You should be ashamed of yourself," "You are just trying to be naughty," "You should know better," destroy the self-esteem of children without setting limits. Such attacks on the child also sever the child-adult relationship, preventing the child from getting attention and his or her needs met. When the relationship is doing well and built on mutual respect, the child has a vehicle for getting attention.

When the relationship is skewed and negative feelings and attitudes prevail, the child is cut off from positive ways of getting attention and power. This pushes both the child and the adult into a cycle of negativity. Some examples of clear and direct limits are:

"My neck is not for squeezing so hard."
"The toys are not for throwing."
"Jeremy is not for hitting."
"The table is not for climbing."
"The window is not for banging with the hammer."
"The book pages are not for tearing."

Step 3: Target acceptable behavior.

Young children act impulsively out of desire and/or need. They do not stop and think. They have a feeling, wish, desire or need and express it in the only way they know. The child may not be aware of any other way to express what is being felt. At that moment the child can think of only one way to express him- or herself. If the child is angry, the child may only know to hit as the expression of that emotion. At this step of the limit-setting process, the teacher must provide alternatives to the child for the expression of the original desired action. This can involve pointing out a variety of different alternatives. A more durable or appropriate object should be selected for the expression. "The doll house is not for standing on. You may choose to stand on the incline or on the climbing stairs." If a child is painting on a wall, a different surface can be selected on which to paint. "The wall is not for painting. You may choose to paint on the easel or on the paper on the table."

A substitute may be needed as an expression of aggressive behavior. "Tammy, I am not for hitting. The pillow in the safe place is for hitting." A nonverbal cue, pointing toward the alternative in conjunction with the verbalized alternative, is especially helpful in diverting the child's attention from the original focus and facilitating the process of choice making. Using the child's name helps to get the child's attention.

In summary, when limit setting is needed, the adult can remember to **ACT** in instituting the steps of the process.

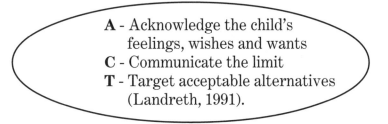

A - Acknowledge the child's feelings, wishes and wants
C - Communicate the limit
T - Target acceptable alternatives (Landreth, 1991).

The following situations will help clarify this basic process of limit setting:

Climbing on the Tables

Kenny and Bud were building a house in the block corner. They almost had the house built when Latisha came rushing in announcing the building was on fire. Kenny and Bud quickly turned themselves into firefighters to assist in putting out the fires. Kenny and Bud proceed to climb on the table to get a shot at the roof of the building. Since this is not safe, the adult must intervene and set limits.

Adult: "Kenny and Bud, I can see your urgency to get up high to save the building. Tables are not for climbing. You may stand on the loft or a pretend ladder to put out the fire. What is your choice?"

Walking on the Cardboard Blocks

Kendra and Jamey worked diligently getting all the cardboard blocks off the shelf and cooperatively building a road for the cars. Once the road was completed, they decided that a balance beam of blocks would be more fun. They began walking on the cardboard blocks, crushing them with their weight.

Adult: "Kendra and Jamey, you are testing your balancing skills on the road you built. The cardboard blocks are not for walking. You may walk on the tape on the floor or the balance beam. What is your choice?"

Throwing Toys

Ben was asked to clean up his toys, but he was reluctant to comply with the request. He decided that he would pick up the toys by tossing them through the air, aiming at the baskets to increase his enjoyment of the task.

Adult: "Ben it was hard to decide to clean up and you thought throwing would help the job become more fun. Toys are not for throwing. You may make your task more fun by singing or getting a friend to help. What is your choice?"

Grabbing a Toy from a Friend

Sherry was playing with the red firetruck and Kevin noticed Sherry with the truck. Once he saw the truck and the fun Sherry was having, Kevin wanted the truck also. He went over to Sherry and began to grab the truck.

Adult: "Kevin, you are excited and really want to play with the red firetruck just like Sherry was doing. You may not grab someone else's toy. You may ask to play with Sherry or find another fire truck. What is your choice?"

Time to Practice

The following scenarios are designed to give you practice in the basic technique of limit setting. A scene is given and space is provided for you to write in the limit-setting phrases you would use in that situation.

Scene 1: **Throwing sand** - Andrea was sifting sand at the sand table. She had been doing this for almost 15 minutes. She started to tire of the activity and began tossing the sand up into the air.
Adult:

Scene 2: **Eating the Playdough** - Lamont had selected the Playdough table during his center time. He decided to use the cookie cutters to make some holiday cookies. Once he got his cookie tray prepared, he began to eat the Playdough cookies.
Adult:

Scene 3: **Walking in front of the swing** - Shawn and Scout were playing chase on the playground. In the excitement of the hunt, Shawn runs in front of the swings, where several children are swinging.
Adult:

How Did You Do?

In limit setting there are no perfect answers. The responses by the adults below may not be identical to your responses. The point is to check and see if the steps of ACT were followed. Did you acknowledge the child's feelings, wishes or desires (overall motivation to act in that specific manner)? Did you set a clear limit so the child knows what is not safe? Did you provide acceptable alternatives for the child to get his or her needs met? Some sample responses to the above scenarios follow:

Scene 1: **Throwing sand** - The adult could respond by saying: "You were bored with sifting the sand and thought throwing would be more enjoyable. Sand is not for throwing. You could fill the cup and turn it over to make hills or use the water wheel. What is your choice?"

Scene 2: **Eating the Playdough** - The adult could respond by saying: "Lamont, you were so excited about the cookies you   baked for the holidays, you thought they would be good to eat. Playdough is not for eating. You could cut cookies out of pieces of bread and eat them or pretend to eat your holiday cookies. What is your choice?"

Scene 3: **Walking in front of the swing** - The adult could respond by saying: "Shawn you were having so much fun playing chase with Scott you ran right in front of the swing and were almost knocked down. You may not play chase in the swing area. You may play chase by the sandbox or climbing structure. Where will you choose to play chase?"

How did you do? Remember, this may be a new skill and any new skill needs practice. A key point in limit setting is getting the child to verbally commit to one of the alternatives. Asking, "What is your choice?" gets that verbal commitment.

When Limits Are Broken

A broken limit can mean anything from mild testing behavior to a battle of wills. Breaking limits is often a cry for help from a child with low self-esteem who really wants the security of knowing definite boundaries do exist. Therefore, at this time perhaps more so than any other time, the child needs understanding and acceptance. The teacher must reflect feelings and desires while stating with firmness the established limit. Debates with lengthy explanations should be avoided. Threatening the child with what will happen if a limit is broken is never acceptable. Limits are never used as a way to punish a child. When children break limits, it is time for the teacher to exercise patience, calm ness and firmness. Even though the limit has been broken, the teacher is accepting of the child.

When the child continues to break an established limit, verbalizing an additional step to the limit-setting sequence may be needed.

Step 4: State the final choice.

At this point, an ultimate or final choice is presented to the child. The adult either indicates the items will be placed off limits for the rest of the morning or afternoon, or presents the child with the option of removing him- or herself to the classroom or home "safe place."

The classroom or home safe place is a section of the room marked off with clear boundaries in which children may retreat when they find themselves unable to function safely in the environment. The safe place consists of non-breakable items such as oversized, soft pillows, a beanbag chair, soft stuffed animals and a couple of hand puppets.

This final step must be carefully worded so that the child knows that she has a choice and that whatever happens will be the result of that choice. "If you choose to throw the blocks again, you choose to (stop playing with the blocks) or (to leave the play area for the safe place)."

Limits presented in this manner are neither punishment nor rejection of the child. If the child throws another block, the child has clearly indicated by action the choice to leave the play area or to stop playing with the blocks, depending on the choice presented by the adult. In this process, leaving the play area or having the blocks placed off limits is not the adult's choice. Therefore, the child is not rejected.

Children need to realize they have a choice and that consequences are related to their behavior. Once the final choice has been presented and the child has indicated the choice by his or her behavior (either stops throwing blocks or throws one more), the adult must follow through and see that the child's choice is carried out. Guerney (1983) pointed out that limits and consequences should be as predictable as a brick wall. If the child chooses to break the limit again, the adult says, "I see by your actions you have chosen to leave the play area and go to the safe place."

Additional Techniques

Limit setting in the form of redirection as described above is an excellent technique to apply before the onset of inappropriate behaviors. Teachers with young children must have a supervision system set up within the classroom to ensure someone is watching the children and assisting in the resolutions of conflicts. This is one of the reasons two adults are needed in classrooms with young children. One adult can be assigned the role of facilitator/teacher and the other adult can be assigned the role of supervisor. The supervisor's duty is to provide and maintain safety in the classroom through prevention and intervention.

Many preschool programs have high adult-child ratios and supervision becomes a problem. Also, since young children are constantly exploring their world and the limits of that world, conflict is inevitable and necessary for the developmental processes to occur. Other limit-setting techniques are needed to facilitate the management of the classroom. In addition to the ACT method of limit setting, there are many more skills available for parents and teachers: giving information, consequences, contingencies, choices and "I" messages. Many times we find ourselves unable to redirect the situation before its occurrence. We find ourselves with two screaming kids or paint on the wall. Let's face it, it would be nice if we were there to catch the mishaps before they occur. Most of the day, however, we are there after the fact. In this case, we need a tool belt of skills.

Giving Information

Since young children retain information in their heads roughly 20 seconds, we adults must do a lot of reminding, prompting and cuing. We can make this a simple task or we can make it a struggle. Many teachers and parents, in an attempt to relay an important message, fall into the trap of lecturing, blaming, warning, using sarcasm and being a martyr. These methods isolate, attack and alienate children and send the message, "You are not good enough." To avoid hearing the "not good enough" message and protect their self-esteem, they tune the adult out. The message falls on deaf ears, as the saying goes. Instead of giving information wrapped in the "attack package," we can communicate differently and elicit cooperation from the child. Faber and Mazlich (1980) suggest giving information by describing what you see ("I see toys on the floor"), saying the reminder with a word ("the toys") or writing a note for those children who are beginning or able to read. In this way the information is sent in a loving, cooperative package that sends the message, "You are capable."

Consequences

Consequences are events that make a particular behavior more or less likely to happen in the future (Marion, 1991). Consequences are discussed in detail in Chapter 14. For now, let it suffice to say that consequences are a form of giving children information about what is most likely to happen if they continue to behave in a certain fashion. In the example of the toys being left on the floor, the adult said, "If the toys are left on the floor and broken, you won't be able to play with them." This is a natural consequence; however, it's unlikely to occur unless a bulldozer runs through the living room. It might be more effective to let the child know what else may happen by saying, "If the toys are left on the floor and I pick them up so I can walk safely in the house, I will put them away and they will not come out until I bring them out." You may then add some choices to your logically created consequence. You may add, "You can be in charge of your toys and put them away, or I will be in charge of your toys and put them away. What is your choice?"

Contingencies

Contingencies are commonly referred to as "Grandma's Law." I suspect this title reflects the wisdom in the technique. It simply means that the child is presented a less desirable task to complete before a more desirable task is offered. Historically, it is the root of "If you finish your meal, then you may have dessert." For a contingency to be effective with a specific child, you must first know the child. Children vary as to what they consider to be more desirable. For example, some children believe that going outside is the greatest thing since squeezed mustard, while others could care less. When using the "If you _____ , then you may _____ " formula, you must be sure that the second option is a very desirable one for the child. If a child is very excited about the possibility of playing in the dramatic play center and ho-hum about picking up the blocks he just played with in the manipulative center, a wise adult could say, "When you pick up these blocks and put them on the shelf, you may go to the dramatic play center." A pitfall to avoid is using this technique with a child who cannot delay gratification long enough to successfully complete the task at hand. What if someone said to you, "I know you've thought your spouse was dead for the past ten years, but he's not. You can see him as soon as you vacuum the living room." I suspect your heart would not be in the Hoover at that moment. Even if you considered vacuuming, you would do it so poorly a conflict would arise over the quality of your work.

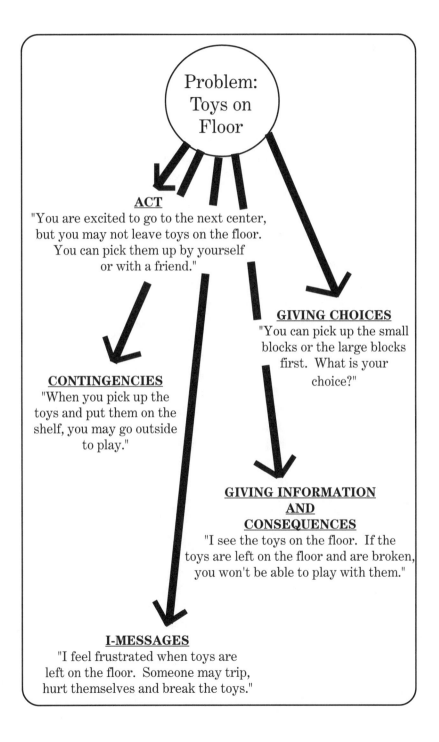

Problem: Toys on Floor

ACT
"You are excited to go to the next center, but you may not leave toys on the floor. You can pick them up by yourself or with a friend."

CONTINGENCIES
"When you pick up the toys and put them on the shelf, you may go outside to play."

GIVING CHOICES
"You can pick up the small blocks or the large blocks first. What is your choice?"

GIVING INFORMATION AND CONSEQUENCES
"I see the toys on the floor. If the toys are left on the floor and are broken, you won't be able to play with them."

I-MESSAGES
"I feel frustrated when toys are left on the floor. Someone may trip, hurt themselves and break the toys."

Giving Choices

Choices empower people and are an integral part of living. When possible, give children choices. Let's use the block example again: "You can begin picking up the large blocks or the small blocks. What is your choice?" In this situation the child is correct no matter which choice he picks. Each is acceptable and each gets the task completed. Chapter 15 provides more comprehensive information about choices, including what to do when giving a choice doesn't work!

I-Messages

"You know, Mrs. Vernon, I really don't mind if Dacia gets angry. I just wish she would do it in a nice way," said Dacia's mom at the school open-house meeting.

"I know what you mean. I said the same thing last year about my children. You know what a friend of mine said to me? She said, ' So Maxine Vernon, how do you get angry?' I thought for a while and realized I didn't really know. It dawned on me that maybe I was expecting the children in my classroom to demonstrate a skill I didn't possess! She continued, "Growing up, when my Dad was mad he would yell. I think I got so scared of being angry I did not allow myself to get angry. I realized I didn't know how to be angry—let alone how to do it nicely."

"I never really thought about it like that. I guess I don't really want Dacia to get angry. Come to think of it, I hate it when anyone gets angry. It scares me too," said Carmen, Dacia's mom.

Carmen and Maxine address a common problem facing many adults. They have come to believe that feelings are okay and need to be expressed, yet they are missing the skills to act on their newly formulated beliefs. The skill they both need is called an I- message.

Thomas Gordon developed a system know as Parent Effectiveness Training and Teacher Effectiveness Training. In his program he developed and utilized the I-message in relationship to problem ownership. According to Gordon

(1989), most parents and teachers look at children's behavior in terms of "behaving" and "misbehaving." These terms are almost exclusively applied to children but seldom to adults. I've never heard people say, "My husband misbehaved at the store today," or "My colleagues at work have been misbehaving lately," or "One guy at the party sure was misbehaving."

It appears only children misbehave. A child is seen to misbehave whenever some specific action is judged as contrary to how the adult thinks the child should behave in a certain situation. Ultimately it is not the child's behavior that bothers adults but the effect of that behavior on the adults. All actions by children are solely for the purpose of getting their needs met.

When a child's behavior is unacceptable to you and has a concrete impact on you, an I- message is a message that tells the child what the adult is experiencing as a result of his behavior. Here are some examples:

"When you talk when I am talking, I feel frustrated because I can't remember what I'm saying."

"When there is so much loud noise in the classroom, I can't hear what anyone is saying to me."

"When I ask you to come in from the playground and you continue to play, I feel angry."

The formula for giving an effective I-message consists of describing the behavior that is bothering you: "When you _____," then expressing your feelings in regard to the behavior, "I feel _____."

I-messages could also be termed responsibility messages for two reasons. First, adults who send an I-message are taking responsibility for how they are feeling, acting and thinking. Second, an I-message leaves the responsibility for changing the unacceptable behavior with the child. More information on how to use I-messages will be discussed in Chapter 15.

Summary

Children must and will test the limits to truly learn the boundaries of who they are. We live in a culture where a significant number of men go to prison and a significant number of women go to therapy. Obviously, something is missing in our ability to set limits for ourselves without hurting ourselves or others. If we want children to learn how to control their impulses, we must control ours and teach them better ways of expressing theirs. Limit setting focuses on teaching and is a prerequisite to understanding and abiding by rules.

Chapter 13

What is the rule in this classroom about running:
Creating Rules That Work

Creating Rules That Work

Think back to when you were a child and entered into your very first school experience. For some of you that would be preschool, kindergarten or first grade, depending on your present age. Do you remember any rules per se of the classroom? Do you remember the teacher ever saying, "the rule is" ...? For many of you, the answer is probably no. The reason is, rules are made for those who break them. If you fulfilled your role as a good little boy or girl, you would have no early memories of rules. With more and more children entering school without the prerequisite foundations of food, shelter and love, more and more children are "breaking the rules." It then becomes vital to understand how to write successful rules and teach the rules to your children.

Writing Rules

There is no one correct way to write rules; however, the following general guidelines will be helpful to insure your rules are clear, specific and concise. Writing rules for older students in elementary school is somewhat different than writing rules for the 5- to 7-year-old primary aged student. Primary children are still very literal in their thinking and have yet to discern the ambiguity present in the English language system. A young child when asked "When will you stop sucking your thumb?" responded, "When I take it out of my mouth." Certainly the same literalness holds true for most children who have English as their second language. Successful rules for younger children contain the following elements:

RULES
- ✔ Are based on sound principles
- ✔ Are behavioral expressions of the principles
- ✔ Are always related to safety
- ✔ Are positive when possible
- ✔ Are brief and specific
- ✔ Are developed with children involvement

- ✔ Have input from parents and administrators
- ✔ Are visually presented to the children
- ✔ Are taught and integrated into the curriculum
- ✔ Are changeable and changed throughout the year
- ✔ Contain a range of consequences for each rule

Sound Principles Are the Basis of Effective Rules

All rules must be based on sound principles. The principles we choose to live by govern our behavior. Our principles come from our values, but sometimes we may value one thing and act another way. This discrepancy, unless identified, can create inconsistencies in the classroom or home.

One way to get at the core of a potential discrepancy is to ask yourself, "What principles do I have that I demonstrate regularly and what principles do I hold in esteem and have trouble living up to?" For example, I value positive thinking about myself and others, yet I catch myself being critical of my weight and the behaviors of others.

Areas where my values do not coincide with my behaviors are called "sensitive points." These sensitive points allow us to see how other people are *not* "doing as they say." People mirror for us our "sensitive points" because it is easier to notice people who are not living up to their own standards of behavior than to notice our own behaviors. If we are not able to live up to our own value system, we will see others who do not live up to their values. In doing this we are apt to be judgmental and critical of others and perpetuate the cycle of valuing one thing and living another.

I have a friend who likes to drive relatively fast. She will almost always be at least 10 miles an hour over the speed limit. As I ride with her, I find it quite humorous to listen to her point out all the people on the highway who are speeding. Every car that passes us gets a comment such as, "What is coming over the world? That person is driving like a maniac. I just don't understand it."

We See In Others What Bothers Us
Most About Ourselves

Exercise: In the space below write down three things about other adults that irritate you the most. It could be talking behind your back, lying, being critical of others, controlling the children, sexism, racism, etc.

1._____

2._____

3._____

Now take this information and see if these areas that bother you so much are not your own "sensitive points." Can you see how these other people are magnifying for you the things you wish you would never do yourself? For example, teachers who are constantly negative about the children in their classrooms may irritate you extremely. Generally speaking then, you find yourself occasionally being negative about children yourself and hate yourself when this happens. To defend ourselves from our own minds, we project the "hate" onto others. In other words, we are irritated at people who are irritated at children, we get mad at children for getting mad, and on and on.

Ms. Oliver has been teaching school for twenty-five years. Each year she is seeing more and more children with more and more problems. She is especially dismayed with the number of children in her class from protective services, especially Lindsey. Ms. Oliver thinks Lindsey is an adorable little girl. If any child in the classroom picks on Lindsey, Ms. Oliver says, "How would you feel if Lindsey did that to you?" The children listen, answer the question appropriately and continue picking on Lindsey . Of course the children know what it feels like; that is why they did it. It has been done to them. Lindsey has just been returned to her home from foster care. Lindsey had been physically abused. Ms. Oliver is furious. She constantly comments on how "Lindsey's parents should be beaten and shown what it feels like."

Ms. Oliver is projecting her hate. She believes that the physically abusive parents should be beaten. She believes this in spite of the overwhelming data indicating that the reason Lindsey's parents beat her is the fact that they were beaten as children themselves. Instead of owning the part of herself, no matter how small or how fleeting, that at moments she herself could just "strangle those children," she projects this onto the abusive parents. We, as teachers or parents, can all relate to those moments when we could "kill them." The thought is so fleeting and scary we immediately make light of it and continue about our business. For many other adults raised in violence, the thoughts aren't fleeting.

To reduce the chaos in your classroom or home you must 1) know what you value; 2) realize you are human and may not always act on your principles; 3) understand that our judgments of others only define ourselves.

Bringing Values and Principles Alive in the Classroom

To bring principles and values alive in the classroom, discuss them with your children. As your class decides on the principles that are important based on their values, write them down. This list of values, along with your personal list, represents what you will be teaching each and every day in your classroom. The list also gives you the principles from which to structure your rules. Principles place rules in a larger context that helps children understand why each rule is selected and needed. Principles are not designed to be enforced because they are too general; they are designed to be taught through modeling and mentoring. Examples of principles primary-age children may suggest are:

✔ Be respectful.
✔ Be prepared.
✔ Treat others as you wish to be treated.
✔ Try your best at all times.
✔ Be honest.
✔ Listen when others are speaking.
✔ Don't take others' belongings.

A similar process can occur at home. Have family discussions about what is really important. Children are surprisingly philosophical when allowed to participate in such discussions. If the family collectively decides they value "being nice to one another," a future discussion of what this means concretely will be helpful.

Writing Rules That Are Clear and Specific

Effective rules are behavioral expressions of the principles that were determined by the class or family. In addition, rules are positive when possible and written very specifically. Rules are to define very clearly what is or is not acceptable behavior in the classroom. Remember, rules are written for those who break the rules—not for those who follow them. The importance of specific rules is related to the need for predictability. For children to develop responsibility for their own behavior, they must experience a predictable environment in their lives. This is an example of a predictable environment: Mr. Hopkins has a fairly fixed routine for his two children. During the week the children rise at regular times and go through a certain sequence of activities before breakfast is served. Upon returning home from school, the children have assigned chores, homework schedules, a sit-down meal and some family play time. Saturday mornings are different, yet a routine exists. On Saturday the children get themselves up, fix their own breakfast, and then watch TV. Mr. Hopkins gets to sleep in.

Many children come from homes lacking in predictability. Here is such an example: Carey wakes up each morning never really knowing what the day will bring. Sometimes she has breakfast and sometimes not. Sometimes when she gets home from school, her mom is there and sometimes she is not. Sometimes she eats dinner with her mom and sometimes she eats cereal in front of the TV.

All children need the primary classroom teacher to write clear and specific rules. Some children need it more than others.

Rules work best when they describe specific behaviors (Curwin & Mendler, 1988).

• •

*Rules are written
for those who break them—
not for those who follow them.*

• •

Exercise: Read the following rules. Decide whether they are too vague, too specific or clear for primary-age children. Beside each rule write a V for vague, S for specific or a C for clear.

1. Students will keep their hands and feet to themselves. ____
2. You may not hit. ____
3. You may not kick, hit, bite, pinch, poke or trip others. ____
4. Raise your hand when you want to speak during large group instruction. ____
5. Raise your hand to speak. ____

> 6. Raise your hand to speak, to go to the bathroom and
>   when you need help. ____
> 7. Use your walking feet. ____
> 8. Use kind hands. ____

In the before-mentioned examples, rule numbers 1, 5,
7 and 8 are too vague for young children. Young children are
very literal. Rule number one would imply you could not
hug your friends. Rule number five would prevent you from
talking with your friends during center time without raising
your hand.

You may think to yourself, "Oh, they know what I
mean." How many stories have you heard about how young
kindergarten and first-grade students misinterpreted the English language because of their literalness? It's just like the
child in kindergarten who was told by the teacher on the first
day of class to "sit here for the present." He waited and waited
and she never brought him a present, so he then began refusing
to go to school. Every time you hear yourself saying, "Oh, they
know what I mean" or "I know they know," catch yourself.
These statements reflect your resistance or reluctance to
change. You want the children to think like you do, and they
don't.

In writing rules for the young primary-age child, as
much ambiguity as possible must be removed. The exceptions to the rules must not be greater than the rules themselves. For example, with the rule *Keep your feet and hands
to yourself*, what exceptions to this can you think of? Some
exceptions to the rule might include:

   ♥ Playing activities or games that require touching
   ♥ Showing affection to your friends or to the teacher
   ♥ Receiving affection from others
   ♥ Sitting or standing close to others
   ♥ Returning items to another
   ♥ Playing cooperatively.

The list of exceptions is lengthy. Now let's look at what
teachers generally intend for the rule to convey to children.
Keep your hands and feet to yourself really is meant for the
following situations:

♥ When hitting or physically hurting others

♥ When other children do not want you to touch them.

As you can see, the exceptions to the rule are greater than the intended rule itself. This ambiguity is difficult for young learners. The consistency and predictability of the environment is reduced.

Rules Are Stated Positively When Possible

It is also important to tell children what to do as opposed to what not to do. If you have ever been participating in sports and someone says to you, "Don't swing too hard" or "Don't hit it to left field," you invariably hit it exactly as you were told not to. The brain can only be programmed with what you want to happen. Similar to a computer, the brain cannot be programmed to do something you wish not to happen. You must tell your brain and the computer what you want it to do. Therefore, whenever possible, write your rules in positive terms.

However, sometimes it is clearer to state them in a negative fashion as in the case with "You may not hit." If the rule will be clearer stated negatively, make sure you use the words "you may not" as opposed to "don't." Contracted verbs are difficult to process for the young learner. State "do not" or "you may not" along with your desired outcome. Rules need to be written both clearly and positively. However, if clarity is sacrificed to write a rule positively, write the rule negatively and preserve the exactness.

"Keep your hands and feet to yourself!"

Rules Are Always Related to Safety

Children relate to safety. On some level, all children understand that in the world they are vulnerable and dependent on adults. Safety provides a bridge between adulthood and childhood. When it comes to safety and feeling safe, we all have a common ground. Safety is a universal language of love. Safety implies the absence of fear. The opposite of fear is love. When rules are written for the primary-age child, they must be based on safety issues. It is important for children to relate to the rules, to see them as a functional part of the social system. Rules based on arbitrary obedience teach children that rules are impositions from the outside placed on fun. Rules not based on safety set up an autocratic system of "us and them." Rules based on safety set up a democratic system of "we."

Think of some commonly held rules in the primary grades. Are these rules based on safety? For example, *Walk inside the classroom* is a rule that can be related to safety. Children may be injured during high excitement times. As you develop your rules, remember to relate them to safety; otherwise, they are not viable for young children. Research indicates that toddlers and preschoolers use "actions of adults" as their main criteria for determining acceptable and unacceptable behavior. As children's cognitive development increases in the primary grades, they determine acceptable and unacceptable behavior in relation to whether it causes physical harm to people and property. It is not until children reach the age of eleven that they perceive the disruption of the social order as inappropriate. Telling young children their behavior is disrupting the classroom or they are bothering their sister or brother means nothing. Rules must be related to safety for them to be meaningful for young children.

Effective Rules Are Brief

Writing rules for classrooms or homes is not like writing legislation. The rules need to be written as briefly as possible. It is also important to keep the number of rules to a minimum. A good rule of thumb is, beginning at age five, have no more than five rules. Six-year-olds may have six rules and seven-year-olds may have seven rules. Seven is as many rules as needed for older primary children. Therefore, eight-year-olds still need only seven or fewer rules. The reason for this has to do with the short-term memory capacity of young learners.

Exercise: Write five or fewer rules you would have in a first grade classroom. Write them clearly and be specific.

1._____

2._____

3._____

4_____

5._____

There are no "right" rules for kindergarten, first, second or third grade. However, there are some general rules seen in classrooms throughout the country. To check your rule-writing ability from the exercise above, see the sample classroom rules at the end of this chapter.

Effective Rules Are Written with Child Involvement

One of the first choices a teacher faces at the beginning of the school year in the primary grades is how to establish rules. Some individuals advocate an authoritarian style. The teacher sets the rules, communicates them to the students and tells them what will happen if they disobey them. In essence the teacher says, "I am the boss. I expect you to follow the rules. If you do not, you will be punished. If you conform to my expectations you will be rewarded."

Historically, this approach has had a great deal of appeal to teachers because it seems to offer teachers security and control.

Research on older students has indicated that this authoritarian style does seem to increase the amount of work produced by learners; however, the side effect is student aggression toward the teacher (Curwin & Mendler, 1980). Similar research on younger children is not available; however, research on child rearing indicates that authoritarian parenting seems to have a negative impact on a child's social and cognitive competence (Marion, 1991). Children of authoritarian parents are not very socially competent with peers, are withdrawn (Baumrind, 1967), tend to have negative self-esteem (Loeb, Horst, & Horton, 1980), and have higher levels of aggression (Patterson, 1982). Placing a great value on obedience, preservation of order, work and controlling children appears to have many negative side effects (Becker, 1964).

Another option in establishing classroom rules is the democratic approach. This method involves shared decision making. It allows learners a voice in establishing the rules. The democratic approach has the advantage of giving students some ownership of the rules and develops a commitment on their part to follow the rules. It also communicates to students a respect for their needs and their ideas. The democratic approach has greater potential for helping students learn self-control (Savage, 1991).

Involving students in the classroom can take many forms. The only limitation is the creativity and risk-taking ability of the teacher. One way to begin is to help children come up with principles. To help them discern their principles, begin a discussion concerning safety. Ask them what they would like to see in the classroom so that it would be a safe, fun place to learn. Ask them how the teacher could help facilitate the class as a safe place. Ask them how each child could help build a safe classroom environment. Once the general guidelines of safety are determined, rules can be decided upon.

If you begin your class discussion with "Let's list some rules for our class," children will more than likely begin parroting back some rote-learned answers to please you or come up with ridiculous ideas to sabotage the discussion. Always begin with a discussion of safety! Many of the safety ideas will be principles such as "be nice." From here, ask the students what "be nice" means to them. From this discussion, many of the actual rules will appear. Once you have a list of rules, elicit student input on the consequences that will occur when children choose to break the rules. Begin the discussion by asking the students, "How can I as the teacher help you obey the rules?" These answers will then add insight as you begin the process of developing consequences for your rules. Listen carefully to your students, especially the ones who suggest severe punitive measures. Children who suggest "locking them in a closet" or "hitting them so they won't forget" are sharing with you their perception of the world and the internal structure they are forming. Children who suggest violence as a solution generally have experienced violence as a guidance measure at home and will utilize that system of problem solving in your classroom.

Modeling the democratic process in action is a wonderful social studies lesson for everyone. When it seems that new rules need to be added during the year or some rules need to be changed, utilize the same democratic procedure.

Parents can follow a similar procedure at home. Many families rely on osmosis. Children are magically supposed to piece all the information together to understand the big picture of what behavior is expected and appropriate and what is not. Bringing the rules out in the open through discussions that focus on safety will provide children a more predictable environment.

Parents and Administrators

Parents and administrators must see the outcome of the classroom process and be invited to add to and join the procedure. This can occur in many different ways: meetings, phone calls, notes and/or newsletters. Parents and administrators need to know and be involved in your classroom. Letters sent home to parents must explain your philosophy of discipline, the goals of your discipline program and, in general terms, how you expect to reach those goals. The letter also must allow for feedback and additional ideas to assist the classroom in being a social system that enhances human interactions. I've included an example you may want to follow.

Sample Kindergarten Letter

Dear Parents,

In this letter I am sharing with you some of the goals I have for my classroom and a few of the tools that will help me reach these goals.

My goal is to create a safe, respectful and material-rich environment that builds self-control, self-esteem and self-reliance.

The skills that our children need are best taught through play and hands-on experiences. My program will encourage children to solve problems by talking about them with the other people involved.

The children will learn to respect others and their feelings as I model and teach active listening. I will listen and accept each child's feelings and provide positive guidance in dealing with them appropriately.

The children will be allowed to make choices and decisions about their work experiences. These reasonable choices will allow them to develop the awareness that they are in control of their own bodies and responsible for their actions. Encouragement will be given as children work on acquiring new skills. If the children do not choose to work within the reasonable choices (limits), then natural and logical consequences will be applied. Rewards, punishments, criticism and comparisons will not be a part of the discipline program. As these goals are accomplished, the children will gain the opportunity to grow to their full potential.

The children in the classroom and I will discuss and determine the classroom rules. I invite you to become a part of this process. If you have certain concerns or suggestions to enhance the classroom, please come visit, call or send a note.

If you are interested in more detailed information regarding how to develop responsibility and self-control in children, there are several helpful books concerning these tools. They are available at neighborhood bookstores or in my classroom library:

- ✔ *How to Talk So Kids Will Listen and Listen So Kids Will Talk* by Adele Faber & Elaine Mazlish
- ✔ *Cooperative Discipline* by Linda Albert
- ✔ *Positive Discipline for Preschoolers* by Jane Nelson
- ✔ *Guiding Young Children* by Eleanor Reynolds
- ✔ *There's Gotta Be a Better Way: Discipline That Works!* by Becky Bailey.

If you have any questions, suggestions or comments, please feel free to schedule a conference at your convenience. Please come in the room anytime and see how we are doing. We can always use another pair of hands.

Sincerely,

Rules Must Be Visually Presented in Writing and Pictures

Young children encode information from the environment visually. That is, they make visual representations of the world in their heads. Children with visual impairments generally encode kinesthetically, auditorially or both. Most young children utilize the "picture" format. It is then necessary for the rules to be displayed visually for the children in picture format as well as in written format. This will allow the child to constantly reinforce the representations in the head and will assist in fostering self-control.

Young children actually create pictures in their heads to guide their behavior. Eventually, they add words to the pictures in their heads and use speech to control their actions and choices. Picture rules are needed all the way to second grade even though the children can read. Young readers still encode visually and need the visual support offered by a picture.

Picture rules for children over five years of age and picture limits for children under five must be displayed in the classroom. These rules must be in picture format and must focus on what the child *can* do instead of what they cannot do.

You may not hurt each other with words or actions.

You may play by yourself.　　You may play with a friend.

Picture Rules Help Young Children

The brain processes information of what to do more efficiently than what not to do. A classic story is told about a baseball pitcher. It was the last of the ninth inning, with the winning run on third base and a heavy hitter approaching the plate. The manager called time out and approached the mound, instructing the pitcher "Don't throw a curve ball." The brain of the pitcher was frantically trying to decode the information saying, "Don't throw a curveball, don't throw a curveball." Well, as you can guess, he threw a curveball. Had the manager told him to throw a fastball, the pitcher would have been programmed to throw a fastball. Instead he was inadvertently programming the brain to throw a curveball. Needless to say, they lost the game. Many classrooms are "losing the game." We must auditorially and visually tell children what to do.

Visual pictures of the rules must be displayed in the classroom at eye level for the children and large enough to be seen. The rules must tell the children what they can do, reminding them of their options. I have developed a set of visual rules to accompany this text. In the back of the book you will find a form to order these prekindergarten to second-grade visual rules or limits:

- ♥ You may clean up your toys with a friend or by yourself. You may not leave your toys on the floor.
- ♥ You may play with a friend or play by yourself. You may not hurt each other by words or actions.
- ♥ You may rest on your cot or sleep on your cot. You may not get off your cot to play.
- ♥ You may walk with me or walk by yourself. You may not run in the classroom or halls.
- ♥ You may eat your lunch/snack while seated or put your tray and food away. You may not move around the room while eating.
- ♥ You may raise your hand to speak in large group time or take turns talking at small group time. You may not talk when someone else is speaking.
- ♥ During teacher instruction you may listen carefully to the teacher or sit quietly. You may not distract your classmates or the teacher.
- ♥ You may work cooperatively in small groups or seek assistance to solve your problems. You may not hurt your classmates with words or actions.
- ♥ You may clean your workspace by yourself or with the help of a friend. You may not leave a messy workspace.
- ♥ You may work on assigned tasks during designated times or you may seek assistance from a friend or teacher to complete your work. You may not play or hang out during work time.

Teaching the Rules/Limits

Teaching the rules can involve a number of strategies. The following examples are to encourage your mind to begin coming up with many ways to teach rules:

Utilize literature to teach rules. Use commercial books, classroom books or teacher-authored books to make a specific point. Mr. Atkins utilized literature a lot at the beginning of the school year to help structure the class. He had come to realize that his kindergarten children needed lots of help in understanding rules. He began the year using limits to keep his classroom safe but also started at the very beginning of the year to teach the concept of rules. He would use books that had a scary part in the story, such as *The Horrible Thing with Hairy Feet* by Joy Cowley, to begin discussions. After reading the book, Mr. Atkins would say, "Was this a safe book?" Generally the children would answer, "Yes." "Why?" asked Mr. Atkins. The responses from the children varied. "No one got hurt," replied Elizabeth. "It is just a book," said Sam. Mr. Atkins then pointed out that even though the horrible thing with hairy feet did not hurt the girl, she was very scared. "If you are scared, do you feel safe?" asked Mr. Atkins. "No," replied the children in unison. Mr. Atkins then proceeded to say, "Rules help keep us safe. What rules could we add that would make the book safer?" The lesson continued as the children explored and formulated their concepts of rules and their uses.

Utilize story telling to teach the rules. The story, *Eating on the Run,* is an example of a story you could tell children. Once you model this creative behavior of making up stories about rules for your children, then the children, individually or as a class, could author some "rule stories." The story that follows explains the rule about why sitting down to eat is important.

Eating on the Run

"Hurry! Hurry! So much to see, so much to do. Hurry! Hurry!" said the brain of the little girl. Kaitlin, a very curious child, enjoyed life so much, had so many toys to play with and so many experiments to test, her brain was constantly saying, "Hurry! Hurry! So much to see, so much to do. Hurry! Hurry!" For the most part this was great. She was learning, she was having fun, she was making friends. She actually was having so much fun she found it hard to sit down and take time to eat. Every time she would sit down to eat, her eyes would catch sight of a toy and her brain would say, "Hurry! Hurry! So much to see, so much to do. Hurry! Hurry!" She would jump up and off she would go, carrying what little food she could in her tiny hand. She would look at things, bend over and get on the floor, all the while carrying her food in her tiny hand, nibbling bits when possible. As she bent over to get the block, some of the food dropped out of her hand. As she bent over to pick up a book, some of the food dropped out of her hand. As she bent over to pick up a puzzle, some of the food dropped out of her hand. As she bent over to pick up a (elicit child response), more food fell out of her hand. As she leaned over to get her picture, what do you think happened? Yes, you are exactly right, more food fell out of her hand! While her brain was going, "Hurry! Hurry! So much to see, so much to do. Hurry! Hurry!" her stomach was going, "S-L-O-W down. I'm hungry, S-L-O-W down."

Well, Kaitlin was so busy playing with sorting seashells, exploring the magnets and having fun, she could not even hear her stomach. So the stomach spoke louder, "S-L-O-W down. I'm hungry, S-L-O-W down." The child still did not hear the stomach. The stomach spoke even louder saying, "S-L-O-W down. I'm hungry, S-L-O-W down." Kaitlin was so busy playing she still did not hear her stomach. However, the teacher did. This stomach was screaming so loud now, people were coming from all over to see what was making such a noise. Many teachers gathered, many moms and dads and aunts and grandmas and cousins gathered. They said, "What should we do? The children are so busy playing they can't hear their own their own stomachs. The noise is driving us crazy—and those poor stomachs." They thought and thought and thought. Then all of a sudden one teacher said, "Let's make a rule. Yes, a rule is perfect. We will make a rule to help the stomach!" And that is how we all got the rule," sit down and eat." HONEST!

Utilize role-playing activities for teaching rules. Have the children act out the acceptable rule choices and the not-acceptable rule choices that are visually represented in your classroom. The positive visual rules will be helpful for the children as they begin "reading" the visual rules. They can do this with assigning roles to themselves or by using puppets. You could create a center called the "safety center."

Utilize small group discussions to help children explore the ways we utilize rules in our society. Help children think if they use rules in their own lives automatically. For example, waking up or brushing their teeth could be an example of a rule that happens automatically. Or another example may be that when you sleep over at someone's house, you take your blanket or doll.

Utilize the visual rules when the rules are broken. The children then know the visuals are there to remind them and help internally represent the rules.

Design games the children can play. These will help them remember and become familiar with the rules.

The following are games teachers can make to help children learn the rules or games parents can do with their children.

• •

Teach children the rules you want them to follow.

• •

Games You Can Make

The Rules Game

Ages: 4-10 years of age
Materials needed: Ten 5" x 8" index cards, markers,
Polaroid camera (optional), 2 shoe boxes.

Object: To teach children the most important rules in the
classroom (or home) and the importance of following
them.

Creating the Deck

On ten 5" x 8" index cards draw a horizontal line
down the middle of the cards on each side. Each 5" x 8"
card now consists of a front and a back divided into two
sections by your horizontal line.

Number the front of cards from one to ten. Do this
by placing a 1 in each half of the first card, a 2 in each half
of the second card, and so on.

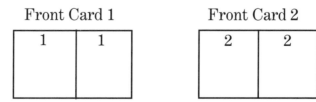

On the back of each card write a rule for the classroom
or home in the one section and a consequence in the other
section.

Back of Card 1

Clean up your toys.	Lose the opportunity to play with toys.

Continue writing rules and consequences for each of the ten cards. You may include natural consequences as illustrated on the next page.

Keep milk in your carton.	Clean up your milk

Beneath each rule and consequence, draw a picture representing each rule and each consequence or take a Polaroid of the child doing something that represents the rule and the consequences if the rule is broken,then paste the photo in its appropriate place on the card.

Now cut each card in two so there are 20 cards (10 rules and 10 consequences), each with a corresponding number on the back. In the classroom have the children make up a deck each of Rule and Consequence Cards for themselves. Have children initial the backs of their cards. When playing in groups, each child should contribute two or three pairs of cards to form a "group" deck.

Playing Some Games

There are many games that you can play with your deck of rule cards. Here are a few; you and the children will think of many more.

✪ First Things First:

It is important for children to learn that some rules are more important than others. Shuffle the 10 rule cards, and have the child select Rules 1-3 and recite them without turning the cards over. Turn the cards over to see if he/she is correct. When this can be done 100 percent of the time, repeat this with the first three consequence cards.

✪ Remembering Rules:

Shuffle the cards and then lay out all 20 cards with the picture sides up. The child now has to match each rule with each consequence. Just turn over the cards to see if the match is right (the number will match; for groups, the numbers and initials will match). This game can be played by one to four children.

✪ Flipping Over Rules:

More active children need active games. Take two shoe boxes and label one Rules and the other Consequences. The child then takes the deck of 20 cards picture side up, and from three to five feet away flips the Rule and Consequences cards into the appropriate box. If this is too easy, move back a few feet.

✪ Exploring Rules and Consequences:

This game is for more verbal children who enjoy telling and hearing stories. Shuffle the deck of 10 Rule Cards or use the Picture Rule Cards and have one member of the group draw a card. She or he must tell a "fairy tale" story about someone who broke the rule and the magical things that happened to the hero in the story. The story should end with an appropriate consequence and a moral. Each player gets five points for telling a story, five points for coming up with a fitting consequence, and five points for the moral or lesson. When everyone in the group has received ten points, the group gets to choose the next school activity.

These four games are just a few of the ways that you can help children remember and follow rules. Each game must be an opportunity for children and teachers to talk about the importance of rules and how they affect all our lives.

Changing the Rules

Throughout the year, the rules must evolve and change to respond to the needs of the classroom or family. It is critical that children learn that rules are created by people, for people, and can be changed by people when they no longer serve a purpose. This social science lesson is best learned through demonstration.

Children who believe rules are made by those in power and changed by those in power eventually disassociate themselves from the responsibility of creating their own world. They believe themselves to be powerless and thus ultimately to have no power to change things in their community or society.

Children must have a voice!

Children who believe rules are created in part by their own participation and can be changed by their actions learn the true meaning of democracy. For this reason the rules need to be examined and reexamined every two months. During this examination time changes must be made even if they are very small.

Children need to know that at any time in the classroom they have the right to request a review of the rules or an addition of new rules. This must be taught to the children. They must be reminded of their rights and responsibilities frequently. Children must be taught and experience the fact that they have a voice and a choice to be true democratic citizens.

Summary

Writing rules is integral in an effective classroom management plan. The discussion and teaching of rules is essential to a healthy family. This chapter focuses on writing rules that are based on safety. If the teacher can logically relate the classroom rules to safety, there is a good chance that the classroom expectations are realistic for the age of the children. Rules must be written so they are brief, specific and positive if possible. If in trying to write a positive rule, it becomes too ambiguous for young children, go ahead and write the rule in the negative form.

Rules must not be written in isolation. It is important to involve the students, the parents, and the administrators in the process. Young children are just developing their reading abilities. Picture rules must be displayed to assist them in internalizing what is expected in the classroom. It is developmentally appropriate to display picture rules that offer children positive choices. Rules must be taught as part of the curriculum just as any content area would be taught. This can be accomplished through writing stories, role-play discussions and puppet shows. All rules need consequences. The next chapter explains the use and abuses of consequences.

Sample Classroom Rules

Prekindergarten and Kindergarten Limits
1. You may clean up your toys with a friend or by yourself. You may not leave your toys on the floor.
2. You may play with a friend or by yourself. You may not hurt each other by words or actions.
3. You may rest on your mat or sleep on your mat. You may not get off your mat to play.
4. You may walk with me or walk by yourself. You may not run in the classroom or halls.
5. You may eat your lunch/snack while seated or put your tray and food away. You may not move around the room while eating.

Kindergarten Rules
1. You may not hit.
2. Raise your hand to speak while in large group instruction.
3. Put all toys and materials back where you found them.
4. Walk from place to place inside the building.

Primary Classroom Rules
1. Raise your hand to speak in large group instruction time.
2. During work time focus on the assigned task.
3. Clean your work space upon completion of projects.
4. Sit quietly while the teacher gives all instructions.
5. When in the school building, walk from place to place.
6. Use assertive words to get your needs met. ("I don't like it when. . . .")
7. You may not hit.

Chapter 14

I don't ever want to see that behavior again:
Enforcing Consequences

Learning Through Experiences:
Natural and Logical Consequences

Ten years ago there were approximately 200,000 people in prison in this country. Today there are over one million people behind bars, a number exceeded only in Germany and Russia during WWII. The cost of incarcerating this many people has a combined federal, state and local budget price tag of $61 billion annually. The United States imprisons more people than any other country, including South Africa and the former Soviet Union.

Ninety-eight percent of all men who commit violent crimes return to jail after being released. Research indicates there is little connection between the length of stay in jail and lower crime rates. For example, in Louisiana the average prison sentence for armed robbery is 17 years, which is twice the national average. Even so, Louisiana has one of the highest rates in this country for armed robbery. Data indicate that incarceration does not deter crime. And it is undisputable that incarceration does not provide rehabilitation.

• •

Many people believe that by getting children to feel bad, they will act good.

• •

What incarceration *does* do is get criminals off the street for a period of time, until they are returned to society where they most often return to crime (Stephenson, 1991). Our prison system is a very large, ineffective, punitive time-out system. Yet we persist in doing what does not work. Our society believes that if we put criminals in jail and they persist in committing crimes, the sentence was not long enough or the jail was too nice a place.

Our "get tough" attitude on criminals has resulted in overcrowding of prisons, early paroles and a huge tax bill that is bankrupting most states. Yet discipline systems in class-rooms and in homes are modeled after this totally ineffective system. Children are placed in "time out" as a cure for misbe-havior. Adults persist in thinking in terms of punishment.

Insane as it may sound, many people believe that by getting children to feel bad, they will act good. Think a moment about your own life. When are you most likely to behave poorly? You probably answered, when you feel overworked, stressed, upset, hurried, harried or "not good enough" in some way. When are you most likely to behave in a more cooperative, respectful manner? You probably answered, when you feel happy, healthy, in a good mood or whatever term you use for feeling peaceful. Internal states are directly related to outward behavior for both adults and children. Yet we go on believing in punishment and rewards as the best system of dealing with children.

Punishment and Rewards

One way to maintain the rules is to reward children when they obey and to punish them when they disobey. This reward-and-punishment system, which is the disciplinary system in which most of us were raised, has many disadvan-tages:

• *It makes the adult in charge responsible for the child's behavior.* Putting someone else in charge of one's behavior is common in our society. The court systems deal with this issue on a regular basis in the form of lawsuits. Lawsuits usually occur when one party decides the other party is at fault. For example, one person sues a tobacco company after being diagnosed with lung cancer. It doesn't seem to matter that this person chose to smoke for over 50 years.

Repeatedly in the family system people make comments such as "I did not do it," "So and so made me," "It wasn't my fault," "She pushed me to the point of drinking," "He would be upset if I went out, so I'd better stay home," and "Look what you have done now; you made your father miss his appoint-ment." All these examples, so prevalent in our society, put *others* in charge of one's behavior. Yet we get angry at young children who blame others and will not accept responsibility.

"He hit me first. I didn't do anything" or "I was just sitting here. She made me talk" are common comments heard from children. The children are merely reflecting our society and its system of socialization. Since the majority of us were raised on the punitive obedience model of rewards and punishments, we can regularly see such examples in our everyday lives or the lives of our friends.

- ***It prevents children from learning from their own decisions and choices in life and consequently, from adopting their own rules for effective behavior.*** The reward-and-punishment system prevents people from learning from their own behaviors. Every behavior has an outcome or a result of that behavior. The adult spends time judging the result of a child's behavior to be "good" or "bad."

For young children who are not able to separate deed from doer, the adult is, in essence, judging the child to be good or bad based on the child's behavior—more specifically, based on the child's behavior outcomes. For example, the children in your first- grade classroom are busy working in groups. The noise in the classroom continues to rise. You, as the teacher, understand that the noise is a direct result of the excitement of learning and the discussion process. You do nothing to reduce the noise level in the classroom. Soon after you make this decision, you see the principal coming toward your classroom. Even though the behavior of talking itself is not annoying you, the behavioral outcome of your possibly being disapproved of by the principal now determines your reaction to the situation.

Adults in the reward-and-punishment system of discipline judge the child based on the consequences of the child's behaviors on the adult, not the child. "What would other people think of me if my children act this way or that way?" is a common unconscious thought that drives the punishment system of discipline.

*People who fear failure
make internal representations
of what might not
work in advance.*

One of my favorite pastimes is to follow families around in the grocery store. I love to watch how families deal with this type of stress. One of the most difficult times is checking out. Candy and children are a volatile combination because generally, the children want candy and the adults don't want them to have any more "junk." Typically, the child has already eaten a donut or cookie prior to checkout, if the store has a bakery. The checkout counter is a prime example of how punishment is driven by the adult's desire to save face among other adults as opposed to *teaching* the child appropriate behavior. As the child starts demanding the candy and the adult starts resisting, the parent starts believing all the public shoppers are watching her or him. The parent focuses on him- or herself, the embarrassment, the humiliation and the inadequacy and just tries whatever is possible to stop the child from making noise.

Children raised in the external discipline system of rewards and punishments are trained at an early age to view the outcomes of their behaviors as either pleasing or displeasing to others or as successes (being good) or failures (being bad). This failure/success belief system is internalized and becomes the way we represent the world to ourselves in our heads as adults. Therefore, when we have a goal we want to achieve and the behavior we activate does not create the goal we wanted, instead of looking at the outcome we did get and changing strategies, we simply view ourselves and the behavior as failures. We become victims. This way of representing the world to ourselves generally prevents us from achieving our goals. It stops the actions we take toward the goal and therefore prevents us from learning from our consequences.

People who fear failure make internal representations of what might not work in advance. This keeps them from taking the action that would ultimately allow them to reach their goals. They become victims to life, unable to risk taking the actions they need to reach their own goals. In my own case, I put off writing this book for a number of years because of my fear of failing. I then put off writing it for another year because of my fear of succeeding!

- ***It sends the message repeatedly that acceptable behavior is expected only in the presence of authority figures.*** The system of rewards and punishments sends a message that rules are to be adhered to only when an authority figure is present. How many adults have you seen observe the speed limit only when a police car is visible? Instilling the belief into young children that acceptable behavior is only necessary when authority figures are visible is dangerous. Notice your own friends and yourself. How many rules do you disregard if no one is there to enforce them?

- *It invites resistance or apathy by attempting to force the child to conform (Dinkmeyer & McKay, 1989).* Apathy, the outward expression of powerlessness, is epidemic in our society. As countries throughout the world fight to have the right to vote, very few Americans are registered to vote. Of those registered, only a small percentage actually turn out at the polls. In 1988 there were 129,800,000 registered voters out of 245,807,000 citizens eligible to vote in the United States. Out of the 50 percent of the population that was registered to vote only 70.6 percent actually voted (U. S. Statistical Abstracts, 1990).

The disadvantages of a reward-and-punishment approach to disciplining young children are phenomenal, not just for our classrooms or home but for *all* of society. It becomes imperative that we utilize a system of discipline that instills in the minds of young children a belief in outcomes or results—as opposed to failures or sins. The child must learn that all behaviors he or she chooses elicit a certain outcome.

As adults it then becomes our job to facilitate children in self-reflecting upon their behavior and the consequences that their behavior produced for themselves and others. Adults can assist students in becoming **scientists of their own behavior.** Did the child receive the outcome he or she wanted? If not, what different strategies could the child try the next time he or she is faced with a similar situation? This system of dealing with behavior teaches children continually to examine their own behavior and make changes until their true goals are reached. The system that builds these beliefs into the mind of the child is based on natural and logical consequences that allow the child to develop her or his own effective rule-governing system based on examining outcomes, not on feeling like a failure.

Steve has forgotten his permission slip for the field trip again. So far this year his class has had four field trips, and Steve has yet to remember to return his permission form. He isn't worried though; he is confident that his mom will bring it to him. Sure enough, Steve's mom takes off from work and brings the permission slip to school. She arrives at the school harried, anxious and disgruntled at having to get off work and burden her colleagues with extra duties. She is short and cross with Steve and fumes, "Why are you so irresponsible? I even reminded you this morning to bring this slip. You never listen. You never think of anyone but yourself."

What has Steve learned in this situation? He has learned to depend on his mother instead of himself. Steve's mom is on the verge of convincing Steve that he is indeed irresponsible and self-centered. Steve also is learning that he is a "bad" person. Instead of experiencing the impact of not being able to go on the field trip, Steve experiences his mother's anger. Anger teaches nothing. It only brings resentment and retaliation. Steve now focuses on "mean Mommy" instead of his own behavior.

Natural and logical consequences help children take responsibility for their own behavior and learn from their choices. The use of natural and logical consequences offers the following advantages over the rewards-and-punishments system. First, it holds the children, not the parents or teachers, responsible for their behavior. In the situation above, if Steve were allowed to experience the natural consequence of his behavior, he would feel his own disappointment of not going as opposed to "mean Mommy." Second, it requires children to make their own decisions about what course of action is appropriate for them. Steve would ultimately learn that it is his actions that create the opportunity to go on the field trip or not. Third, it allows the children to learn from the outcomes of their choices. Steve, after experiencing the loss of the opportunity, would be on his way to learning the skills he needs to get future permission slips signed and returned. Natural and logical consequences permit children to learn from the natural and social order of events, rather that forcing them to comply with the wishes of other people (Dinkmeyer & Mckay, 1989). Last, consequences of actions are embedded in a belief in the social order and a sense of belonging and community, as opposed to the belief in obedience.

Natural and logical consequences are outgrowths of the child's behavior, and the result usually follows the action. This is a concrete way to teach children cause and effect as it applies to their own behavior as well as to teach the need to accept responsibility. Here are a few examples of logical consequences:

"Looks like your milk spilled; here's the sponge."

"When kids throw their toys, they pick them up."

"When I get kicked when I am holding you, I put you on the

floor. Kicking hurts me."

Natural Consequences

Natural consequences represent a natural flow of events. It is the direct result of behavior without prearranged consequences. For example, if a child runs and falls, she may bruise her knees; if a child does not tie his shoes, he may trip over them; if a child repeatedly treats her friends poorly, she may find herself without many friends. These consequences are not arranged or imposed by anyone; they just occur.

The adult simply allows the children to learn from their own consequences. The role of the adult is to provide information to the child, by bringing to the child's awareness the behavior and the result of that behavior. The adult may also offer assistance to children who wish to try another behavioral strategy to avoid producing the same consequences repeatedly. For example, let's take a child who treats her friends poorly. We start by offering information: "When you call your friends names, it may hurt their feelings." Then we add the possible consequence of that behavior: "If you continue to treat them that way, they *may* choose not to play with you." Finally, we offer assistance if the child wants to change the behavior: "Would you like to learn other ways of getting angry that may help you tell you friends how you are feeling but maintain the friendship?"

• •
Accepting responsibility for one's choices and behaviors is much easier in an environment of understanding and warmth.
• •

If the answer is yes, then teach the child other strategies; if the answer is no, wait and begin the process over again. Another example involves a child who brought an airplane to school to play with on the playground. The teacher gave the child information, saying, "If the airplane flies into the street, you may lose the plane." The child continued to fly the plane by the fence close to the street. Eventually the plane went over the fence and was crushed by a car. **The teacher must not lecture, argue or preach, just offer sincere regrets.** Accepting responsibility for one's choices and behaviors is much easier in an environment of understanding and warmth.

Rudolf Driekurs warns that adults may tend to use consequences as punishments. This can be done by pointing out the error of the child's way with such comments as "I told you so," "See what happens when you do not heed my advice," or "I tried to warn you, but no, you were too stubborn" (Dreikurs & Grey, 1968).

Natural consequences are generally a matter of getting out of the way and allowing children to learn from their own experiences. Too often adults deprive children of the chance to experience the consequence of their actions. Adults do this because they care about children and don't want them to have unpleasant or disappointing experiences. As adults, we try to save children from their own feelings because we were raised to be afraid of our own feelings. Unfortunately, the result is that the children don't become responsible for their own actions. They learn to fear their own feelings and they, in turn, grow up trying to control the feelings of others. The cycle continues generation after generation.

The Role of the Adult in Natural Consequences

The role of the teacher in natural consequences is to:

✔ Allow the child to experience the consequence of the child's choice.

✔ Provide information to the child about the actions

the child is taking and the possible outcomes. It is extremely important that we refer to outcomes as possibilities. We need to refrain from such comments as *If you run, you **will** fall down and hurt yourself.* Instead ,use comments such as, *If you **choose** to run, you **may** fall and hurt yourself.*

✔ Offer assistance to children who wish to learn new strategies to get their needs met in ways that are socially acceptable.

✔ Offer empathy and understanding to children who make choices that have disappointing outcomes.

✔ Natural consequences work for children of all ages. Read the following discipline examples and decide if the adult is facilitating learning responsibility or if the adult is creating dependency on the teacher.

Lunch-time situation: Karri has placed her drink on the edge of the table and is waving her arms as she enthusiastically tells Marcus, her cousin, about how big her dog has become.

The mom says, "Karri, put your drink in the middle of the table or else you are going to spill it." Karri ignores her mom's request and eventually knocks over the drink. Mom, frustrated and a bit self-righteous that her prediction has come true, says to Karri, "See, I told you it would spill. You **must** learn to listen. Get something and clean it up!"

Show-and-tell situation: Etta has brought a special, delicate model of a butterfly to school for show-and-tell. In order to keep items safe in the classroom, children are instructed to keep their show-and-tell items in their cubbies until the actual show-and-tell time. Etta was so pleased with her butterfly, she wanted to play with it and show her friends throughout the day. She is now walking around the room during center time carrying her butterfly.

The teacher says, "Etta, I see you are carrying your special butterfly. You seem so proud of your show-and-tell item it is hard to wait until show-and-tell time to take it out of your cubby. If you continue to carry your butterfly and show it to your friends, it may get broken. Put your butterfly in your cubby so it will be safe."

Etta ignores the teacher's comments and secretly continues to share her show-and-tell butterfly during center time. Eventually the butterfly is broken as two children try to look at it at the same time. Etta is hysterically crying. The butterfly is lying on the floor in millions of little pieces.

The teacher says, "Oh, Etta, How tragic! Your precious butterfly is broken. You must feel terribly sad and maybe really angry at your friends who wanted to see your beautiful butterfly. How hard to lose something you care so much about!"

The scene at the dinner table built dependency. In this scenario, the parent sent the message to the child, *I can predict the future and if you would only listen to me, I could keep you safe from being "bad."* The show-and-tell example builds responsibility. The teacher gave the child information as to how to keep herself or her toys safe. The child chose otherwise and the teacher allowed the child to feel the impact of her choices, while empowering her to gain control through empathetic listening.

Can you remember times in your own life when you made a decision that caused you great pain? Which type of person would you prefer to be around—the "I told you so" or the empathetic listener who stays with you as you process your pain? Would the "I told you so" prevent you from ever making a similar decision? We all make poor choices. To learn from these mistakes, we must accept them without blame. To facilitate this acceptance, an empathetic, understanding adult can truly work miracles.

As a university professor I have many graduate students who are juggling full-time work and family with part-time graduate school. Many of the students get overwhelmed and unable to turn in assignments when due. Amy Turner was one such student. She came to my office with "a prepared list of excuses." As she began to blame the world for her late work, I gently gave her ownership of her choices and understanding of her situation. "Amy, you have so many things going on in your life right now it must be difficult for you to prioritize what to take care of first." She responded and expounded on her life events. "What I am hearing is that you are choosing to focus on your family first and postpone your graduate obligations." She began to cry and become apologetic. "Amy, I sense you feel I may be disappointed in you. Difficult choices require courage, and you definitely are in a situation that requires making difficult choices." Amy went on to complete the course at her own pace and wrote me a letter a year later. She said she learned the most about working with children the day she came to my office and felt the power of an empathetic, understanding teacher.

• •

To learn from mistakes we must accept them without blame.

• •

Logical Consequences

The real world offers much more opportunity for natural consequences than school. By its nature, school is an artificial environment that doesn't allow much opportunity for natural consequences. At home, a parent can allow children much more freedom to learn from their own mistakes than a teacher can at school. At home, if the children don't put away their toys, eventually pieces get lost. At school, the custodian finds the pieces and gets frustrated with the teacher. At home, if children go out in the cold without a coat, they realize they are cold and can go back in and get a jacket. At school, a teacher may feel that a parent will think the teacher is being irresponsible by letting the children go outside without a coat when it is cold. School rules also prevent a child from returning to the classroom to get a coat without supervision.

While school is an artificial environment that may

restrict some experiences with natural consequences, children still manage to experience them often. They will build an unstable block tower and experience its collapse. From this natural consequence they begin to learn about balance, physical limits and maybe how hard blocks are if they land on their body. Social behavior and friendships are also molded a great deal by natural consequences. A child who repeatedly hurts others physically or hurts them emotionally will reap the consequences of rejection.

Logical consequences are useful where natural consequences will not work. It is not just the artificial environment of school that makes natural consequences impossible at times. In some instances natural consequences are unacceptable, such as situations in regard to life or death for the child. These situations demand the use of logical consequences instead of natural consequences. As adults we would not let a child run into the street to learn the consequence of that behavior. When it comes to safety in a social system, the adult is responsible for arranging the consequences of certain behaviors. The link between rules and logical consequences is safety. Rules not related to safety invite punishments instead of logical consequences.

Logical consequences are those events that are guided and arranged by teachers (Savage, 1991). Driekurs and Grey (1968) point out that there is a fine line between logical consequences and punishments. The line is one of attitude or belief. Punishment aims to "hurt" the child in some way. The goal is to make them feel bad about what they did in order to stop them from doing that behavior again. Consequences aim to *teach* the child in some way. The goal of consequences is to have children make choices and learn from those choices in order to shape their own behavior.

Logical consequences, as the name implies, refer to the use of *logic* in arranging consequences for young children. Since young children under six are in what is termed the preoperational stage of cognitive development (Piaget, 1963), they are not logical. Young children are constructing reality in order to develop logical operating systems in their brains. Therefore, logical consequences have minimal effectiveness in facilitating the development of the child five years of age and younger. Instead of using logical consequences, it is more effective to use a series of limit-setting or problem-solving techniques. (See Chapters 12 and 15.)

Requirements for Effective Logical Consequences

- All logical consequences must be discussed and understood by the students as being related to safety.
- Logical consequences must be related to the misbehavior.
- Logical consequences must be arranged when the adult is modeling self-control.
- Logical consequences must involve a choice.
- Logical consequences are concerned about the present or future behavior of the child.
- Logical consequences must be nonjudgmental; that is, they imply no element of personal moral judgment as to good or bad, right or wrong.
- Logical consequences grounded in safety are arranged and maintained in a manner that acknowledges mutual rights, respect and understanding.

Safety

Logical consequences must be related to safety to have meaning for young children. Kindergarten and first grade are transition times for young children in their perception of the world. The experiences, patterns and beliefs instilled in them through their interactions are being internalized. Children during this time are just beginning to develop internal speech, so they are able to talk to themselves in their head to manage, guide and control their behaviors. This self-talk was previously the talk of others (i.e., parents and teachers). Children now take ownership of many of the beliefs held by others by mentally representing the world in their own heads as it has been presented in the earlier stages of development. In essence, the children are making decisions about programs they will instill in their own belief systems that will guide their behavior consciously and unconsciously for a lifetime.

As children make this transition in personality development and cognitive development from prelogic to logic, the use of safety is the link. Safety, in which limits are grounded, provides the scaffold upon which rules can be built and logical consequences understood. Having a rule of not talking in line is difficult to understand for young children. Having a rule of not stealing other children's belongings is much easier for young children to understand. Rules that have little meaning to children are harder to remember and follow.

Rules not based on safety are also difficult for adults to model. A teacher would never steal in front of the children; however, he or she may talk with other teachers in the halls when the rule is no talking. If your rules are related to safety, the logical consequences are more likely to be meaningful to the young student in kindergarten through third grade.

Related to Misbehavior

Each logical consequence you arrange for your children must also be related to the misbehavior. If the consequence is not clearly related to the behavior, then the child is likely to view the consequence as a punishment.

Nick's mother returns home from work and finds his toys are in the driveway, preventing her from parking the car. Nick is nowhere to be found. She moves the toys and parks the car. Upon locating Nick she says, "Nick, I cannot park the car with all the toys lying around. You can pick them up before I come home, or I will remove them and put them in the shed." This is a logical consequence arranged on the spot by the mother to deal with the toy situation. She would have used punishment instead of logical consequences if she had said, "You either pick up those toys or there will be no soccer game for you on Saturday." The soccer game is not related to the toys in the driveway.

The younger the child, the stronger should be the relationship between the inappropriate behavior and the consequence. If this relationship is not made in the mind of the child, the child will see the consequence as a punishment and focus his or her energy on changing the punisher as opposed to changing one's own behavior. Many adults comment, "I just cannot think of a logical consequence for so and so." A good rule of thumb is that if you can't think of a logical consequence for a certain behavior, then consequences are not needed. Turn your attention to problem solving. (See Chapter 15.)

Exercise: In the following situations write C for consequence and P for punishment after the statements made by the teacher.

Situation # 1: While eating lunch in the cafeteria, Carl engages in a belching and giggling contest with Marcus.

Teacher Statements

1. I see by your actions you have completed eating your lunch. Take your tray to the window. _____
2. You boys are being rude to your classmates. You lose 5 points for the class. _____
3. Lunch is supposed to be a pleasant, social time for all. Your behavior is not pleasant for others. You may not sit with each other. _____
4. Since you are choosing to be disruptive, you will not be going to recess today. _____
5. Your actions are disrupting the ability of others to enjoy their lunch. Tomorrow you will eat in the office. _____

In the situations above, the consequences are numbers 1,3 and 5. Numbers 2 and 4 are punishments. Two and four were not related to the inappropriate behaviors that the teacher desired to change.

Situation # 2: Kenneth repeatedly "forgets" to clean up his toys.

Teacher Statements

1. Kenneth, you were told to clean up all the toys and you disobeyed me. You are to sit in time out. I will set the timer. _____

2. Kenneth, you are being irresponsible and a spoiled brat, just trying to get your own way. You may not watch TV tonight. _____

3. Kenneth, you have a choice—pick up the toys or lose the opportunity to play with the toys for the rest of the day. _____

4. Kenneth, since you have been unable to remember to clean up the toys you use, you can only play with these toys under my supervision. _____

5. Kenneth, since you have not been remembering to clean up when you are finished playing with the toys, you will not be able to go to your friend's house. _____

   In the above situation, the consequences were numbers 3 and 4. Numbers 1, 2 and 5 were punishments. However, there are more to consequences than just being related to unacceptable behavior. Calling children irresponsible and spoiled brats is an attempt to hurt them. Anytime your goal is to hurt, you are punishing. If your goal is to teach, you probably are using consequences.

Choice

   Choices are integral parts of logical consequences. Alternative actions are proposed by the teacher, and then the teacher accepts the child's decision. This ensures that the child makes a choice with just external structure. Two things are important when giving choices: the tone of voice of the teacher must reflect an attitude of respect, acceptance and good will (Dinkmeyer &McKay, 1989). Screaming choices at children puts the external pressure back in the situation. The teacher becomes controlling instead of structuring.

There are two levels of choices that can be offered to a child:

• A choice to be a part of the group and stay in relationship with the teacher and classmates.

• A choice to remove oneself from the group or situation.

Choices that include the option to stay in relationship:

"Nicole, we are at the rug for story time. Everyone has a right to hear the story. You may listen to the story from the brown rug or from the yellow rug. What is your choice?"

Choices that include the option to remove yourself:

"Nicole, we are at the rug for story time. Everyone has a right to hear the story. You may sit in the group quietly or remove yourself to your table. What is your choice?"

Get in the car or I'm leaving you!

Excellent Choices - NOT!

When teachers present children with choices that ask them to choose to remove themselves from the group or from the activity, it is critical that they invite them back. In the level two example above, if the child chooses to remove him- or herself, the teacher would say, "When you are ready to listen to the story, join us at the rug." If the child returns to the group and continues to be disruptive, inhibiting the learning of others which is unsafe, the teacher must hold the student accountable to the choices offered. "I see by your actions that you have decided to remove yourself from the group again. You may come to story time tomorrow. You have decided not to be a part of this group today."

Opportunity = Responsibility = Consequences

For every opportunity children have, there is a responsibility. The obvious consequence for not accepting the responsibility is to lose the opportunity. The opportunity of having toys requires the responsiblity of taking care of them. When children don't take care of them, the consequence is to lose the opportunity of having the toys they didn't take care of. Children have the opportunity of using the school playground during recess. The responsibility is to treat the equipment and other people with respect. When people or things are treated disrespectfully, it would be logical to lose the opportunity of using the playground and sit on a time out bench until he or she is ready to be respectful again. Children must know that they will have another chance as soon as they are ready for the opportunity. It is important to verbally invite children back into the group. A teacher might say, "When you are ready to use your words instead of hitting your friends, please join us."

Present or Future Behavior

Punishment generally deals with past behaviors. For example, if a student does not turn in an assignment, a punishing teacher would say, "Betty, you are always turning in your papers late. How many times do we have to go through this? You failed last grading period. Is that what you want to happen now? You can just stay in from recess for the next two weeks." By constantly relating the present behavior to the past, students are assured they are not changing and the teacher does not expect them to change. A strong self-fulfilling prophecy is set in motion and reinforced with each misbehavior.

Logical consequences are concerned with present and future behavior. A teacher using logical consequences with Betty would say, "Betty, your assignments were due today. You have a choice of getting them to me by the end of the day or receiving a zero for the work. The next assignments are due on Friday. I am confident you can meet that deadline. What could you do to ensure the work will be ready by Friday?" Logical consequences facilitate students in taking different strategies in the future.

HOPE

This concept of "crystal balling," as I call it, is a difficult habit for me to break. I catch myself constantly projecting the past into the future. Riding in the car to the grocery store, I hear myself saying "Oh no, it's two o'clock. There are always lines at two o'clock." Traveling to give a workshop, I will catch myself thinking, "I just know the traffic is terrible. It always is." Predicting the worst based on a past experience was so much a part of my life, one friend of mine finally said, "If you are going to crystal ball the future, at least make it hopeful." Hope means having only positive expectations.

Imply No Element of Moral Judgment

Logical consequences are nonjudgmental; they imply no element of personal moral judgment. There is no reference to being good or bad or right or wrong. The student simply demonstrates a behavior.

Punishment is personalized and implies moral judgment. For example, a student borrows the stapler from the teacher without permission. A punishing teacher might angrily lecture the student by saying, "You took my stapler without my permission. Don't you know that is like stealing and stealing is wrong! I am ashamed of you, and I'm sending a note to your parents."

A teacher using logical consequences would give the student information, request the stapler be returned and assist the student in formulating a new strategy to obtain a stapler when needed in the future. The teacher might say, "Juan, return the stapler to my desk. When you borrow materials from another person, you must first ask permission. What could you do when you need the stapler again?"

Writing Logical Consequences

Consequences are an essential part of rule writing when working in a public school setting. Each rule you have in your primary classroom must have consequences.

Traditionally, classroom teachers have listed their rules and their consequences. Usually there is one consequence for one rule. You might have seen the following in classrooms:

Rule	Consequence
Keep hands and feet to one's self.	Time out.
Turn work in on time.	Receive zero on assignment.
Walk in the halls.	Lose 10 minutes of recess.

In this setup, each and every time the child breaks the rule, the specified consequence must be applied. This leaves no room for teacher flexibility and/or meeting the individual needs of children.

Michelle was a quiet, timid child in Mrs. Brown's first-grade classroom. She was what Mrs. Brown would call a "good student." The class had been studying insects, and on Monday morning a homework assignment called "Weekend Bugs" was due. To Mrs. Brown's surprise, Michelle did not have her work. She had forgotten and left it on the kitchen table. Of course, Bobby had said the same thing. Mrs. Brown knew Bobby had to be lying, but what would she do with poor little Michelle? The consequence of not having the work was to give the student a zero. That was fine for Bobby; he got them regularly. Mrs. Brown felt herself in a dilemma. She resolved her conflict by thinking *a rule is a rule*. She gave Michelle a zero. Michelle cried and became very depressed. As the days went on, Michelle became more and more withdrawn from the class. Later in the year, a parent conference was called to see what was "wrong" with Michelle.

When you have one consequence per rule, the teacher is limited in meeting the individual needs of his or her children. A smorgasbord approach to utilizing consequences is more effective. A smorgasbord represents a variety of generic consequences from which the teacher may select the most appropriate one for a given situation and a given child.

With young learners the following four generic consequences will work for any rule:

Reminder of the rule and its relationship to safety: "Carmen, the rule is walk in the classroom. It is not safe to run." Sometimes you may want to add problem-solving techniques to your reminder. In this case you would say, "Carmen, what could you do to help yourself to remember to walk in the classroom?"

Choice of options that enable the student to function within the rules: "Carmen, you must walk in the classroom. You may choose to walk or stay at your seat. What is your choice?"

Contingency option—when you do this, then you can

do that: "Carmen, when you show me you can walk from your table to the story area, then you can join us."

Loss of privilege or removal to safety: "Carmen, if you continue to run in the room, creating an unsafe place, you will no longer be able to participate in center time."

● ●

Adults often use choices to manipulate children.

● ●

An example of utilizing the above generic consequences with young learners in a rule-governed system would be as follows:

Rule: Clean up your work space

Consequences:

Reminder: "Clean up your work space. Clutter in the room makes it unsafe." ("Where could you store your work?" could be utilized if problem solving is needed.)

Choices: "It is time to clean up. You may pick up the large items first or the small items. Which ones will you pick up first?"

Contingencies: "When your work space is cleaned, you may move to another area."

Loss of Privilege or Removal: "Your refusal to clean up your work space creates an unsafe classroom. I am here to keep it safe. You may not work at a center today. Work quietly at your table. Tomorrow you will be able to join the class at center time."

Exercise: Write four consequences for the rule *Do not hit.*

1._____

2._____

3._____

4._____

Consequences for the hitting example could look like the following:

1) *Reminder:* "Stop! I will not let you hurt yourself or anyone else in this classroom. When someone pushes you say, "I do not like it when you push me.' Stop Now!" A reminder would also be given to the child pushing. (Both children would be required to practice using their words as opposed to actions.)

2) *Choices:* "Jamey, hitting is not allowed in this classroom. You have a choice to keep your hands to yourself or leave the area. What is your choice?"

3) *Contingencies:* "When you have calmed down enough to solve your problem without hitting, then you may return to your work table."

4) *Loss or Privilege or Removal:* "Hitting hurts. I will not allow you to hurt anybody. You must stay in the quiet space until you believe you can join the class and contribute to its safety." (Or you could say, "If you hit to be first in line to go to recess, you will not go at all.")

Some students may just need a reminder to assist them in functioning within the classroom rules. Some children need removal and loss of privilege to get the point across. With generic consequences the teacher then has the option of giving a reminder or having the child lose privileges. The teacher then can individualize the behavioral plan for each child within his or her classroom. The same is true for parents.

You may be saying to yourself, "What if this," or "What if that" or "This lady has never seen my Jason." Consequences are effective tools for children doing what children do (i.e., testing the limits, exploring cause and effect, etc.) However, children who have behavior problems may or may not respond to the generic consequences as outlined. Many teachers fall into the trap of structuring the classroom around the needs of the children with behavior problems as opposed to a developmentally appropriate structure. Reynolds (1990) gives teachers four questions to ask themselves to discern if a student has a behavior problem:

1. Is the student exceeding limits or rules chronically, severely, knowingly and purposely? When the child exceeds the limits or rules, is the child harming other children?
2. Does the behavior appear to cause harm to the child? Is the child's self-esteem at risk?
3. Do one or more adults perceive the behavior as problem behavior? Because of this, is the child receiving negative reinforcement more often then he or she is receiving positive reinforcement?
4. Is the child's behavior indicative of an unmet need? Does the child attempt to meet his or her needs in inappropriate ways?

If the answer to the above questions is yes, the child has a behavior problem. Teachers must not structure their classrooms to meet the needs of children with behavior problems at the expense of those who need a developmentally appropriate structure!

It is generally assumed that most of the students in your class (85% of them) work well under any guidance system. Not true. If you use a punitive system in an attempt to control two or three students with behavior problems, you are putting your total class at risk in the area of competence and esteem. Would it not be better to structure your classroom on developmentally appropriate principles and then create a special system to meet the individual needs of all your students with severe behavior problems?

Summary

Consequences, whether natural or logical, are ways of helping children learn from their experiences and their choices. Like teaching through example, teaching through experiences is an extremely powerful technique. Experience alone is not enough to teach young children; the role of the teacher is critical in the process. The child must reflect upon his or her experience, the choices made and the outcomes obtained. The adult must facilitate this process. It is this process of thinking about the experience that produces the learning. Children then are capable of constructing an internal sense of right and wrong or safe and hurtful, or even effective and ineffective. Moral concepts such as these have true meaning to the child, as opposed to being told what to think or what to believe. Children will remember concepts they themselves construct, and in addition those concepts are more likely to be used to guide their behavior.

Consequences teach children self-discipline. They not only help children take responsibility for their own choices and behaviors, but they also assist in the development of autonomous behavior. Children will eventually be able to function constructively and caringly without adult supervision. Instead of order being imposed from the "authority," order is maintained by each person for the benefit of the group. Children learn how to handle freedom with responsibility, and a democratic classroom is created and maintained by all members.

Writing rules is part of the school culture and accountability for primary-age children. Writing effective rules and consequences is part of the responsibility of the teacher. In order to do this, the teacher must be able to discern rules from principles and write effective consequences for each rule that allows the teacher flexibility in meeting the needs of the individual children in the classroom. One of the most popular questions I am asked is, "What would be the logical consequence for _____?" The answer is, "If the consequence is not obvious, then a consequence is not appropriate." One of the most effective things to do instead of looking for logical consequences is to look for solutions. It's a mistake to think there must be a logical consequence for every behavior. It's time to put less emphasis on consequences and more emphasis on problem solving.

Chapter 15

You have a brain, please use it:
Problem Solving Skills

Adult/Child Conflict Techniques

Child/Child Conflict Techniques

Child/Child Problem Solving
  (Adult did not see what happened)

Child/Child Problem Solving
  (Adult sees what happened)

Resolving Conflicts

Once we abandon the search for the magic consequences we believe are necessary to change children's behavior, we free ourselves to solve problems. Problem solving involves bringing solutions to conflict situations. Conflicts can be classified as occurring between the adult and the
child or between the child and another child. This chapter
offers some beginning skills needed for problem solving.

Adult/Child Conflict Techniques

When the adult has a problem with a child or a group
of children, four options are available as solutions:

**1) The adult can change his or her expectations so the
behavior is no longer perceived as unacceptable.**
Mr. Greer had a terrible time getting one child to
come to circle; he had always required that all children must
come to circle; and had tried everything he knew to get Mica
to come to circle. Eventually, he reevaluated his routine
and decided that as long as a child was not disturbing the
circle time routine, he or she could choose to come to circle
or not. The very next day, Mica came to circle.

**2) The adult can change the routine or situation to
better accommodate the needs of the children.**
Mrs. Canipe had the same problem as Mr. Greer.
Actually, they were helping each other come up with ideas of
what to do with the children who refused to come to circle.
Mr. Greer told Mrs. Canipe of his success with Mica, yet
Mrs. Canipe just could not allow circle time to be a choice. It
was too valuable an experience for one child to miss and "if
you let one child get away with it, all the children will want
to stop coming!" Mrs. Canipe decided to change the situation. She shortened her circle time and made it more lively
and child-centered. Ben, her straggler, decided circle time
wasn't such a bad place after all.

3) The adult can give the children the necessary information so that they can successfully respond to the adult expectations.

"Use your inside voices. If the classroom does not get quiet you will lose fun Friday. This is it! You are being rude to me and the other classes. Do you want to lose your special time on Friday? What is the matter with you today? Why can't you be like Ms. Williams' classroom?"

As teachers attempt to get children to comply with their wishes, the above comments can be heard in classrooms throughout the country. Instead of giving the children the information they need to make a decision about their own behavior, adults tend to threaten, lecture, compare and name-call in hopes the children will finally be forced to listen and obey. This form of disciplining creates conflicts. Adele Faber and Elaine Mazlish (1980) in their wonderful book, *How To Talk So Kids Will Listen & Listen So Kids Will Talk,* suggests five ways of giving information to children that will elicit *cooperation* as opposed to *resistance.*

✔ Describe what you see - *I see a room full of children shouting.*
✔ Give information - *The noise in the room is disrupting the other classrooms and making it difficult for you to hear each other.*
✔ Say it with a word - *Children, the noise!*
✔ Describe what you feel - *I feel frustrated when I repeatedly ask you to be quiet and I am ignored.*
✔ Write a note - *The noise is pounding on my eardrum and it is hurting me. Please talk softly. Love, your ear!*

For many children, adults just talk too much. Once children learn the schedule and the daily routine, it becomes imperative that the adult refrain from long lectures and keep things simple. However, some children with special needs may need more guidance and information than others. For example, Sarah, a typically developing five-year-old, has forgotten to get her lunch from her cubby. The teacher might just say, "Sarah, your lunch," to prompt her memory, while the same teacher may comment to Peter, a highly distractible, developmentally delayed child, "Peter, it is time to get your lunch from the cubby (point to the area). Ralph is getting his. Do what Ralph is doing." Children vary with the amount of information they need to be successful in school environments.

The role of the teacher is to empower the children with the least amount of information necessary. In this way, the children are constantly asked to think about their own behavior and become more and more self-reliant. Always remember, when you do something for persons that they are capable of doing for themselves, you disempower them and make them dependent on you.

4) **The adult can give the child I-messages.**

In white middle-class America "you" messages are used to convey messages to people who are bothering us: "You are driving me crazy" ; "You are making it impossible for me to finish this lesson" ; "You are disrupting the entire classroom" ; "You are totally out of line with that behavior" ; "You are forcing me to put you in time out."

You-messages send a very powerful message to young children. They say **you, the child, have the power to make me, the adult, act in certain ways.** In other words, not only do you- messages blame children for adult actions, they also send a constant message to the children that they are in charge of the adult. Many children who repeatedly are told they are in charge of the adult, begin acting as if it were true. At this point, many adults then feel out of control.

Mrs. Dodge and Ian had a special relationship in the class. They both were able to irritate each other relatively easily. Mrs. Dodge would say to Ian, "Now look what you made me do. You are making me angry. You are disrupting this class. You are causing the class to miss their lunch time." Ian had tons of power. He was in control of everyone and everything—even lunch time. Ian was learning how to be in charge of everyone except himself.

All adults get frustrated with children. All adults have a right to be angry. All adults also have a responsibility to display their frustration to the children in a socially acceptable way.   All adults have an obligation to model for the children positive ways to express anger.

An I-message gives the children the description of the behavior that is annoying or disruptive, the tangible effect of that behavior on the adult and the feelings the adult is experiencing. Here are some examples:

- ✔ When your toys are left on the floor, I might trip, and I am afraid I will fall and hurt myself.
- ✔ When you talk when I am talking, I forget what I was saying, and I feel terribly frustrated.
- ✔ When you do not come in from the playground when I call you, you may get hurt, and I feel scared some thing bad could happen to you.
- ✔ When the noise in the room gets louder and louder, the other teachers may think I can't do my job, and I feel embarrassed.

I-messages relate the following information sequence: behavior, effect, feeling. The secret to I-messages is they must be an honest reflection of what is really going on with the adult. I remember when I first learned of I-messages. I was anxious and curious to try them with the children and actually went to work excited about getting angry. I also was so nervous that I would say the I-message wrong, I wrote, "When you ___ I feel ___ because ___" on the back of my hand with an ink pen (kind of like a cheat sheet). Jeremy was my first practice case. He kept crawling all over me when I was reading. It didn't bother me at first, but as he continued, I felt claustrophobic and simply pawed to death. My first words were "Jeremy, stop it!" I realized I did not give an I-message nor did I give him any useful information. I then said, "When you climb on me, you are bothering me." Jeremy, of course, was still climbing all over me as I fumbled through another bunch of meaningless words. I finally just got so frustrated I said, "Jeremy, I can't read this book with you climbing on my back! I feel frustrated!" He stopped. I was elated. From then on I tried not to make my I-messages so perfect.

There are some general principles in regard to I-messages that will help you on your journey.

✔ Use I-messages only when you have a problem with a child's behavior or the behavior of the classroom. Always ask yourself, is this my problem or is it the child's problem? The key to answering this question is generally who is bothered by the behavior. For example, if at story time you are reading a book and the children are more interested in talking to each other, who has the problem? You do. The children are very happy and content to talk to each other. You are the one who is frustrated and have your veins popping out of your neck. It is *your* problem.

✔ If you are frustrated or angry, let your tone of voice demonstrate this as you deliver your I-message. Children will learn that frustration and angry emo tions are okay and that there are acceptable ways to express them without hurtful words or actions.

✔ I-messages are relationship specific. If you are in relationship with children and you give them an I-message, they probably will choose to change their behavior once they understand the impact the behavior is having on you.

✔ I-messages can measure the connectedness of your relationship with the children at any given moment. Use how they respond to I-messages as an assessment technique. Know that those children who do not respond to your I-messages are "out of relationship" with you at that moment. The best cure for getting back into relationship is to spend some time playing with them. If a child is not responding to your I-messages, make a point on the playground to play tag, push the swings, toss the ball or during center time play with him or her.

✔ I-messages modeled for children will eventually be used by children. What you do to and with children is eventually what the children will do with and to you and each other. One day I visited a kindergarten classroom where Lee Canter's Assertive Discipline was in use. On the playground two girls were in a fight over who got to the swing first. One of the frustrated girls said, "I am going to put your name on the board," and walked off. At first I laughed to myself, then I thought how sad that this young girl had no other skill to resolve her conflict. She was modeling how the teacher in her classroom deals with conflict and frustration.

✔ Simpler versions of I-messages can be used to model assertiveness skills and ways to express anger. The simplest form of an I-message is "I don't like it when you _____." Teachers may model this for children as well as directly teach the skill to children.

Time for an I-Message!

I-messages taught to young children do not generalize from situation to situation, they are very specific. The poem below demonstrates the specificity and power of giving information to another person in the form of I-messages.

Maria hit me on Sunday.
She hit me on Monday, too.
She hit me on Tuesday,
I was turning black and blue.

She hit me twice on Wednesday,
And Thursday even more.
But when she hit me on Friday,
She began to get me sore.

"Enough's enough," I said to her,
"I don't like it when you hit me!"
"Well, then I won't!" Maria said.
That Saturday, she bit me.

Then . . . .
Maria bit me on Sunday.
She bit me on Monday, too.
She also bit me on Tuesday,
I was turning black and blue.

She bit me twice on Wednesday.
And Thursday even more.
But when she bit me on Friday,
She began to get me sore.

"Enough's enough," I said to her.
"I don't like it when you bite me!"
"Well, then I won't," Maria said.
That Saturday she hugged me.

Child/Child Conflict Techniques

Child/child conflicts are common occurrences when young children are placed in group situations. Typical problems arise over property ("It's mine. I had it"), territory ("I was sitting here"), attempts to influence others ("I won't invite you to my birthday party if you don't play with me!") and feeling valued and important ("I was here first!").

Children are egocentric. This simply means they see the world from their own perspective. Coupled with egocentrism, young children have magical thinking. They believe that just because they want something a certain way, therefore it is.

For example, if you tell a four-year-old child that she cannot go outside because it is raining, she will simply tell you, "It is not raining." If you tell the same child she cannot go outside because she would get wet, she will respond, "No, I won't." At this point you are very tempted to put the child out in the rain. Even so, once the child is allowed out in the rain and returns inside all dripping wet and you comment, "I see you are wet," the child will simply reply, "No, I'm not."

This is magical thinking. As you can imagine, it is very difficult to reason with magical thinking. Young children are just as likely to turn their socks into "little bunny fu fu" as to put them on their feet when getting dressed in the morning. Magical thinking can be frustrating for adults.

Young children may focus on one aspect of a situation and disregard other information. Children will focus on what is of interest to them and ignore all other information. For example, I once took a group of young children to the movie *101 Dalmatians*. After returning to the school, the children talked of their experience. One girl kept talking about the cats. We tried to convince her it was a movie about dogs but to no avail. She had focused on the one five-second scene in the movie where cats appeared and then disregarded the dog story. She had just gotten a new kitten at home and was concentrating on this part of her life.

Whenever two children are in conflict with each other, it becomes the adult's job to relay the big picture by giving information from both children's perspective to the children involved. The following conflict over cotton balls gives an inside view of egocentrism. The situation is viewed from Marsha's perspective, Kareem's perspective and the teacher's perspective.

Marsha's Egocentric View of the Situation

Marsha was busy working on a drawing for her mommy. She was missing something in her picture but could not quite put her finger on the missing piece. Suddenly she saw the glue stick and some cotton balls. She thought, this is perfect! I want the glue stick and the cotton balls. She excitedly scurried across the room to gather her needed items. When she got the glue stick and cotton balls, for no reason Kareem hit her. Marsha ran to the teacher, crying.

Kareem's Egocentric View of the Situation

Kareem was working at the art center making a design with cotton balls. He was busy with the glue stick as he precisely and carefully selected the location of his next cotton ball. As he was about to place the last cotton ball on his picture, Marsha grabbed the glue stick and the cotton balls from his hand. Angry and shocked at the disruption, Kareem hit Marsha in an attempt to maintain possession of the items.

Teacher's Egocentric View of the Situation

These children are driving me nuts. "Marsha, what is the matter? Kareem hit you? Why? You don't know? Kareem, why did you hit Marsha? She took your cotton balls? Marsha, did you take Kareem's cotton balls? No? What is going on here? Both of you go back to work. I'm too old for this kind of work."

In the above examples, it is clear that each child had his or her own perception of the events that occurred and the teacher didn't have a clue. Most of the day-to-day conflict situations that occur, the adult does not see. The adult is then left with the magical, egocentric thinking of both children to try and piece together the puzzle and figure out what actually happened. In the above situation, Marsha wanted a glue stick and cotton balls and therefore obtained them, unaware that Kareem was using them. Kareem was shocked at the intrusion and became violent. Both children needed information. This was the adult's role. The adult could intervene in one of two different ways, depending on whether she or he actually saw what happened.

The following responses and dialogues will demonstrate the information the adult can give the children when she or he does not witness the event.

Child/Child Problem Solving
(Adult Did Not See What Happened)

Adult:	Marsha, you seem very upset.
Marsha:	He hit me!
Adult:	Kareem hit you and you are very upset. Do you like it when he hits you?
Marsha:	No.
Adult:	Then tell him, "I do not like it when you hit me."

The teacher stands beside Marsha as she goes to tell Kareem, "I don't like it when you hit me."

Kareem:	Well, you can't take my glue stick. It is not fair.
Adult:	Kareem, you didn't like it when she took your glue stick?
Kareem:	No.
Adult:	Then tell her.
Kareem:	I don't like it when you grab things out of my hands.
Adult:	So the problem is, Marsha, you want to use the glue stick that Kareem has. What could you do to solve the problem without hurting each other?

The adult in this situation was teaching each child to be assertive. By teaching children assertiveness skills (I-messages), they are empowered to solve their own problems. Marsha started the process by bringing her first problem to the adult. Being hit by Kareem was her first immediate problem. The teacher set Marsha up to listen to her by validating her feelings: "You seem upset." Then the teacher set Marsha up 1) to know it was her problem instead of the adult's, and 2) to be able to access her assertive energy by asking, "Did you like it when he hit you?" This is a crucial step in the process. The teacher put Marsha back in charge. Marsha and most children would answer, "No." This gets their energy moving. Kind of like, "No, I didn't and, by George, I am going to do something about it."

The teacher then followed Marsha to Kareem, giving her the exact words to say. Tell him, "**I** don't like it when **you** hit **me!**" Notice the teacher did **not** say, "Tell him, **you** don't like it when **he** hits **you!**" The teacher must give the child the exact words to say so the child can imitate the teacher. The pronouns must be ordered from the child's perspective.

After completing a workshop in Florida, I discovered the pronoun issue. Following the workshop, I had the opportunity to visit the classrooms of some of the teachers who had attended the workshop. The teachers were dedicated and committed to changing some of their discipline practices. Shortly after my arrival, a young boy approached the teacher and despondently said, "Alfred took my picture!" The teacher eloquently responded, "You seem really sad. Did you like it when he took your picture?" Alfred perked up a little and said, "NO!" "Well, go tell him YOU DON'T LIKE IT WHEN HE TAKES YOUR PICTURE!" Alfred seemed empowered, his body posture became erect and he marched over to Alfred and said, "YOU DON'T LIKE IT WHEN HE TAKES YOUR PICTURE!" Alfred looked at this kid as if he were crazy, and I had a very good laugh with the teacher.

As Marsha began asserting herself with Kareem, Kareem began to speak up on his own behalf. Another piece of the puzzle was presented to the teacher. The teacher then repeated the process with Kareem. The beauty of this technique is that both children learn assertiveness skills and the adult learns what probably occurred in the original conflict. The process is ended by the teacher presenting the children with the original problem and asking for socially acceptable solutions.

Summary of conflict resolution practices when the adult does not see what transpired.

☑   Validate the feelings of the child if a strong feeling is present:
       You seem really angry.
       You seem really sad or upset.

☑   Provide assertiveness for each party by:
       a) setting the child up: Did you like it when . . . ?
       b) giving the child the exact words to say: I don't like it when you . . . .

☑   Piece together the original conflict and present this back to the children by:
       a) defining the problem: So the problem is . . . .
       b) seeking solutions from the children: What could you do to solve the problem of . . . ?

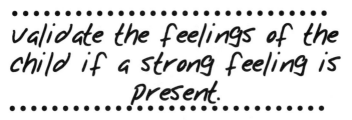

Validate the feelings of the child if a strong feeling is present.

Exercise: Practice giving children information so they may solve their own problems.

Situation # 1: The teacher is busy reading a story in the library corner of the room. Suddenly, Maria appears very upset. Amidst the tears the teacher hears, "Sam took my baby."

Write your response:

Sometimes it does actually occur that a adult witnesses a conflict between two children. When an adult sees what actually transpired, another approach is more effective. Following are the comments from a teacher who witnessed Marsha and Kareem.

Child/Child Problem Solving
(Adult Sees What Happens)

Adult to Marsha: Marsha, I see you are very upset that Kareem hit you. When you took the glue stick and the cotton balls from his hands without asking, he became angry and hit you. You may not grab things from others in this classroom! What could you do besides grab the glue stick from Kareem?

Adult to Kareem: Kareem, you seemed shocked and angry when Marsha grabbed the glue stick and the cotton balls from you. When you became angry, you hit Marsha to stop her from taking your things. You may not hit people in this classroom! What else could you do when you are angry besides hit her?

The teacher in this situation was teaching the children alternative strategies for getting their needs met. Marsha needs to learn to ask instead of grab. Kareem needs to learn to talk instead of hit. To do this, the teacher must connect the children's internal states with their external behavior. For example, think about your own life for a minute. What do you typically do when you become extremely happy? Do you tend to smile and want to talk with or hug somebody? Whatever you do, you probably have done it similarly all your life. Your internal state of happiness triggered the program, "hug."

Children learn early how to express or repress their internal states. Children who see anger expressed as violence generally express anger as violence. In the above situation, Marsha has a "grab it program." Every time she wants something, she takes it. Kareem has a "hit program." When he gets angry, he will hit most of the time.

Our role as adults is to instill into children the socially acceptable alternative programs to get their needs met. The adult in the above example illustrates the problem solving process by:

✔ Describing the children's immediate feeling states: "Marsha, you seem upset! Karee, you seem angry!"

✔ Describing the children's incorrect behavior that was utilized to get their needs met. "Marsha, when you took Kareem's things, he became angry and hit you. Kareem, when you became angry, you hit." The aggressive child needs to be given the complete information of the cause and effect of their behavior so they know it was not an effective strategy. In this case Marsha needed to be told that when she took the glue stick, she was hit. This was not what Marsha was expecting. She truly thought she could just take the items and all would be well. The aggressive child needs to learn that aggressive behavior will get the child into trouble with his or her peers. The victim who retaliates with aggressive acts needs to learn that using aggression instead of assertiveness skills will get that child into trouble with the adult.

✔ Stating the classroom rule or limit. "You may not hit in this classroom. You may not grab somethingfrom another person in this classroom."

✔ Seeking alternative strategies from the children involved. "What else could you do besides hit? What else could you do besides grab?"

Exercise:

Situation # 2: In this scene the teacher observes the following: Marty sees Dan and Steve building blocks in the block area. She seems excited about their structure and appears to want to play with them but seems hesitant. In her excitement to play she runs over to the block area and knocks the building down. Dan throws a block at Marty in his anger, while Steve calls her a "nerd." Write your response:

How Did You Do?

There is no one absolutely correct way to give information to children. It depends on the situation and the children involved. The idea is to give the children the information they need to choose an acceptable way of expressing their needs and achieving their goals. Below is a sample adult response to the situations in which you practiced.

Situation # 1: The adult is busy reading a story in the library corner. Suddenly, Maria appears very upset. Amidst the tears the adult hears, "Sam took my baby."

Information and dialogue by the teacher:

Teacher:	Maria, you seem very sad. Sam took your baby from you?
Maria:	Yes.
Teacher:	Did you like it when Sam took your baby doll?
Maria:	No.
Teacher:	Then go tell Sam, "I don't like it when you take my baby."
Maria:	Sam, I don't like it when you take my baby.
Sam:	You can't hog the wagon.
Teacher:	Sam, you wanted to use the wagon to carry something too, so you took the baby out?
Sam:	Yeah!
Teacher:	When you want something another person is playing with, what could you do besides grab it?

In this situation the story unfolded as each person began assertively standing up for him or herself. As the teacher gave information to each child and empowered the child, eventually what happened began to make sense to the teacher. However, there are times when the teacher does not see a conflict, and she or he will never truly know what happened.

Situation # 2: Marty sees Dan and Steve building blocks in the block area. She seems excited about their structure and appears to want to play with them but seems hesitant. In her excitement to play she runs over to the block area and knocks the building down. Dan throws a block at Marty in his anger, while Steve calls her a "nerd."

Information and dialogue by teacher:

Teacher: Marty, you were so excited about playing with Dan and Steve you couldn't think of the words to use to get to play with them. When you knocked down their building, they became angry and hurt you. What else could you do besides knock down the building when you want to play with another child?

Teacher: Dan and Steve, you seem very angry that your wonderful building was destroyed. You were having so much fun and were just about fin ished building. Dan, when you get angry, you may not throw the blocks. That is not safe. Steve, when you get angry, you may not call someone names. That hurts. What else could you have done to let Marty know you're angry without hurting her?

In this case the teacher gave the children information regarding internal states and the actions they produced. The teacher then moved into problem solving to elicit from the children new skills to go with their internal states.

I'm First: A Common Child/Child Problem

The most annoying problem for teachers throughout this country appears to be the "I'm First" issue. Teachers complain they are constantly trying to convince children that "first" is not "that important." Let's drop in on a typical kindergarten classroom and see just how unimportant "first" is. "Good morning, boys and girls. Hello, Michael, I see you got here early before Jeffry this morning. Today we have a special visitor coming to the classroom. The table that is ready first will be called to sit up front. Oh! I see the blue table is first;

come on up." After the guest leaves, the teacher continues: "What a wonderful treat we had this morning. Who can remember what our guest did first? Yes, Karri! Excellent. You are exactly right. You were really paying attention. Now, boys and girls, who can remember what happened next? I see so many hands. Jacob, your hand was up first. Yes, we touched the snake. You also were paying very close attention. It is now time for lunch. The children who are sitting up tall and quietly will be called first to line up. Tamara, Lamont, Jessica." The teacher begins to call out the names of the children sitting correctly. Tamara and Lamont race to the door pushing and screaming, "I was first, I was first!" The teacher goes to the door and sends them both to the end of the line, saying "I don't know why you think being first is so important."

To address the "first" issue the teacher must reflect upon how often she or he uses being first as a motivator in the classroom. When being first is used throughout the day as the motivator to get children to behave correctly, the "first" problem is going to increase. Since the dominant culture in our society values competition, winning and individualism, the value of first will be absorbed by many children. Classrooms who value competition, winning and individualism will compound the problem. It is important for teachers to know that many cultures, including Native Americans, Koreans, Chinese, many African peoples, and Japanese, value cooperation above competition and individualism. These children would not respond to competitive "first" types of classroom motivators.

As teachers learn they are sending contradictory messages to children on a regular basis about being first, some become baffled as to other ways of managing the classroom. Some teachers are so embedded in the culture of competition and individualism that it appears like "human nature."

I Was Here First: Solving the Problem

The following dialogue provides an example of how to solve the problem of "I was here first."

"Okay, what is happening?" Mrs. Benson asks as she approached two children pushing and shoving.

"I was here first; I had it first. No way ! I was here first. It is mine," screamed the two children.

Mrs. Benson calmly said, "You two are extremely angry with each other and have a big problem."

The children simultaneously reiterated, "I was here first. I had it. No, it is mine. I was here first."

"Hold up," responded the teacher. "I can't hear but one person at a time, but I do hear both of your frustrations. What I hear is you both want the Batman cape."

"Yeah and I was here first," pouted Jack.

"The problem is you both want to play with the same item. What could you do to solve this problem?"

"I could have it since I was first," responds Jack. "No way, that is stupid. I could have it first since I was first," snapped Beau.

"I can see you both are not ready to solve the problem

of the cape. I will keep the cape, and when you both have decided to solve the problem as opposed to fight over who was first, come and see me. Jack what are you going to do until you calm down?"

"Build with blocks," Jack answers.

"Beau, what are you going to do until you calm down?" "Write a story," responded Beau.

"As soon as you both are ready to solve the problem, I am ready to help you," Mrs. Benson reminded the boys as she moves to another conflict in the room.

Mrs. Benson demonstrates how to handle those "I was first" issues. Both boys hold the belief that the one who gets something first has the right to possess the object or the area. It is a conquering idea, similar to planting the flag and claiming the land for the United States. The belief does not take into consideration that we all are connected and must share resources. To begin helping children redefine the power of "first," the teacher must:

✔ Validate the feelings of the frustrated and angry children. "You both seem really angry. It is so difficult when two people want the same thing so badly."

✔ Let the children know they have a problem. It is not the adult's problem, it is indeed a problem *they* have, and the adult will help them solve it if they are willing. "You have a big problem."

✔ Define the problem for the children by stating the true dilemma. Do not include "first" in your statement. *The children who get into "first" issues start out wanting the object and end up wanting to win the battle.* "The problem is you both want to play with the _____ at the same time" or "You both want to be in the same space at the same time."

✔ Facilitate the children's attempt to come up with solutions to the real problem. If the children refuse to let go of their power struggle to be first, simply remove the item or the children until they are ready to solve the real problem.

Remember the value placed on being first is cultural. The value you place on being first in your own classroom is up to you. The way you deal with solving "first" problems will add fuel to the belief that first is best or will spark the belief that cooperation and equality offer an alternative approach to being "better than."

• •

The value you place on being first in your own classroom is up to you.

• •

Using Choices to Prevent Conflicts

"What movie do you want to see?" asked Pat.
"Whatever," responded Jan.
"Doesn't matter to me either. Really, Jan. Whatever you decide is fine." reiterated Pat.
"You're driving. You decide," concluded Jan.
You have probably experienced the above conversation sometime in your life, especially if you are a woman. Women in our society are raised to please others. As you can imagine, it is difficult to make choices and simultaneously please others. Children in our society are raised with the same double-bind situation. They are asked to think for themselves and solve problems yet please the adults all at the same time. Since this task is impossible, children eventually begin to feel "bad" about themselves and their self-esteem suffers.

A person's ability to make choices and accept the ones he or she makes is a measure of self-esteem. Making choices bolsters self-esteem while the inability to make choices lowers self-esteem and creates "other esteem." If you will not make choices for your own life, eventually someone else will.

To completely make a choice, you must first make a decision and then accept the consequences of that choice. For example, pretend you are at a restaurant. You have just eaten a delightful meal of heavy pasta. You are so full you couldn't eat another bite, yet the server brings around the dessert tray. You hesitate slightly as your belt digs into your stomach, yet the double chocolate cake calls to you gently. You then make a choice to have the cake (possibly splitting it with a friend).

Later, as you drive home in a state of total agony, you complain excessively about yourself to yourself with your own inner speech. "I knew better than to eat that cake. I always do this. I am so stupid and overweight. I hate it when I do this. My pants are gagging me. It's my own fault. I am just worthless." In this case a decision was made to eat the cake, yet another choice was made not to accept the decision. To bolster self-esteem, choices must be made *and* accepted.

The same thing can be seen with children. A child is offered two choices, A or B. Many children will simply make their choices. However, some children will choose C almost every time. Given the choice of orange juice or milk, the answer could easily be soda. The child uses choices as a means to draw the adult into a power struggle, in hopes of winning. By winning the power struggle, the child believes he or she would feel better about him- or herself.

Maria's mom says she comes from the "old school." She quickly tells Maria what to do and how to do it. If Maria tries to make her own decisions, her mom is generally critical of these choices. Comments such as, "Those two colors don't match. Here, let Mommy do it" are often heard at their house. When Maria arrives at school, she becomes the "boss." She quickly tells her playmates what to do and how to do it: "I am the mommy and you are the baby."

Ms. Kelly asked Maria at circle time which song she would like to sing, "Alice the Camel" or "Wheels on the Bus." She quickly snapped back her answer, "Ms. Mary Mack." Ms. Kelly just sighed. Every time she structures some options for Maria, she refuses to accept the structure. Today she is just not going to let her get away with it anymore, thus beginning a power struggle.

Other children, when given the choice of A or B, may say A; no, B; no, A; no, B, never truly deciding on either one. At last, some children may just shrug their shoulders and refuse to make any choices. How children respond to choices reflects their self-esteem and the current amount of stress in their lives. Children who chronically have difficulty making choices probably have low self-esteem. Children who previously have been able to make choices but currently are unable to make them are experiencing a great deal of stress. Think in your own life. There are some days when the stress has built up to such a degree that deciding whether to watch one TV show as opposed to another is an overwhelming decision. Sometimes adults are so stressed that when asked if they would like cream or sugar in their coffee, tears can result. The same is true for children.

Natasha appeared "off" this week. The teacher could not put her finger on what it was. She just seemed irritable, inattentive and fidgety. The teacher, in her attempt to help Natasha focus, decided to offer her some choices. "Natasha, we have two new centers in the room today, the post office and the farmyard. Which one would you like to play in?" Natasha, instead of selecting a play area, broke down in tears and repeated the word "no" several times.

Natasha was showing signs of stress. Teachers and parents can utilize the information on how children make choices as a measure of self-esteem and stress. In addition, once a diagnosis is made, the adult must then begin administering some helpful prescriptions.

Offering Choices to Help Children Focus

Choices can be used effectively as a discipline technique and as a means to help children focus. Mr. Adams had announced to the class that in five minutes it would be cleanup time. He personally got Jason's attention and told him face to face. After the five minutes had passed, the class began singing the cleanup song and putting the toys away. Jason had trouble redirecting his focus from playing to cleaning up. "Jason, you have a choice. You can pick up the big blocks first or the little blocks first. What is your choice?" Excitedly Jason said, "The big blocks because I am strong."

All children benefit from classrooms that offer rich and diverse curriculum options. Most children can benefit from using choices as a guidance tool, especially children who need additional structure to function in the classroom. Jason is a good example. He needs more direction than some of the other children. Since he needs more guidance, the teacher is prone to giving him a lot of commands. "Jason, get your lunch. Jason, get in line. Jason, wait until the door is opened," are commands representative of what Jason might hear over and over throughout the day.

Jason, in his need for external structure from adults, misses out on some of the choice-making decisions other children acquire on a regular basis. So, instead of constantly directing Jason throughout the day with commands, choices would give him the structure he needs, provide him practice in making decisions and ultimately build his self-esteem.

Choices are also helpful in getting children to comply with adult wishes. A teacher is less likely to get resistance with "Katie, you have a choice to sit on the red tape or the blue tape," than if the teacher simply said, "Katie, it is circle time; sit down." Since preschool children are developing autonomy and initiative skills, they sometimes like to assert themselves in response to adult commands. Choices provide the child the option of complying with adult wishes while still maintaining the "last word," so to speak.

In order for the adult to deliver choices to children on a regular basis, two things are required.

1.   The adult must think in terms of what he or she wants the children to do. We have been conditioned to think negatively—what we *don't* want them to do: Don't run, Don't walk, Don't talk when I am talking, etc. This type of thinking is detrimental to giving choices.

2.   The adult must give the children two positive choices. Typically, adults have been trained to give the child one "good" choice and one "bad" choice to coerce the child into picking the one the adult wanted. For example, children have been given choices to pick up their toys or lose recess time. This is not a choice; this is a manipulation. A true choice is given when we as adults do not care which option the child selects.

To create choices for children, think first, *what do I want them to do?* Then create two positive options to accomplish that goal. If you want a child to wipe off the table, you could create the options of "with a towel" or "with a washcloth." If you want a child to pick up some trash on the floor, you could give the options of "putting it in this trash can or that one."

When I first tried giving choices as opposed to manipulating children, I kept saying, "You have a choice. You can clean up before snack or after snack. What is your choice?" It seemed that when I was faced with thinking on my feet, I could only think of changing the time frame. Do it now or do it later. Well, as you may guess, the children ran all over me. They chose to do it later and later never came. I chose to revert back to good old force techniques. My days became longer and my headaches pounded intensely to every beat of "If You're Happy and You Know It." Avoid at all costs giving them positive choices of doing it now or doing it later!

Practice Time!

In the following situations, you have decided that giving choices would be an effective technique to utilize. Instead of writing your responses, rehearse them out loud to yourself or a friend. To help you in getting started, pattern yourself after this: My dear reader, you have a choice. You can rehearse the choice situations out loud, alone or with a friend. What is your choice?

Situation #1: Casey has gone into the bathroom to blow his nose. He has been in there quite a while. You notice he is making paper airplanes with the paper towels.
Response:

Situation #2: Kelvin is wandering around the room when he is supposed to be at circle time.
Response:

Situation #3: Melissa has just awakened from nap time. Her tasks are to put her shoes on and pick up her mat. She is just sitting there, singing "The Ants Go Marching One By One."
Response:

Situation #4: Marietta is playing with her food at lunch time. Response:

How did that feel to you? Most of the time new skills feel awkward. Below are some responses given by an adult to the above situations. Remember, there are no right answers.

Situation #1: Casey has gone into the bathroom to blow his nose. He has been in there quite a while. You notice he is making paper airplanes with the paper towels.
In this situation the adult decided her goal was to get the child out of the bathroom. "Casey, you have a choice. You may put your planes in the trash can and come out of the bathroom or you may come out and put your planes in your cubby. What is your choice?" This adult could have easily had another goal for Casey, such as to blow his nose. "Casey, you have a choice. You may blow your nose with a

paper airplane or with another paper towel. What is your choice?" **Your options all depend on the goal you have for the child.**
Situation #2: Kelvin is wandering around the room when he is supposed to be at circle time. "Kelvin, you have a choice. You can sit on the blue tape at circle or the red tape. What is your choice?"
Situation #3: Melissa has just awakened from nap time. Her tasks are to put her shoes on and pick up her mat. She is just sitting there, singing "The Ants Go Marching One By One." "Melissa, you have a choice. You can put this shoe on first or that one. What is your choice?"
Situation #4: Marietta is playing with her food at lunch time. "Marietta, you have a choice. You can eat your food or put your food back in your lunchbox. What is your choice?"

Dealing with Children Who Have Difficulty Making Choices

Children who have difficulty making choices fall into four categories. Those who refuse to make a choice, those who developmentally do not understand what a choice is, those who like to make their own options and those who change their minds.

Helping Those Who Refuse

Children who are overwhelmed by choices need , in their world. This can be accomplished by both teaching the routine and by the other techniques suggested in Chapter 9. To assist children in beginning to make choices, do the following:

✔   Point out to the children that they are always making choices. For example, when the child goes to the art center say, "I see you made a choice to draw today." Whenever possible, let the child know he or she is always making choices. "I see you made a choice to put your backpack in the cubby. I see you made a choice to do your homework," etc.

✔   Offer the child small choices that involve intimacy with the adult. For example, "Beth, it is time to go outside. You have a choice to hold this hand or this hand. Which do you pick? You chose my right hand. I like holding hands with you." Another example would be, "Beth, I would like you to sit next to me during story time. Would you like to sit on my left side or my right side? Oh, you picked my right side." Making choices is an autonomous activity. For some of these children, autonomy is frightening. So to ease the journey into independence, the teacher can use the "relationship with the adult" as a transition. Once the child is able to make structured relationship choices with the adult, begin offering the child more independent choices.

✔   Model making mistakes for the child. These children are typically afraid of not pleasing or being wrong. It becomes important for the teacher to model the fact that all people make mistakes. The child needs to see the adult make a mistake, forgive him- or herself, and choose a different strategy without any negative ramifications. It is most authentic when the adult "thinks aloud" his or her thinking about a true mistake instead of inventing a contrived example. "Today, children, I'm going to read a favorite of yours, *Goodnight Moon* (1975) written by Robert Munsch. Oops, that is not correct. I made a mistake. The author is not Robert Munsch. I must look it up to correct my mistake. Here it is. The book is written by Margaret Brown. All people make mistakes."

Helping Children Who Are Developmentally Delayed with Choices

Special needs children with developmental delays need structured assistance in understanding the concept of choices. To assist in this process, the teacher can do the following:

✔ Point out to the children they are always making choices (as explained above). All behavior is a result of choices. This just needs to be brought to the attention of the child.

✔ Observe children playing to see the toys they prefer. Some children prefer playing with vehicles, others with blocks, etc. Once you know his or her favorite toy type, present the child with a favorite toy and another type of toy. Generally, the child will select his or her favorite toy by eye gaze, pointing, touching or verbalizing. As the child makes the selection, reinforce the idea the child has made a choice. The same exercise can be done with pictures of toys.

✔ Karri loved horses. She would spend her entire day with horses if the teacher would let her. Ms. Walsh knew this and used this information to assist Karri in understanding the concept of choice. She would hold up a firetruck and a horse in front of Karri. "You have a choice of playing with the firetruck or the horse. What is your choice?" Karri wo¡uld look at the horse, reach and make a loud squealing noise. "I see you are choosing the horse. Here it is. You made a choice all by yourself. How exciting!"

Helping Children Who
Make Up Their Own Options

Some children will use the structured choices of adults as opportunities to engage the adult in a power struggle. If the teacher were to say, "Dana, you have a choice. You may walk with a friend or walk with me down the hall. What is your choice?" Dana would respond, "I will walk by myself." Dana is a child who, when given two parameters by an adult, constantly creates a third option for himself. We all have a need to feel that we have some power.

We need to believe we have some control and that we can manipulate the environment to some degree. Children who have been frustrated in gaining power through acceptable means may discover that their only way of feeling powerful, and therefore significant, is through socially unacceptable means. Through their inappropriate behavior, children are trying to prove that they are the boss and that the adult is powerless to force them to behave. These children believe that they are inadequate, and they have very low self-esteem. To compensate for these self-loathing feelings, they seek to obtain power from others in the form of winning. A general rule is that the more adults try to control the child, the more the child feels powerless and tries to control the adult. A vicious cycle is set, in which neither child nor teacher ultimately win. The following suggestions are helpful in dealing with these children:

✔ Discuss in your classroom the concept of power and the concept of strong. Attempt to redefine the concepts for all children. Television presents the children with the idea that to win or to beat up the bad guys is being strong or powerful. These definitions must be actively challenged at school. To challenge a child's concept, you must first discern the child's belief system and then offer other, more socially acceptable options for the child. This can be done through a technique called "mutual storytelling" (Gardner, 1986). Ask the child or children to tell you a story about a person who was powerful. This way you can elicit from the child his or her definition of powerful. After the child tells his or her story, ask the child to give the story a name, and a lesson of the story or a moral, depending on the age of the child. Then the role of the adult is to retell the child's story with the same characters in similar settings but introducing the concept of personal power to the child, as opposed to Power Over or Power Under.

Child's story: Hulk Hogan! He would take the bad guys and beat them up. The bad guys had stoled the money. Hulk was strong and got the money back.

Teacher's retelling of child's story: One time these guys were getting real hungry and they decided to steal some money so they could eat. Hulk Hogan heard this. He thought, I must help! I am strong. I know I can think of a plan. He decided to get the guys a job and then they would earn money and not steal it. Hulk had saved the day.

✔ Give the child direct commands. Children who tend to bring adults into power struggles respond better to commands than structured choices. To give a child a command simply state, "Dana, walk beside me." This of course is no guarantee the child will comply with the command, but it does reduce the amount of power struggles. Commands must be given, not requested. A request would be "Dana, would you walk with me?" or "Dana, please walk with me." or "Dana, walk with me, okay?" A request is something we ask children to do in which they have a choice of responding yes or no. "Please pass the salt" is a request. The person has the right to pass the salt or not. A command is a directive statement that does not present the other person with choices. It simply states "This is what you are to do." Women are not socialized to give commands. It is generally taught that women who give commands are rude or aggressive. However, men are taught to give commands, and men who are unable to give commands are considered weak and unreliable. Many children respond to the commands given by men better than the request given by women. Commands are easier for literal children to understand. Mrs. Baer could not understand why James would comply to the music teacher, Mr. Robbins, and not to her. She would say to James, "Would you line up by the door?" and James would just ignore her. Mr. Robbins would say, "James, go line up at the door," and James would walk across the room and lean against the wall. This was baffling to her. She couldn't understand why, when they both told James "the same thing," he would only listen to Mr. Robbins. Mrs. Baer did not realize she was requesting James to line up and Mr. Robbins was commanding. They were not saying "the same thing."

✔ Once in a power struggle, get out quickly. Every morning say to yourself, "Would I rather be right or happy? Today I will choose not to get into power struggles with Jason." Many adults rationalize their desire to be right by saying, "If I give in, the child will think he or she can control me." This is not true. The child is after power in the form of winning. If you do not engage in the struggle with the child, no one can win and no one can lose. Four ways to deal with children who attempt to engage you in power struggles frequently are: 1) ignore the child's initiating attempts to get you into a power struggle; 2) acknowledge the child's feelings; 3) refuse to play; and 4) remove the child or yourself to a safe place to calm down if needed.

"Harris, it is time to clean up." Harris responds to the teacher by saying, "I didn't play here. I don't have to clean up." "Harris, it is time to clean up. You have a choice. You can pick up the vehicles first or the blocks. What is your choice." Angrily Harris retorts, " I don't have to and you can't make me!" The teacher now is sure of her intuitive feeling of being hooked into a power struggle. She feels frustrated and angry. She catches herself thinking, "I'll show you who's boss in this classroom. I certainly *can* make you, you little brat!"

At this point she realizes she is hooked in. She pauses a moment, takes a deep breath and changes the thoughts in her head. "All right, pull it together. He is just baiting me. I must stay calm. Would I rather be right or happy? I choose to be happy and let go of making this child do anything." She now can turn around and ignore Harris and start focusing on the children who are cleaning up.

This is an example of ignoring the child's hook. The teacher could also say to Harris, "You seem really determined not to clean up, and you are frustrated with me. I will not fight with you over this matter. I will talk to you later when you are calm."

In this situation the teacher decides to acknowledge the child's feelings and postpone the confrontation in hopes the child will be calmer. Another option, one of my favorites, is to acknowledge the child's power and simply refuse to play. This is done by saying to Harris, "You are right. I can't make you clean up the toys. You are in charge of your own actions. You are the only one who can decide whether you will clean up or not." I prefer this approach because it works so well. The child is given power and responsibility for his or her own actions.

Some children exert their power over the teacher through tantrums, screaming and other out-of-control behaviors. In this case, removing the child is probably the best option. The teacher can simply state, "You are right. I cannot make you clean up. However, I will not let you hurt yourself or anyone else in this classroom." The child is guided or physically placed in a safe place area. This method is the least effective because the child is "forced" to be removed. The child has created another situation in which he or she is totally powerless. Now the child will eventually want that power back and will try to hook the adult again.

Helping Children Who Change Their Minds

Chelsea was given a choice of milk or juice for snack. She selected milk. Then she changed her mind, refusing to drink the milk and calling for juice. The adult wanted to dump both the milk and the juice on top of her head.

Once again, children such as Chelsea have self-esteem issues. They attempt to control their environment by being indecisive and by whining. Whereas the power-struggle children could be called "aggressive," these children could be called "passive aggressive." Helping these children involves holding them to their original choice. The adult responded to Chelsea by saying, "Chelsea, you chose milk. That was your decision and that is what you will get."

By this time Chelsea was in a full-blown tantrum, throwing the milk off the table, screaming passionately for juice. The adult had to stay calm, validate the child's experience, hold the line and if necessary, restrain the child. This was done by saying the following: "Chelsea, you are furious with me now. You really wanted me to let you change your mind. You asked for milk. That is what you got. It is hard to be in charge of what happens to you. I know you are really angry and want me to go away. I will stay with you until you get calm." The adult needed to stay with Chelsea for a while. When she had regained her composure, the adult then gave her milk with a choice to drink it or to put it in the trash.

The above situation is called a "showdown." The child is held to the first decision no matter how long or severe the resistance and/or tantrum. The child must learn he or she has power and that power comes from making and accepting choices. This does not mean that ALL children cannot change their minds. This means that children who chronically act like Chelsea must be taught the power of choosing.

Summary

At any given moment, we examine problems to find solutions or assign blame. Those who choose to look for solutions need skills in facilitating problem solving. This chapter explored looking for solutions to conflicts. If the conflict involves an adult and a child or group of children, the adult can change his or her expectations, change the routine by structuring the situation differently, give I-messages or give the children the necessary information they need to function more successfully.

Child/child conflicts are everyday occurrences for young children. You were given problem-solving strategies for situations in which you see what happens and those in which you did not see what happens. The child/child problem of "I'm first" was specifically addressed. Sadly, we have managed to instill in the minds of young children that being first is equal to being special and better than others. To change this, adults must learn how to motivate themselves and children through techniques other than the drive to be special or first.

This last chapter concluded with an understanding of

the power of choice and how to use choices effectively as a discipline technique as well as a self-esteem assessment tool.

• •

A general rule is that the more adults try to control the child, the more the child feels powerless and tries to control the adult.

• •

AFTERWORD

With every ending there is a new beginning. I hope this book has offered you some endings and some new beginnings. I know I am starting a new beginning in my life. The writing of this book helped me become aware of how little I really know and just how willing I am to continually learn. My intent was to make conscious the beliefs that govern our behavior and to offer alternative beliefs and skills that create more peaceful and loving relationships. As old beliefs die, new beliefs are allowed to grow. I often say to myself, "Go conscious, not crazy."

In essence, the whole book is about choices. The choice between looking for solutions or looking for blame. The choice between awareness or denial. The choice between resentment and forgiveness. The choice between using structure or control. Underlying all this is a choice between judgment and acceptance. I would like to close by sharing with you a poem I wrote, " A Gift of Acceptance." My dream is that we all learn to receive and give this gift.

A Gift of Acceptance

If I constantly see what children can't, won't or don't do, I may be overly critical of myself.

If I judge others to be not caring, I may be feeling under-valued and undernurtured in my own life.

If I blame others for restricting my creativity, I may be feeling inadequate, out of balance and unable to express myself.

If I view the children as mean or bad, I may be feeling "not good enough" as a person.

If I constantly feel a need to get control of the children, I may be unaware of my own self-punishing thoughts and feelings.

If I believe I know best what others should choose to do or not do in their own lives, I may be uncertain as to what I myself want or need.

If I have a need for the children to be right and to do perfect work, I may be terrified of making mistakes in my own life.

If I have a need for the children to be quiet and obedient, I may be frightened of my own power.

If I see the beauty in all children, their parents and all people, I know I am love and extend it graciously.

If I see the intelligence and creativity in all children, I have discovered my own wisdom.

If I value and see the unique radiance of all children, even those who lash out, I have accepted myself.

Becky Bailey
1996

Dr. Becky Bailey, University of Central Florida professor of Early Childhood Education and Development, is a dynamic speaker and the author of numerous research articles, audio tapes and five books, including the recently published and highly acclaimed, *I Love You Rituals: Activities to Build Bonds and Strengthen Relationships* (Loving Guidance Publishers, 1997).

Positive thinking has fueled Dr. Bailey's life since her childhood. A near-death experience, the result of a car accident at age 16, forever changed her life and outlook on living and relationships. Her message involves helping others shift from a life based on fear to one full of love.

CONSCIOUS DISCIPLINE

Dr. Bailey has designed a four-part discipline program for elementary schools. The four parts consist of:

1. becoming conscious or aware of beliefs that limit or prevent teachers from letting go of control and changing outdated practices;
2. creating a conflict resolution curriculum based on cultivating a school family;
3. creating a structure that allows the school family to grow and teaches children responsibility;
4. learning the ten basic skills of discipline to maintain the school family.

This program is a developmentally appropriate discipline system that integrates the academic curriculum with teaching children socially acceptable behaviors.

For more information about seminars in your area, please call 1-800-842-2846.

Teach Only Love For That Is What We Are

APPENDIX

LETTERS TO PARENTS
(English and Spanish)

Dear Family,

Many times in our educational system, only one cultural point of view is presented in teaching our children. Unfortunately as a consequence of this, children of other cultural roots do not have the opportunity to identify completely with what is being taught. In my classroom, I would like each and of my students to feel valued for his or her own particular view of the world, as well as for his or her own family customs and cultural heritage. I would also like to create an atmosphere in the classroom where all students are able to share and celebrate their diverse cultures with respect and honor.

With this in mind, I am asking you to share with me your culture and customs. In this way, you will be able to help me improve the educational experience of your child. I would like to thank you for your help, support and participation in ensuring that this school year will be a positive one that allows for the teaching of all children.

Cultural Information

Please answer the following questions to the best of your ability:

1. What is your cultural heritage?
2. Do you identify with this cultural heritage?
3. What languages are spoken in your home? What is the predominant language used?
4. Are you comfortable speaking and reading English?
5. What are the traditions, objects or foods that most reflect your culture?
6. Why are these traditions, objects or foods important? What values or history do they represent?
7. What is your religious background?
8. What values do you want us to teach your children?
9. In what way can we here at school support and continue your cultural values?
10. What celebrations, heroes, music, stories, traditions and games could we include that represent and support your heritage?
11. Does your family celebrate birthdays? If so, how?
12. Would you be willing to come and share your family's ways of celebrating holidays with your child's class?

Sincerely,

Estimada Familia,

Muchas veces en nuestro sistema educación, se presenta un solo punto de esto, las enscñanzas de los niños. Desafortunadamente como consequencia de esto, los niños con otras raices culturales no tienen la oportunidad de identificarse completamente dentro de la enseñanza. En mi salón de clase, deseo que cada uno de mis alumnos se sienta valorado por su propia perspectiva cultural y por sus diferentes costumbres familiares. También quisiera crear un ambiente en el salón de clase donde todos los estudiantes puedan compartir y celebrar sus diversas culturas con respeto y honor.

Con ese fin, voy a necesitar que cada uno de ustedes me deje conocer acerca de su cultura y costumbres. Asi podrán ayudarme a mejorar la experiencia educational de sus hijos. De antemano, les agradesco por su ayuda, apoyo y participación de esta manera asegurando que este año escolar sea muy positivo y deje enseñanza para todos.

Información Cultural

Por favor, trate de contestar las siguientes preguntas dejando en blanco las que no pueda. Añada una hoja si es necesario.

1. ¿Cuál es su decendencia cultural?
2. ¿Se identifica usted con su decendencia cultural?
3. ¿Qué idiomas se hablan en la casa? ¿ Cuál es el principal?
4. ¿Se siente usted bien hablando y leyendo el inglés?
5. ¿Cuáles son las tradiciones, o comidas que reflejan mas su cultura?
6. ¿Qué representativos tienen estos en su cultura?
7. ¿Qué religión practica su familia?
8. ¿Qué valores quiere que le enseñemos a su hijo o a su hija?
9. ¿De qué manera en la escuela podemos apoyar a continuar sus valores culturales?
10. ¿Qué personajes, celebraciones, música, historias, tradiciones y juegos podemos incluir aqui en la escuela para mantener viva su cultura?
11 ¿Celebra su familia los cumpleaños? ¿ De qué forma?
12. ¿Está dispuesto usted asistir al salón de clases para compartir con nosotros su forma de celebrar sus tradiciones y fiestas culturales?

Sinceramente,

CHILDREN'S LITERATURE THAT SUPPORTS LIMITS AND RULES

Alexander and the Terrible Horrible, No Good, Very Bad Day
by Judith Viorst
Macmillan Publishing Company
ISBN 0-689-71173-5

Bad Mood Bear by John Richardson
Barron's
ISBN 0-8120-5871-2

Bootsie Barker Bites by Barbara Bottner
G. P. Putnam's Sons
ISBN 0-399-22125-5

I Like Me! by Nancy Carlson
Viking
ISBN 0-670-82062-8

I Don't Eat Toothpaste Anymore! by Karen King
Tamarind Books
ISBN 1-870516-16-8

If I Ran the Family by Lee and Sue Kaiser Johnson
Free Spirit Publishing
ISBN 0-915793-41-5

I'll Do It Myself by Jirina Marton
Annick Press
ISBN 1-55037-063-4

It's Hard to Share My Teacher by Joan Singleton Prestine
Fearon Teacher Aids
ISBN 0-86653-924-7

The Kissing Hand by Audrey Penn
Child Welfare League of America
ISBN 0-87868-585-5

Little Beaver and the Echo by Amy MacDonald
G. P. Putnam's Sons
ISBN 0-399-22203-0

Love You Forever by Robert Munsch
Firefly Books
ISBN 0-920668-37-2

Miss Nelson Is Missing by Harry Allard
Houghton Mifflin Company
ISBN 0-395-40146-1

Mufaro's Beautiful Daughters by John Steptoe
Lothrop, Lee & Shepard Books
ISBN 0-688-04045-4

No Jumping on the Bed! by Ted Arnold
Dial Books for Young Readers
ISBN 0-8037-0038-5

Owl Babies by Martin Waddell
Candlewick Press
ISBN 1-56402-101-7
Purple, Green and Yellow by Robert Munsch
Annick Press Ltd., Canada
ISBN 1-55037-256-4
So Much by Trish Cooke
Candlewick Press
ISBN 1-56402-3443
Sometimes I Feel Awful by Joan Singleton Prestine
Fearon Teacher Aids
ISBN 0-86653-927-1
Sometimes I Like to Be Alone by Heidi Goennel
Little Brown
ISBN 0-316-31842-6
Sometimes I Get Angry by Jane Werner Watson
Crown Publishers
ISBN 0-517-56088-7
Swimmy by Leo Lionni
Alfred A. Knopf, Inc.
ISBN 0-394-82620-5
The Day Jimmy's Boa Ate the Wash by Trinka Hakes Noble
The Dial Press
ISBN 0-140-54623-5
The Temper Tantrum Book by Edna Mitchell Preston
Puffin Books
ISBN 0-14-050181-9
Tough Borris by Mem Fox
Harcourt Brace & Company
ISBN 0-15-289612-0
When Emily Woke Up Angry by Riana Duncan
Barron's
ISBN 0-8120-5985-9
Where's My Teddy? by Jez Alborough
Candlewick Press
ISBN 1-56402-280-3

REFERENCES

Baumrind, D. (1967). Child care practices anteceding three patterns of preschool behavior. *Genetic Psychology Monographs*, 75:43-88.

Beck, A. (1972). *Depression: Causes and treatment.* Philadelphia: University of Pennsylvania Press.

Becker, W. C. (1964). Consequences of different kinds of parental discipline. In M. L. Hoffman (ed.), *Review of Child Development Research* (vol. 1). New York: Russell Sage Foundation.

Bradshaw, J. (1990). *Homecoming: Reclaiming and championing your inner child.* New York: Bantam Books.

Brown, N. W. (1975). *Goodnight moon.* New York: Harper & Row.

Clarke, J. I., & Dawson, C. (1989). *Growing up again: Parenting ourselves, parenting our children.* New York: Harper Collins Publishers.

Corsaro, W. A. (1981). Friendship in the nursery school: Social organization in a peer environment. In S. R. Asher and J. M. Gottman, eds., *The development of children's friendships.* New York: Cambridge University Press.

Curwin, R. L. & Mendler, A. N. (1980). *The discipline book: A complete guide to school and classroom management.* Reston, Va.: Prentice-Hall Company.

Curwin, R. L., & Mendler, A. N. (1988). *Discipline with dignity.* Association for Supervision and Curriculum Development.

Dinkmeyer, D., & McKay, G. D. (1989). *The parent's handbook.* Circle Pines, Minn.: American Guidance Service.

Driekurs, R. (1964). *Children the challenge.* New York: Hawthorne Press.

Driekurs, R., & Grey, L. (1968). *Logical consequences.* New York: Meredith Press.

Ellis, A. A. (1969). A cognitive approach to behavior therapy. *Interactional Journal of Psychotherapy, 8:* 896-900.

Ellis, A. A. (1962). *Reason and emotion in psychotherapy.* New York: Stuart.

Faber, A., & Malish, E. (1980). *How to talk so kids will listen and listen so kids will talk.* New York: Avon Books.

Firestone, R. (1985). *The fantasy bond: Structure of psychological defenses.* New York: Human Sciences Press.

Gardner, R. A. (1986). *Therapeutic communication with children: The mutual storytelling technique.* Northvale, N.J.: Jason Aronson, Inc.

Glenn, H. Stephen (1989). *Developing capable people.* Provo, Utah: Sunrise Books, Tapes & Videos.

Gordon, T. (1989). *Teaching children self-discipline: At home and at school.* New York: Times Books.

Guerney, L. (1983). Client-centered (nondirective) play therapy. In C. E. Schaefer & K. L. O'Conner, eds., *Handbook of play therapy.* New York: John Wiley & Sons.

Hart, L. (1983). *Human brain and human learning.* New Rochelle, N.Y.: Brain Age Publishers.

Hodapp, R., Goldfield, E., Boyatzis, J. (1984). The use and effectiveness of material scaffolding in mother-infant games. *Child Development,* 55(3):17-32.

Hoffman, M. L. (1970). Moral development. In P. Mussen, ed., *Carmichael's manual of child psychology.* 3rd ed., New York: John Wiley & Sons.

Hughes, P. (1991). *Human development across the life span.* New York: Macmillan Publishers.

Landreth, G. L. (1991). *Play therapy: The art of the relationship.* Muncie, Ind.: Accelerated Development Inc., Publishers.

Loeb, R. C., Horst, L., & Horton, P. J. (1980). Family interaction patterns associated with self-esteem in preadolescent girls and boys. *Merrill-Palmer Quarterly,* 26: 203-217.

Marion, M. (1991). *Guidance of young children.* 3rd ed. New York: Merrill, an imprint of Macmillan Publishing Company.

Maultsby, M. C., Jr. (1975). *Help yourself to happiness.* New York: Institute for Rational Living.

Miller, A. (1990). *For your own good: Hidden cruelty in child rearing and the roots of violence.* New York: Farrar, Straus and Giroux.

Miller, D. F. (1990). *Positive child guidance.* New York: Delmar Publishers.

O'Conner, K. (1991). *The play therapy primer: An integration of theories and techniques.* New York: John Wiley & Sons.

Patterson, G. R. (1982). *Coercive family process.* Eugene, Ore.: Castalia Press.

Peck, M. S. (1978). *The road less traveled: A new psychology of love, traditional values and spiritual growth.* New York: Simon and Schuster.

Piaget, J. (1963). *The psychology of intelligence.* Patterson, N.J.: Little-Adams.

Reynolds, E. (1990). *Guiding young children: A child centered approach.* Mountain View, Calif.: Mayfield Publishers.

Ross, S., & Lollis, P. (1987). Communication within infant social games. *Developmental Psychology,* 23(2): 241-48.

Savage, T. V. (1991). *Discipline for self-control.* Englewood Cliffs, N.J.: Prentice Hall.

Snyder, R. (1982). *Three differing systems of discipline and their impact on conscience and culture.* Unpublished manuscript, Albuquerque,N.M.

Stephenson, J. (1991). *Men are not cost effective: Male crime in America.* Napa, Calif.: Diemer, Smith Publishing Company, Inc.

Williamson, P. (1990). *Good kids, bad behavior: Helping children learn self-discipline.* New York: Simon and Schuster.

Young children (March 1992). National Association for the Education of Young Children. Washington, D.C.: (Vol. 47 n.4)

Thank you for purchasing this book
from Dr. Becky Bailey's Loving Guidance.
Please visit us at www.beckybailey.com
We encourage you to continue your journey of growth
with the following materials:

Books:

Easy to Love, Difficult to Discipline: The 7 Basic Skills for
        Turning Conflict Into Cooperation
I Love You Rituals
Conscious Discipline: Seven Basic Skills for Brain Smart
        Classroom Management

Musical Recordings:

It Starts in the Heart (with Jack Hartmann)
Songs for I Love You Rituals Volume 1 (with Mar. Harman)
Songs for I Love You Rituals Volume 2 (with Mar. Harman)

Lecture Recordings:

Loving Guidance: Setting Limits Without Guilt
10 Principles of Positive Discipline
Brain Smart
Conflict Resolution
Preventing Power Struggles
Transforming Aggression Into Healthy Self-Esteem

These and other materials are available for purchase
on our website at www.beckybailey.com
or by calling Loving Guidance at 1-800-842-2846.